Palgrave Studies in Economic History

Palgrave Studies in Economic History is designed to illuminate and enrich our understanding of economies and economic phenomena of the past. The series covers a vast range of topics including financial history, labour history, development economics, commercialisation, urbanisation, industrialisation, modernisation, globalisation, and changes in world economic orders.

More information about this series at
http://www.palgrave.com/gp/series/14632

Lei Sun

Economic Growth and Development

Chinese Agribusiness Enterprises Development

palgrave
macmillan

Lei Sun
Shandong University of Finance and Economics
Shandong, China

ISSN 2662-6497 ISSN 2662-6500 (electronic)
Palgrave Studies in Economic History
ISBN 978-3-030-46098-3 ISBN 978-3-030-46099-0 (eBook)
https://doi.org/10.1007/978-3-030-46099-0

Cover illustration: nevodka / Alamy Stock Photo

This Palgrave Macmillan imprint is published by the registered company Springer Nature Switzerland AG.
The registered company address is: Gewerbestrasse 11, 6330 Cham, Switzerland

Acknowledgments

This book introduces the combination development approach with its associated inclusive growth of agribusiness and rural enterprises. China's rural enterprise development affects both industrial and service industries. This development approach can transfer rural workers and farmers into industrial and service industries in rural areas during upgrading economic development in developing countries and transitional economies. When institution and property rights are incentives for private agribusiness management, prices allocate resources and factors of production efficiently in markets.

I express my thanks to the team members of Palgrave Macmillan for their professional work in publish this book.

Contents

List of Graphs

List of Tables

List of Boxes

CHAPTER 1

Introduction

1.1 Introduction

This chapter examines the role of agribusiness and rural enterprises in economic growth and development in developed countries, transitional economies and developing countries. Some countries upgraded into industrialized economies from agricultural-backbone economies through sustainable economic development and growth over more than 200 years. The role of agribusiness enterprises was important to industrial development and economic growth in developing countries. There are debates on the role of agricultural sector in progress towards industrialization and economic development. Some suggest that the agricultural sector provided surplus rural labor to work in the industrial and services sectors during the process of industrialization and economic development. Further, agricultural exports often supplemented capital accumulation for industrialization. The development process involves the transfer of surplus capital from agriculture to the non-agricultural sector (Ghatak and Ingersent 1984). The sources of agricultural growth were and remain science and technology in discovering new farming methods and a unique combination of private and public endeavor. Land improvement, new farming methods and more research have all been necessary requirements for agricultural growth (World Development Report 1982). However, sources of growth in agriculture are not based in or on the land, given that the non-farming sector contributed to agricultural productivity at the times when

L. Sun, *Economic Growth and Development*, Palgrave Studies in Economic History,
https://doi.org/10.1007/978-3-030-46099-0_1

structural changes were adopted in agriculture. Schultz highlights the importance of modernization of traditional agriculture and believes that agriculture can become a powerful engine in promoting economic growth (Schultz 1964).

The share of agricultural production to a country's gross domestic product declines after the increase of the industrial and service sectors in the development process from agricultural-backbone to industrialized economy. The traditional agricultural sector played an indispensable role in maintaining livelihoods in developing countries in the past. Evidence shows that many developing countries have made significant progress towards a modern, commercial agricultural economy, increasing farmers' income in the past three or more decades. During this period, agricultural development has contributed to economic growth and poverty reduction in some developing countries. Agricultural development retains an important role in sustainable economic development and food security for many developed countries.

The share of the population in rural areas is declining, because some developing countries are undertaking the process of urbanization. With urbanization, the rural share of poor households will decline, but based on current trends that share will not fall below 50% before 2035 (Ravallion 2001). As global extreme poverty has fallen, by one measure, from close to 2 billion people in 1990 to about 700 million today, the world has learned about anti-poverty strategies that work (Gill and Revenga 2016). The concentration of the world's poorest shifted from East Asia in the 1990s to South Asia in the following decade. At present, the most severe poverty regions are Sub-Saharan Africa and South Asia. China's rapid economic growth and a remarkable reduction in poverty has contributed to the overall development figures for poverty alleviation in the East Asia region, because China's rural poor residents made up large proportion of the total poor in the region. China's rapid economic growth and poverty-reduction success has been the major contributor to the reduction in world poverty (Roser and Ortiz-Ospina 2017).

Agricultural development will play very important role in economic growth and alleviating poverty for many developing countries in the future. In 2018, 820 million were hungry, up from 785 million just three years previously. In terms of United Nations Report 2019, world hunger is on the rise in absolute numbers. After decades of steady decline, the trend in world hunger, as measured by the prevalence of undernourishment, reversed in 2015, according to "The State of Food Security and

Nutrition in the World 2019" report launched at the UN headquarters in New York. A World Bank report recommended inclusive growth to alleviate poverty. Even in those countries which have seen significant growth, a disproportionate share of the gains have gone to the better off, the upper 30%, or even the upper 10%, with many of the poor actually becoming worse off (Stiglitz 2017). In order to mitigate inequality, governments need to apply policies to stimulate adequate employment opportunities and improve the chances of decent livelihoods for the poor in a context of sustainable development.

Growth and development of agribusiness and rural enterprises are critically important to achieving the Sustainable Development Goals advocated by the United Nations. Successful agricultural development is essential to overall economic development and to meet the targets for poverty reduction and sustainable development. Agricultural development is central to the provision of food and the eradication of poverty and hunger. Agribusiness development plays an important role in increasing income for farmers, and it can create more work opportunities for rural labor.

Kirkpatrick and Nixson (1983) suggested that although attention has been focused in recent years on the need for agricultural development and rural rejuvenation, policy statements still emphasize the argument that industrial development is necessary to achieve high rates of economic growth and create more employment opportunities: industrialization is still the fundamental objective of economic development for the great majority of less developed countries (LDCs).

With increasing globalization and trade liberalization, more countries have been paying attention to agribusiness and markets for agricultural products. Stiglitz (2002) pointed out that focusing on the economy, globalization has three advantages: the demand for a country's products is no longer constrained to its own markets; a country's investment is no longer constrained to what it can save itself; and country's producers can have access (at a price) to the most advanced technology. Smallholder farmers in developing countries have had difficulties in doing their agribusiness, playing a full part in international trade, in the past—it was large-scale agribusiness enterprises and adequately capitalized agribusiness enterprises that were able to access global value chain. However, when transaction costs are higher than profits for small-scale agricultural production for domestic markets, farmers are not incentivized to trade in agricultural products.

There is a gap in empirical study addressing the question of how agribusiness and rural enterprises drive inclusive growth to help developing countries to upgrade into emerging countries and then developed countries. Market and firms are critically important in allocating market resources efficiently and coordinating economic activities. Nevertheless, it is important to analyze how institution facilitates inclusive growth that could help a majority of the poor escape from poverty and help sustain economic development. Some institutions arising in response to information-based market failures may actually lead to Pareto-inferior outcome (Stiglitz 2017).

International trade expanded rapidly after 1990, powered by the rise of global value chains (GVCs). This expansion enabled an unprecedented convergence: poor countries grew faster and began to catch up with richer countries. Poverty fell sharply (The World Bank 2019). Developing nations' role in global trade grew. Agricultural trade has also grown during the last 50 years, but only at about the same rate as global economic output. Notable among the factors that contributed to this relatively slow growth in trade was the failure to include agriculture fully in the multilateral trade negotiations under GATT that were so successful in reducing industrial tariffs (FAO 2003). Among developing countries, there are now considerable differences between the catching-up countries (e.g. newly industrialized countries) and the less developed countries. These changes have helped to transform the opportunity sets of both multinational enterprises (MNEs) and host countries, with the consequence that the competences of multinational enterprises are becoming increasingly mobile and knowledge-intensive (Narula and Dunning 2000).

Globalization and information as well as technology bring new opportunities to agribusiness, trade and economic development in developing countries. Although small and medium-sized enterprises (SMEs) represent the vast majority of firms worldwide, their participation in international trade remains limited relative to their share of overall economic activity and employment. The rise of the digital economy could, however, open a range of new opportunities for small firms to play a more active role in GVCs (Ganne and Lundquist 2019). The evidence so far suggests that the emergence of new products, new technologies of production such as automation and 3D printing, and new technologies of distribution such as digital platforms are enhancing trade and GVCs (World Development Report 2019). New technologies have impacted on patterns of commerce and trade in developing countries. It is time to study how these new technologies and information can help smallholder farmers to make profits from existing opportunities of agribusiness both in local and international markets in the context of globalization.

A successful agricultural and rural transformation is a foundation for overall economic transformation in developing countries. Agricultural transformation is largely characterized by modernization, commercialization and marketization. Successful agricultural transformation should also be linked to industrial development in the development process. Importantly, the development of agribusiness enterprises and rural enterprises are key components of industrial development leading to rural industrialization in developing countries.

A dual economy consists of two sectors: agricultural and industrial. A dualistic model of economic development highlights the role of agriculture in the progress of industrialization. Such dual economic models with agricultural and industrial sectors exist economically successful developing countries. Lewis (1954) indicated that the model of economic development with unlimited supplies of labor illustrated the important role that surplus labor in agriculture (and other sectors) plays in the development process and in fueling industrial growth (Thirlwall and Pacheco-López 2017).

In many developing countries the majority of the population lives in rural areas and they largely work in the agricultural sector before substantially moving to industrialization and urbanization. These structural changes contribute to the economic growth and progress of industrialization in developing countries—rapid economic growth is accompanied by significant structural change (Kirkpatrick and Nixson 1983). Table 1.1 shows that the share of the agricultural sector in gross domestic production declined in low-income and middle-income countries between 1960 and 1978, and the shares of industry, manufacturing and services increased during the same period.

Structural changes are one source of growth during the economic transformation of developing countries. Economic transformation has been slow in many developing countries, although some of them have moderate levels of economic growth. The structural changes link economic adjustment and reallocation of labor. Economic development as a dynamic process entails structural changes, including industrial upgrading and diversification and corresponding improvements in hard and soft infrastructure. Such upgrading and improvements require coordination and go hand in hand with large externalities to firms' transaction costs and returns on capital investment (Lin 2011).

Table 1.1 Less developed countries: structure of production, 1960 and 1978; distribution of gross domestic product (%) (weighted averages)

	Agriculture		*Industry*		*Manufacturing*[a]		*Services*	
	1960	*1978*	*1960*	*1978*	*1960*	*1978*	*1960*	*1978*
Low-income countries[b]	50	38	17	24	11	13	33	38
Middle-income countries[c]	22	16	31	34	22	25	47	50

Source: World Bank (1980), Annex, Table 3

[a]Manufacturing is part of the industrial sector, but its share in GDP is shown separately because it is typically the most dynamic part of the industrial sector

[b]Thirty-eight low-income LDCs with per capita incomes in 1978 less than $360

[c]Fifty-two middle-income LDCs with per capita incomes in 1978 greater than $360

The weight of agricultural production to total gross domestic product should be decreasing during the progress of industrialization, while the industrial and manufacturing sectors as well as the service sectors should increase as a proportion of GDP. At the same time, the surplus rural labor will tend to transfer into industry, manufacturing and services sectors, driven by and driving structural changes in the economy.

Nevertheless, empirical evidence demonstrates that successful development of agribusiness firms and rural enterprises is vital in balancing agricultural and industrial development, and this process can facilitate a development strategy of rural and urban integration. Because a majority of poor people live in rural areas in many developing countries even though they move into urban areas migrant rural laborers remain poor and precarious in status in cities, failing to find work. Many developing countries experience severe urban poverty during the progress of industrialization and urbanization. Therefore, the development of agribusinesses and rural enterprises that can absorb a large amount of surplus rural labor squeezed out of a traditional agricultural production system can mitigate inequality between rural and urban areas.

Existing literature has extensively focused on the important role of technological change in agricultural productivity and rural industrialization as well as economic growth. Technology change is recognized as one of the main drivers of long-term economic growth (UNIDO 2016). Griffin (2018) suggested that new technologies long held a central position in interpretations of industrial revolution. Many developing countries have accelerated their industrialization. New technology has changed to information technology, technological innovation in agricultural production, green technologies in sustainable development and biotechnology applications in agricultural transformation. Global market and technological competition has brought new opportunities and challenges to international cooperation in respect of the development and adoption of technology among developing and developed countries.

Technological innovation needs to be combined with a commercial structure for sustainable development of agribusiness. Development of agribusiness firms drives technological innovation in meeting market competition. Agricultural commercialization can upgrade the supply chain of high -agricultural products and increase income for farmers. On the one hand, agribusiness and international trade companies stimulate development of agricultural processing enterprises and commercial/ business management structures. The emergence of global value chains has also had an impact on workers in developing countries. Higher earnings and employment within sectors and firms is associated with global value integration, which also supports other spillovers that operate through labor markets (Hollweg 2019). On the other hand, local agribusiness and rural enterprises can create job opportunities for skilled rural labor with flexible working hours, and this skilled rural labor can also work on their household agricultural productions at different times. Job growth has occurred directly in the export sector, as well as indirectly through linkages of exporting firms to domestic, input-supplying firms. Employment creation and wage gains have been biased towards more skilled workers in developing countries, which contrast with the predictions of trade theory (Hollweg 2019). Therefore, the development of agribusiness enterprises could improve agricultural productivity and efficiency in labor allocation.

Oyvat (2015) noted that in the latter phases of development in the developing countries structural changes contribute to economic growth, and labor becomes mainly medium- /higher-skilled and moves towards the urban formal sector. The structural changes drive technological innovation—prioritized development issues in economic transformation in developing countries. (Lyu et al. 2019) analyzed migration over a 30-year period and found that rural migration to urban locations is clear linked with unemployment, and not with better income in urban areas or poor rainfall, thus providing conclusive evidence in support of policy interventions that focus on generating employment opportunities in rural areas to reduce migration flow to urban areas in China. The numbers of rural laborers have significantly decreased during the progress of industrializing development in the countries with the economic transformation in China.

Section 1.2 analyzes the role of agribusiness and rural enterprises in economic growth and development; Sect. 1.3 examines the role of agribusiness in upgrading developing countries to developed status; Sect. 1.4 analyzes the role of agribusiness and rural enterprises in economic growth and development of developing countries; and Sect. 1.5 presents a summary of this chapter and introduces the structures and contents of the remaining chapters of the book.

1.2 Role of Agribusiness and Rural Enterprises in Economic Growth and Development in Developing Countries and Transitional Economies

This section reviews the role of agribusiness enterprises in the development process through comparisons between development experiences in transforming developing countries into emerging economies. It analyzes how agribusiness enterprises contribute to industrialization and economic growth in upgrading developing countries into developed countries.

There are different facts and path of economic development for different countries. Some development economists advocate that the key role of agriculture is to provide surplus capital and labor transferred from agriculture to industry to support capital accumulation for industrialization (Lewis 1954; Fei and Ranis 1964). In developing countries, a key challenge is solving problems of dual-structural economies in respects of surplus rural labor, income inequality and obstacles to structural changes.

Difficulties of structural change include demand by different markets and newly developing industries. One such dilemma is that the allocation of labor can hardly reach optimized status in corresponding with market demand when information asymmetry exists in an infant market. Structural changes can help to transfer surplus rural labor into the industrial sector at the early phase of economic transformation. However, structural change can fail to create s work opportunities for a large proportion of rural labor at the time when the economic development stage demands an upgrade to the economic structure. Even though some developing countries have a moderate level of economic growth, structural changes cannot help but upgrade the value chain of agricultural products, which will cause severe unemployment problems in a transitional economy. Institutional innovation helps structural changes through incentive policies. Incentive ownership of farming land is important for farmers, and they can become stakeholders in a value chain of agribusiness to increase profit and income. In addition to encouraging an effective market mechanism, a government should play an active role in facilitating structural change (Lin 2011).

In much of the orthodox literature on economic development, industrial development is discussed in the context of the trade and commercial policies pursued by the leased developed countries). Many developing countries have adopted policies of agricultural import and export to accumulate capital for the process of industrialization. Some countries have adopted import-substitution industrialization and export-oriented trade policies at different economic development stages as they seek to progress toward industrialized economy status. Agricultural trade and export also contribute to capital accumulation of foreign exchange receipts.

Table 1.2 shows the share of developing and industrial countries in world exports between 1980–81 and 2000–2001. These differential growth rates are reflected in developing countries' share of exports in world trade (Aksoy 2005). (1) Industrial countries had high rates of agricultural exports and manufacturing exports to the industrial countries in 1990–91 and 2000–01. But industrial countries' share of manufacturing sector exports to industrial countries fell between 1980–81and 2000–2001. Developing countries exported more agricultural product to industrial countries than to developing countries, though (2) in agricultural trade, developing countries lost market share during the 1980s and barely recovered during the 1990s to their 1980–81 level of around 36% (Aksoy 2005). Agricultural exports by developing countries to developing countries did not increase significantly between 1990–91 and 2000–2001, nor was there any improvement in their market share of agricultural sector exports to the industrial countries in the period between 1990–91 and 2000–2001. However, the developing countries have increased their manufacturing sector exports to developing countries and industrial countries from 1980–81 to 2000–2001.

Vogel (1994) suggested that strong production linkages to the rest of the economy help make low-income, agricultural countries prime

Table 1.2 Shares of developing and industrial countries in world exports, 1980–81 to 2000–2001 (per cent)

	Developing countries			*Industrial countries*		
Sector by Destination	*1980–81*	*1990–91*	*2000–2001*	*1980–81*	*1990–91*	*2000–2001*
Agriculture						
Total	37.8	33.0	36.1	62.2	67.0	63.9
To developing countries	13.4	10.5	13.7	18.9	14.5	15.6
To industrial countries	24.3	22.4	22.4	43.4	52.5	48.3
Manufacturing						
Total	19.3	22.7	33.4	80.7	77.3	66.6
To developing countries	-6.6	7.5	12.3	21.7	15.2	19.0
To industrial countries	12.7	15.2	21.1	59.0	62.1	47.6

Source: Global Agricultural Trade and Developing Countries, The World Bank (2005)

candidates for implementing a rural-based industrialization strategy. Agribusiness and rural enterprises are a form of rural industrialization with respect to a combination of operation and management, as well as industrial development and application of technology. Agribusiness and rural enterprises are also the development strategy of rural industrialization, which can help structural changes in agriculture, shifting from low and primary agricultural production into high value added agricultural products. And industrial development in the agricultural sector drives increasing factory farming, in which rural labor faces changes in the workplace, forcing agribusiness enterprises to adapt. Industry also needs a market for its industrial goods, which, in the early stages of development, must largely come from agriculture (Thirlwall and Pacheco-López 2017).

The ratios of rural labor to total number of employees are much higher in low-income countries than high-income countries, that is, in developed countries the proportion of rural labor is much smaller than in developing countries. A large proportion of rural surplus labor will transfer to other industrial sectors in the process of development. Development of agribusiness and rural enterprises can absorb a large amount of rural surplus labor during economic transformation in developing countries.

1.3 Role of Agribusiness in Upgrading Developing Countries to Developed Countries

Britain had similar characteristics to other countries when early industrial development began from agricultural sector. In pre-industrial societies, a large numbers were typically engaged in agriculture, their lives devoted to procuring the food, shelter, heating and clothing necessary to sustain human life (Griffin 2018). The British agricultural revolution changed from traditional production system to modern farming system that improved agricultural productivity and is considered one of major causes of the industrial revolution. Technological progress improved agricultural productivity and contributed to the industrializing process in British agricultural production, and facilitated processing of raw materials like cotton by newly adapted manufacturing technology in the textile industry (Griffin 2018). The cotton industry commanded the central role in Britain's early industrialization. In the eighteenth century, Britain's cotton industry charged ahead of other countries. Technological innovation was vital to the scale of development of Britain's textile industry, which created a large number of work opportunities for rural labor in the period of progressive industrialization.

Britain's industrial revolution accelerated its economic transformation into a developed country. The economic transformation shifted employment into the industrial sector: Britain's economic transformation was driven by its agricultural industrialization and by concomitant urbanization resulting in large population shift from the countryside to the cities during the early of nineteenth century. O'Brien (2017) suggests that England's agriculture, coal mining and the state all continued to support urbanization, structural change and occupational diversification, and the economy reached a plateau of possibilities for an accelerated rate of economic growth, based increasingly on technological innovation. The growth of Britain's per capita output and labor productivity accelerated from 1763 to 1846 (O'Brien 2017).

Importantly, agribusiness and international trade expanded Britain's international markets, and Britain's success in international trade led to a high-wage, cheap-energy economy at home, which in turn created a demand for new technology – the famous inventions of the industrial revolution (Allen 2009). Allen argues that the British industrial revolution was a successful response to the emergence of a global economy in the seventeenth and eighteenth centuries. The upshot of Britain's success in the global economy was the expansion of rural manufacturing industries and rapid urbanization (Allen 2009). The industrial revolution was a process of household-based resource reallocation that increased both the supply of marketed commodities and labor and demand for market-supplied goods (Vries 1994).

Textile-based industrial development helped economic growth in the towns and cities in Britain. Industrial textile production adopted technology which created more rural skilled labor opportunities in the period of the British industrial revolution. And technological innovation helped the industrial development accelerate the transformation from labor-intensive agricultural sector to the industrial-sector production.

The development of trade and the rise of business accelerated the progress of the industrial revolution in Britain. As Britain industrialized, urbanization speeded up. The prominent textile-industrial development boomed, fueled by trade and expanding markets. Britain's industrialization relocated millions of people by drawing workers into big cities and industrial towns. Industrialization is partly integrated with urbanization.

Secondly, many economists have reached a consensus that technological change is vital to long-term economic growth in the United States. It has significantly contributed to economic growth and transformation in America, contributing significantly to the development of US agribusiness in the late nineteenth century, and playing a major part in driving the corporations and big business that make the US food industry what it is today. During the economic transformation of America between 1880 and 1929, industrialization and urbanization expanded in the United States faster than ever before, and the tendency for new industrial factories to be located in or near urban areas meant that cities grew much faster during the late nineteenth century than ever before (Rees 2016).

American agrarian reform evolved from collectively owned property rights to individual ownership. At the time of accelerating industrialization and urbanization, the percentage of tenant farmers within the whole of agricultural producers rose from 25.6% in 1880 to 42.4% in 1930: tenant farming was becoming a step toward ownership (Delahaye 2002). By 1959, the percentage of tenant farmers had dropped to 19.8%, and in the 1960s and 1970s, the state ceased playing any direct part in rural development programs and the reinforcement of individual ownership and market transactions in farming land (Delahaye 2002).

Global value chains have driven the rapid development of American agribusiness enterprises and food industry in both domestic and international markets. For example, the world's leading food manufacturer and agribusiness enterprise, a successful agribusiness enterprise that strengthened the integration of a local supply chain and a global value chain, is the Coca-Cola company, founded in 1886. McDonald's, a large chain fast-food group, was founded in 1955 and has set up branch restaurants in more than 120 countries in six continents. Many famous international brands of American agribusiness and food industrial companies have implemented successful corporate strategies and set up global value chains, effectively managed over a long period. Importantly, the multinationals and global value chains promoted successful agricultural transformation of the commercial and modernized agricultural sector in a sustainable way in the United States.

The 2012 census of Agriculture estimated 3.2 million self-described "operators" on the nation's 2.1 million farms in U.S.A. (Nesheim et al. 2015). Combined with unpaid family labours and paid employees, the study estimated a total of nearly 6 million workers in the farm sector (ibid). However, in terms of employment, agriculture indirectly accounts for much employment in other industries such as manufacturing and processing, wholesaling, and retailing. In 1985, agriculture employed 3.2 million people in farm production, 16.3 million in marketing farm products, and 2.0 million in the production of farm equipment and supplies in U.S.A (Cramer and Jensen 1994). Agriculture is thus responsible for employing approximately 21% of the labor force of the United States. In addition, the farm and food system accounts for 18% of the nation's gross national product in 1985 in U.S.A. (ibid).

Most of the farms in the United States are classified as family farms. In 1982, individual proprietorships or family farms accounted for 87% of all farms, partnerships accounted for 10%, corporations 3%, and others (estates and trusts) less than 1% (Cramer and Jensen 1994). Since many of the partnerships and corporations are family organizations, about 98% of US farms are really family farms. Of 2.3 million farms, 59,792 were operated under a corporate management. The number of corporate farms in agriculture has increased by 19% since 1978 (ibid). Of the corporations, a very large percentage had 10 or fewer shareholders. This also tends to indicate a family type of structure (ibid).

Thirdly, Germany successfully speeded up its industrialization during the nineteenth century, and agricultural reform was one of main foundations of its successful industrialization. The agricultural sector was the economic backbone of Germany before the economic transformation moving the country to industrialization. German agricultural transformation was driven by modernization, and development of industrial enterprises at an early phase of its industrialization. Technological innovation has historically contributed to inclusive economic growth in Germany. In more recent decades, however, this contribution has weakened due to the declining impact of technological innovation on labor productivity growth (Naudé and Nagler 2017), which has been taken as evidence of the need for an appropriate industrial-innovation policy.

Simultaneously, German progress through industrialization has driven its development of urbanization. Urbanization in this context was more than simply the growth of individual towns. To understand the process, we must bear in mind two contrasting phenomena: the statistically measurable expansion of already existing towns with concomitant development of an essentially industrial urban landscape; and the gradual evolution of a specifically urban way of life, characterizing a highly civilized industrial society (Reulecke 1977). German industrialization led to the migration of a large proportion of the rural population between the late 1800s and the early 1900s. That is, a great deal of surplus rural labor migrated into cities due to combined agricultural transformation and industrialization. At the same time, structural changes in agricultural production were being driven by international trade and enterprise. Ogilvie (2006) examined state corporatism and proto-industry in the industrial countryside of south-west Germany, where a dense worsted industry dominated the rural economy from 1580 to 1800. One example of proto-industry is dense, export-oriented rural manufacturing, which arose throughout Europe before factory industrialization. Corporate institutions such as guilds, merchant companies, village communities and manorial systems retained enormous power. Around 1830s, Germany also quickly became a center for business combination. Though many small firms continued to operate in crafts and retailing, Germany's big companies helped the process of industrialization (Stearns 1993).

Fourthly, Japan upgraded into a capitalist, industrialized country from agricultural-backbone status very quickly. Japan's industrial revolution began to take shape in the 1870s, and it became the first Asian industrialized country. Rural-based industrialization was a notable feature of Meiji Japan (1869–1912), with striking success in balancing rural–urban growth (Hayami 2007). Wade (1990) showed the importance of the role of government in emerging market economies through the evidence derived from investigation of the rapid development of new industrial countries in East Asia. Japan has little cultivable land area, compared to its population, so the Japanese government established private land property rights between 1868 and 1912. Land reform improved efficiency in the utilization of land and facilitated the agricultural growth rate. Growth in the agricultural sector laid the foundation for economic take-off in the early development stages in the process of Japan's industrialization.

Fifthly, agribusiness facilitated the process of industrialization and economic growth in an early development stage of Singapore, including agricultural manufacturing sector, food-processing firms and industrial development of agricultural resources. Singapore's industrialization took off in the late 1960s and accelerated in the 1970s. During this period, agricultural industrialization significantly contributed to the overall progress of its industrialization. The strategies of economic development were adopted by industrialized agricultural and manufacturing firms (Chen et al. 1991). There were only a small number of firms processing food and raw materials such as rubber and wood before the1960s. The country implemented a plan of industrialization in the 1970s, and there were 21 export-led processing industrial bases to supply international markets; the processing sector, including food processing, developed rapidly (Yu 1988).

Local enterprises adopted labor-intensive industries, such as food manufacturing. In 1966, the food sector was 13.6% of gross output of manufacturing industries, which was the largest element of the manufacturing sector in Singapore (Chen et al. 1991). Agriculture and food-processing companies contributed hugely to the industrialization of Singapore.

1.4 Role of Agribusiness and Rural Enterprises in Economic Growth and Development in Developing Countries

This section analyzes how agribusinesses facilitated the development process and economic growth in developing countries. Some developing countries have had a moderate level of economic growth and agricultural transformation over the past four decades. Asia has grown faster than any other developing region during this period, and a few of its economies have undergone a rapid and remarkable transformation. However, the pace of economic transformation of other economies has been slow. In many of them, agriculture is the largest employer and workers are moving from agriculture into low-productivity services, bypassing high value-added industrialization (Asian Development Bank 2013).

The key challenges are: how to increase farmers' income through sustainable agricultural transformation while countries are undertaking the process of industrialization; and how to create more work opportunities for large numbers of rural migrants in cities undergoing rapid urbanization. For the transitional countries with a majority of population in rural areas, agricultural and rural transformation are priorities for overall economic transformation. The agricultural sector has remained a very important component of the economy in developing countries such as China, India, Vietnam, Burma, Bangladesh and the Philippines.

Some developing countries have achieved remarkable progress in poverty reduction over the past four decades. Estimates of undernourishment rose from 777 million people in 2015 to 821 million people in 2017 (FAO, IFAD, UNICEF, WFP and WHO 2017). Table 1.3 shows that Africa has the highest number of people affected by food insecurity, followed by Asia. In Table 1.3, prevalence is calculated as the number of people living in households where at least one adult has been found to be severely food insecure, as a percentage of the total population (FAO, IFAD, UNICEF, WFP and WHO 2017).

Table 1.3 Percentage and number of people affected by severe food insecurity in 2016

	Percentage	*Millions*
World	9.3 (± 0.4)	688.5 (± 27.6)
Africa	27.4(± 0.7)	333.2(± 8.6)
Asia	7.0 (± 0.6)	309.9(± 26)
Latin America	6.4(± 0.3)	38.3(± 2.0)
North America and Europe	1.2(± 0.1)	13.0(± 1.3)

Source: FAO, IFAD, UNICEF, WFP and WHO 2017

The gradual shift in residence of the human population from rural to urban areas, combined with the overall growth of the world's population could add another 2.5 billion people to urban areas by 2050, with close to 90% of this increase taking place in Asia and Africa, according to United Nations data (UN 2014, *World Urbanization Prospects*). Agricultural transformation and rural industrialization should strengthen rural urban integration to mitigate inequality between rural and urban areas.

There have been valuable development experiences of poverty reduction and economic development in a few emerging economies such as China, India, Brazil and South Africa, as well as some developing Asian countries. Emerging or transition economies offer the world great opportunities. Producers can look to new markets, and consumers can benefit from new products. Increased efficiency and resource mobilization in transition economies will expand the global supply of goods and services (World Development Report 1996).

China's development experience demonstrates that the development of rural enterprises and agribusiness firms helps to mitigate inequality of rural and urban areas through creation of large numbers work opportunities for surplus rural labor at an early stage of economic transformation. The role of agribusiness enterprises is important for economic development in balancing agricultural and industrial sectors in the economic transformation of developing countries.

Furthermore, international markets and trade drive agribusiness enterprises to adapt new technologies and to access global value chains, which can promote structural transformation and industrial development in both the agricultural and industrial sectors. Multinational agribusiness companies help to increase profits through comparative advantage in international trade. Multinational companies also can help to upgrade technological progress in the food industry and to access global value chains. And management of agribusiness enterprises is very important for raising agricultural productivity, because effective management of agribusiness can bring profitable business opportunities for the stakeholders from agribusiness firms in linkage with global value chain.

China's own experience with moving out of extreme poverty through a carefully calibrated series of reforms has direct relevance for developing countries. Forty years ago, China was in a similar situation to many developing countries. In 1979, the average annual income was only USD182, and 70% of the population was employed in the agricultural sector and living in rural areas (Lin 2011). China's net average farmers' income increased by 7.1% per year between 1978 and 2007 (*Chinese National Bureau of Statistics* 2008).

China's development of agribusiness firms and transformation of rural enterprises are valuable cases in respect of development and poverty reduction. The transformation of rural enterprises has evolved from the collective ownership of firms to dominant private management of rural enterprises in the past four decades. China's town and village enterprises were collectively owned and played a dominant role in China's agricultural transformation during the take-off stage of economic growth. Now, privately owned enterprises have mainly replaced collective ownership/ management of town and village enterprises and China's agribusiness and rural enterprises have heavily contributed to the growth of the agricultural sector during a period of agricultural and economic transformation. A comparison of rates of growth of output in agriculture and township village enterprises (TVEs) highlights the extent to which rural economic expansion has become increasingly dependent on non-farm activities in the countryside. Thus, between 1978 and 2007, agricultural GDP grew, on average, by 12.1% annually, while the gross output value (GVO) of TVEs rose by 24% per year (Ash 2010).

China's rapid economic growth and remarkable achievement in poverty reduction offers valuable lessons to other developing countries. China has succeeded in balancing the agricultural and industrial sector over the past four decades. The dynamic development of agribusiness enterprises and rural enterprises has been the major component of China's agricultural and rural transformation over the past four decades. Agricultural transformation has largely shifted away from traditional agricultural production toward commercialization and modernization. The development of agribusiness enterprises has laid the foundation of successful agricultural transformation in China. These agribusiness enterprises are mainly involved in processing agricultural raw materials, active in the food industry, food manufacturing and forestry. The development of China's agribusiness firms and rural enterprises has contributed to its agricultural productivity, upgrading to high-value products as well as developing value chains.

Rural transformation mainly has progressed toward rural industrialization, as an important blueprint of development. Rural enterprises have been established in villages and towns all over China, not only engaged in agribusiness but also in other industries or services sectors located in rural areas. This remarkable rise of rural enterprises has absorbed a great deal of the surplus rural labor and many migrants, and played an important role in integrating rural and urban China.

Vietnam was largely an agrarian society before the market-oriented economic reforms of Doi Moi. Its economy has been in transition from socialist central planning to a market economy since 1986. At the outset, the population was 70% rural (Liu and Zhang 2011); the poverty rate has decreased from 59% in 1998 to 15% in 2008 (Liu and Zhang 2011). Vietnam's agricultural production and trade has increased rapidly since its accession to the World Trade Organization in 2006. It is now one of the large exporters of agricultural products in Southeast Asia. To reach its development objectives in economic growth and poverty reduction, the government indicated that its structural reform priorities were to change the country's trade and financial policies, liberalize the climate for private investment, increase the efficiency of public enterprises, and improve governance (Auffret 2003). Vietnam is now one of the largest exporters of several agricultural products in the world, notably rice, coffee and rubber. High economic growth, on average 6.1% a year between 1993 and 2008 helped Vietnam reduce its poverty rate by average of 2.9% a year (The World Bank 2012). The development of agribusiness helped to create more work opportunities for rural labor. Multinational agribusiness companies have involved local agribusiness in Vietnam, including the American Cargill Vietnam, Thailand's Charoen Pokphand and China's East Hope Group. Liu and Zhang (2011) found that some rural migrants found it difficult to find suitable jobs after they moved into cities, because of the generally low educational level of the rural population. In Vietnam, state enterprises have been playing important role in industrial growth.

The majority of India's population live in rural areas. The rural population was nearly 80% of the whole in 1975, and was still 65.5% in 2019. Agricultural development is critically important for overall Indian economic growth: Kalamkar (2009) observed that agriculture is the mainstay of Indian economy because of its high share in employment and livelihood creation, notwithstanding its reduced proportional contribution to the nation's gross domestic product. According to the World Bank report, India's rapid economic growth has helped accelerate poverty reduction. Between 2004 and 2011, poverty declined in India from 38.9% of the population to 21.2% (2011 purchasing power parity at $1.90 per person per day). There were 70.6 million living in extreme poverty in 2018 at India. According to a Sustainable Development Goals report of the United Nations Development Program, India has made significant progress: "between 2005–2006 and 2015–2016, the incidence of multi-dimensional poverty in India was almost halved, declining to 27.5 percent from 54.7 percent according to the 2018 global Multidimensional Poverty Index report" (Kaur 2019).

India has been experiencing an unprecedented rate of urbanization over three decades, and has had to face severe challenges in its economic transformation with regard to development and creation of suitable work opportunities for rural migrants. The level of urbanization in India has increased from 27.81% in 2001 to 31.16% in 2011. Urbanization in India is a consequence of demographic explosion and poverty-induced rural–urban migration (Sharma 2017). In other words, India, where the majority of the population is still dependent on agriculture, is no exception to the global trend. The large numbers of rural migrants who have moved into cities within a short period lacked a social welfare support, resulting in more urban poverty in a transitional time in cities. Urban poverty in India remains high, at over 25%, and this form of rural–urban development has resulted in significant barriers to economic transformation. India needs a balanced rural and urban policy for a smooth rural–urban transformation (Tripathi and Rani 2018). As the population grows, more work opportunities need to be created for migrant rural labor in cities and surplus rural labor in rural areas (ibid.).

Agriculture is an important economic sector for most regions in Africa. Many countries in African continent have undertaken agricultural transformation in the past two or three decades, and urbanization has also made fast progress in many African countries: sub-Saharan Africa (SSA) is often regarded as the world's fastest-urbanizing region. Urban areas currently contain 472 million people, a figure that will double over the next 25 years (Saghir and Santoro 2018). Even so, 57% of the population of the African continent lived in rural areas in 2019. Although some African countries have been accelerating their economic transformation for more than 10 years, agricultural transformation has been slow in most countries of sub-Saharan Africa, and the agricultural sector has essentially remained the backbone of Africa's economic development. Large numbers of smallholder farmers are dependent on food production through farming or livestock husbandry for most of their livelihood. Diao et al. (2010) suggested that agricultural growth is more pro-poor than industrial growth and it allows for greater participation of the poor in the growth process in low-income African countries.

There are questions on how economic growth can help to reduce poverty significantly during economic transformation. Approximately 27.4% of the population in Africa was classified as food insecure in 2016, which is almost four times higher than any other region (FAO, IFAD, UNICEF, WFP and WHO 2017). Food insecurity is on the rise, specifically in sub-Saharan Africa: from 2014 to 2016, food insecurity increased by about 3% (FAO, IFAD, UNICEF, WFP and WHO 2017). Africa's share of the world's urban residents is projected to grow from 11.3% in 2010 to 20.2% by 2050. Urban centers play a critical role in fighting poverty and sustaining economic growth in sub-Saharan Africa (Saghir and Santoro 2018).

In sub-Saharan Africa, youth are facing high levels of under-employment and unemployment and many move away from rural areas because of the unattractiveness of low-productivity agriculture. With around 380 million people entering the labor market by 2030 (of which about 220 million will come from rural areas), the challenge for sub-Saharan Africa in the next decades is to generate enough employment to absorb its booming labor force (FAO 2017). Further, as many countries have accelerated urbanization, urban poverty and urban slums have become serious challenges to the process of urbanization itself.

However, sub-Saharan Africa's opportunities are vast, and its challenges persistent. Home to the world's largest free trade area and a 1.2 billion-person market, the continent is poised to create an entirely new development path, harnessing the potential of its resources and people (The World Bank 2020). Several African countries have enjoyed rapid growth in recent years: for instance, Ethiopia's economy experienced strong, broad-based growth averaging 9.9% a year from 2007–09 to 2017–18, compared to a regional average of 5.4% (The World Bank, Ethiopia Overview 2019). Agribusiness enterprises are, however, underdeveloped, and there is great potential to create more work opportunities for smallholder farmers and surplus rural labor. Ethiopia's main challenges are sustaining its positive economic growth and accelerating poverty reduction, both of which require significant progress in job creation as well as improved governance (ibid).

Investment in agriculture must be increased substantially and made to work more effectively, if poverty in Africa is to be reduced. Africa's foreign direct investment (FDI) stock in agriculture accounts for just 7% of the total stock in developing countries-compared to 78% for Asia and Oceania, and 15% for Latin America and the Caribbean (OECD 2010). Investment in agriculture in Africa can be more effective to solve the problems of development. After almost two decades of neglect and dis-investment in the agricultural sector in Africa, there is a resurgence of interest, focusing on agriculture as a conduit for reduction of poverty and hunger.

In addition, policies to invest in the development of business and trade sectors are essential. Intra-African trade has consistently remained low, averaging about 10–12% of trade in the last decade (Mkandawire et al. 2014); this is low when compared with intra-European trade (73%), intra-Asian trade (52%), intra-North American trade (48%) in 2009 (WTO 2011) and intra-South and Central American trade (26% in 2009) (Mkandawire et al. 2014). Intra-African trade in agriculture and food is relatively low (estimated at 15%), a somewhat paradoxical situation when examined in the context of the potential of the sector as a key driver of growth, trade, employment and poverty-reduction in Africa (Mkandawire et al. 2014).

In Brazil, one of major development tasks is how to manage the dual economic structure in Brazilian economic development. Brazil adopted the import-substitution model of industrialization when the Brazilian industrial revolution began in July 1983 (Wirth and Bresser-Pereira 1985). Export receipts have promoted industrial development in Brazil.

International trade and global markets help promote structural change between the agricultural and industrial sectors. The terms of trade improvement, however, benefited mainly large farms that used imported inputs. Large-farmer agriculture has grown for decades, but, the level of poverty reduction is modest. And the challenge is still serious for labor productivity in the dual-structural economy of agricultural and industrial sectors in Brazil (Tsakok 2011). Big scale commercial farmers occupy 75%

of cultivated land areas in Brazil. These are high-growth and largely export-oriented businesses, co-existing with the smallholder farm household type, either subsistence or domestically oriented (Tsakok 2011).

Urbanization has contributed to economic growth, but there are serious social and economic obstacles to development. Rapid urbanization has led to very high levels of rural–urban migration, but without stable jobs in the destination cities. Brazil's economic and social progress between 2003 and 2014 lifted 29 million people out of poverty, and inequality dropped significantly. The income level of the poorest 40% of the population rose, on average, 7.1% (in real terms) between 2003 and 2014, compared to a 4.4% income growth for the general population (The World Bank 2019). A large number of smallholder farmers are poor, and they lack capital and technology to start their agribusiness. Brazil needs government development strategies to pave the way for smallholder farmers to be integrated with agribusiness. Institutions and policies designed to create a development environment conducive to investment and development in small agribusiness enterprises and smallholder-managed firms should take center stage. Institutions and policies determine the economic and political environment within which individuals accumulate skills, and firms accumulate capital and produce output (Besley and Burgess 2003).

1.5 Summary

Some developing countries have achieved economic growth and poverty reduction since the 1990s. Sustainable and inclusive development of agribusiness enterprises has played a vital role in economic growth and poverty reduction in developing countries. It is important to recognize that inclusive development of agribusiness enterprises can drive technological innovation. A revealing case is China which has only 9% of the world's cultivated land area but feeds 20% of the world population. Some 80% of the population lived in rural areas and rural poverty was extensive in 1978. China has lifted 700 million people out of poverty, contributing more than 70% of global poverty reduction. In the past four decades, China has had the fastest sustained economic growth in the world: it is a case of successful development experience from a low-income country to the world's second-largest economy consequent upon a period of economic reform. Since 1978, China has transformed itself from a low-income to an upper-middle income country with average annual GDP growth of 9.4% (Zhang 2018). Its remarkable contribution to world poverty reduction has led to its experience being recommended by development economists, policy makers and development practitioners.

The dynamic development of agribusiness and rural enterprise, as well as technological innovation, has contributed to a successful agricultural transformation and overall economic transformation in a number of transitional economies and developing countries' economies. There are many developing countries that have also undertaken agricultural transformation. There are opportunities and challenges for development by transitional economies and developing countries, but only a few transitional economies have achieved rapid economic growth and massive poverty reduction through sustainable development in recent decades. Sustainable development aims to create suitable work opportunities for a large amount of rural surplus labor in a period of agricultural transformation. Industrial development and agribusiness management are important for increasing farmers' income and the improvement of agricultural productivity. In addition, the development of rural enterprises can help a scale economy and upgrade value chains as well as creating work opportunities in manufacturing and service industries in rural areas during the economy's transitional period.

Developing economies have different paths of economic development to upgrade into industrialized economy from a pre-industrial economies. Technological innovation has contributed to improvement of output value of agricultural production and industrial development. Nevertheless, agribusiness and rural enterprises have helped in the development of industrial economies in different ways, helping to transform agricultural-backbone economies to industrialized economies.

The rest of the book deals with the following topics:

- An in-depth analysis of China's economic growth and the development path of agribusiness and rural enterprises;
- An introduction to a theoretical framework on development economics, and an illustration of the extent to which inclusive development of agribusiness and rural enterprises has helped to solve dilemmas of development in a sustainable way in developing countries;
- An analysis of the contribution of technical efficiency to China's agricultural growth, and institutional impacts on technical efficiency;

- Evidence that industrial development and technological innovation are necessary development strategies for inclusive growth during the period of economic transformation in developing countries—many developing countries have failed to upgrade into an industrialized economy from a low-income, developing economy;
- An examination of China's industrial development and the role of rural enterprises in the success of the scale economy and its domestic economic take-off nationwide-range—institutional innovation has facilitated rapid development of inclusive business and rural enterprises at a national scale;
- An examination of the relations between China's agricultural growth and technological change and the way that the market and consumption have driven agricultural growth and structural change;
- An analysis of barriers to development and how to succeed with industrial development through development of agribusiness and rural enterprises;
- An introduction to the combination development approach as applied to the dynamic development of agribusiness and rural enterprises in economic development;
- Case studies analyzing how China's agribusiness enterprises have contributed to economic growth and agricultural productivity, and international economic cooperation in respect of international development
- An introduction to the role of global governance in sustainable development;
- An examination of the role of China's international trade in its industrial development and agricultural growth;
- An analysis of China's agricultural investment and rural enterprises from the perspective of international development.

References

Aksoy, M. A. (2005). The Evolution of Agricultural Trade Flows. In M. A. Aksoy & J. C. Beghin (Eds.), *Global Agricultural Trade and Developing Countries*. Washington, DC: The World Bank.

Allen, R. C. (2009). *The British Industrial Revolution in Global Perspective*. Cambridge: Cambridge University Press.

Ash, R. (2010). The Chinese Economy after 30 Years of Reform: Perspectives from the Agricultural Sector. *The Copenhagen Journal of Asian Studies, 28*(1), 36–62.

Asian Development Bank. (2013). Asia's Economic Transformation: Where to, How and How Fast? – Key Indicators for Asia and the Pacific 2013 Special Chapter. Mandaluyong: Asian Development Bank.

Auffret, P. (2003). Trade Reform in Vietnam: Opportunities with Emerging Challenges. Policy Research Working Paper, No. 3076. Washington: World Bank.

Besley, T., & Burgess, R. (2003). Halving Global Poverty. *Journal of Economic Perspectives, 17*(3), 3–22.

Chen, E. K. Y., Nyaw, M.-K., & Wong, T.Y.C. (1991). Industrial and Trade Development in Hong Kong, University of Hong Kong Centre of Asian Studies.

Chinese National Bureau of Statistics. (2008). Beijing, http://www.stats.gov.cn/ztjc/ztfx/jnggkf30n/200811/t20081105_65694.html

De Vries, J. (1994). The Industrial Revolution and the Industrious Revolution. *The Journal of Economic History, 54*(2), 249–270.

Delahaye, O. (2002). Agricultural Land and the Law of the United States of America. Origin of the Washington Consensus. http://www.agter.org/bdf/es/corpus_chemin/fiche-chemin-454.html

Diao, X. S., Hazell, P., & Thurlow, J. (2010). The Role of Agriculture in African Development. *World Development, 38*(10), 1375–1383.

FAO, IFAD, UNICEF, WFP and WHO. (2017). *The State of Food Security and Nutrition in the World 2017. Building Resilience for Peace and Food Security.* Rome: Food and Agriculture Organization of United Nations.

Fei, J. C. H., & Ranis, G. (1964). *Development of the Labour Surplus Economy: Theory and Policy.* Homewood: Richard A. Irwin, Inc.

Food and Agriculture Organization of the United Nations. (2003). World Agriculture Towards 2015–2030. http://www.fao.org/3/y4252e/y4252e00.htm#TopOfPage

Ganne, E., & Lundquist, K. (2019). The digital economy, GVCs and SMEs. In *Global Value Chain Development Report 2019-Technological Innovation, Supply Chain Trade, and Workers in a Globalized World.* Geneva: World Trade Organization.

Ghatak, S., & Ingersent, K. (1984). *Agriculture and Economic Development.* Britain: Wheatsheaf Books LTD.

Gill, I. S., & Revenga, A. L. (2016). *Grow, Invest, Insure: A Game Plan To End Extreme Poverty by 2030.* New York: Social Science Electronic Publishing.

Griffin, E. (2018). *A Short History of the British Industrial Revolution.* London: Macmillan Palgrave.

Hayami, Y. (2007). Rural-Based Development in East Asia under Globalization. *East Asian Versions: Perspectives on Economic Development*. The World Bank and the Institute of Public Policies of Singapore.

Hollweg, C. H. (2019). Global value chains and employment in developing economies. In *Global Value Chain Development Report 2019-Technological Innovation, Supply Chain Trade, and Workers in a Globalized World*. Geneva: World Trade Organization.

Kalamkar, S. S. (2009). Urbanization and Agricultural Growth in India. *Indian Journal of Agricultural Economics, 64*(3), 442–461.

Kaur, R. (2019, September 2). *Poverty and Its Causes in India*. India Society Blogs.

Kirkpatrick, C. H., & Nixson, F. I. (1983). *The Industrialization of Less Developed Countries*. Manchester: Manchester University Press.

Lewis, W. A. (1954). Economic Development with Unlimited Supply of Labour. *The Manchester School, 22*(2), 115–227.

Lin, J. Y. (2011). New Structural Economics: A Framework for Rethinking for Development and Policies. *The World Bank Research Observer, 26*(2), 193–221.

Liu, H. D., & Zhang, C. X. (2011). Vietnam Environmental Issues in Rural Areas: Current Situation and Solution Measurement. In *Journal of Around Southeast Asia* (Vol. 7). GuangXi: GuangXi Academy of Social Science.

Lyu, H., Dong, Z., Roobavannan, M., Kandasamy, J., & Pande, S. (2019). Rural Unemployment Pushes Migrants to Urban Areas in Jiangsu Province, China. *Palgrave Commun, 5*(92), 1–12.

Mkandawire, P., Nyantakyi-Frimpong, H., Armah, F., & Arku, G. (2014). Regionalism, Food Security and Economic Development. *Occasional paper* No. 23. Zimbabwe: The African Capacity Building Foundation.

Narula, R., & Dunning, J. H. (2000). Industrial Development, Globalization and Multinational Enterprises: New Realities for Developing Countries. *Oxford Development Studies, 28*(2), 141–167.

Naudé, W., & Nagler, P. (2017). *Technological Innovation and Inclusive Growth in Germany*. Bonn: Institute of Labor Economics, IZA. DP No. 11194.

O'Brien, P. K. (2017). Was the First Industrial Revolution a Conjuncture in the History of the World Economy? In *Economic History Working Paper No: 259/2017*. London: London School of Economics.

Ogilvie, S. C. (2006). *State Corporation and Proto-Industry: The Württemberg Black Forest, 1580–1797*. Cambridge: Cambridge University Press.

Organization for Economic Co-operation and Development. (2010). FDI in Africa–Policy brief no. 4-October 2010, https://www.oecd.org/daf/inv/investmentfordevelopment/46148740.pdf

Oyvat, C. (2015). Structural Change and the Kuznets Hypothesis. *Greenwich Papers in Political Economy* 14074. University of Greenwich, Greenwich Political Economy Research Centre.

Ravallion, M. (2001). *On the Urbanization of Poverty.* Washington, DC: The World Bank.

Rees, J. (2016). Industrialization and Urbanization in the United States, 1880–1929. https://oxfordre.com/americanhistory/view/10.1093/acrefore/9780199329175.001.0001/acrefore-9780199329175-e-327. Accessed Jul 2016.

Reulecke, J. (1977). Population Growth and Urbanization in Germany in the 19th Century. *Journal of Urban Past and Present*, (4), 21–32.

Roser, M., & Ortiz-Ospina, E. (2017). Global Extreme Poverty. *Our World in Data*. https://ourworldindata.org/extreme-poverty

Saghir, J., & Santoro, J. (2018). Urbanization in Sub-Saharan Africa-Meeting Challenges by Bridging Stakeholders. *Center for Strategic and International Studies.* Assessed 12 Apr 2018.

Schultz, T. W. (1964). *Transforming Traditional Agriculture*. New Haven: Yale University Press.

Sharma, K. (2017). India Has 139 Million Internal Migrants. They Much not be Forgotten. *World Economic Forum*. Accessed 1 Oct 2017. https://www.weforum.org/agenda/2017/10/india-has-139-million-internal-migrants-we-must-not-forget-them/

Stearns, P. N. (1993). *The Industrial Revolution in World History.* Boulder: Westview Press.

Stiglitz, J. E. (2002). Development Policies in a World of Globalization. The Columbia University https://www0.gsb.columbia.edu/mygsb/faculty/research/pubfiles/1454/Stiglitz_DevelopmentPolicies.pdf

Stiglitz, J. E. (2017). The Revolution of Information Economics: The Past and the Future. NBER *Working Paper 23780.* Cambridge, MA: NBER.

The World Bank. (1980). World Development Report 1980, Washington: The International Bank for Reconstruction and Development/The World Bank.

The World Bank. (1982). Sources of Agricultural Growth. In *World Development Report 1982.* Washington, DC: The World Bank.

The World Bank. (1996). World Development Report 1996 from Plan to Market, https://doi.org/10.1596/978-0-1952-1107-8

The World Bank. (2005). Global Agricultural Trade and Developing Countries, The International Bank for Reconstruction and Development/The World Bank.

The World Bank. (2012). Well Begun, Not Yet Done: *Vietnam's Remarkable Progress on Poverty Reduction and the Emerging Chanllenges*, Hanoi: World Bank in Vietnam.

The World Bank. (2019). *The World Bank in Ethiopia-Overview*. Addis Ababa: The World Bank in Ethiopia. https://www.worldbank.org/en/country/ethiopia/overview

The World Bank. (2019). *The World Development Report 2019: The Changing Nature of Work*. Washington, DC: World Bank.

The World Bank. (2019). *Poverty Continues to Decline, but Pace of Poverty Reduction is Slowing in Central Asia, Infographic: Poverty in Central Asia*. Washington, DC: World Bank.

The World Bank. (2020). *The World Bank in Africa*. Washington, DC: The World Bank. https://www.worldbank.org/en/region/afr/overview

Thirlwall, A. P., & Pacheco-López, P. (2017). *Economics of Development*. London: Palgrave Macmillan.

Tripathi, S., & Rani, C. (2018). The Impact of Agricultural Activities on Urbanization: Evidence and Implications for India. *Journal of International Journal of Urban Sciences, 22*(1), 123–144.

Tsakok, I. (2011). *Success in Agricultural Transformation-What Its Means and What Makes It Happen*. New York: Cambridge University Press.

United Nations. (2014). World's Population Increasingly Urban with More Than Half Living in Urban Areas. https://www.un.org/en/development/desa/news/population/world-urbanization-prospects-2014.html. Accessed 10 Jul 2014.

United Nations Industrial Development organization. (2016). The Role of Technology and Innovation in Inclusive and Sustainable Industrial Development. In *Industrial Development Report 2016*. UNIDO. Vienna.

Vogel, S. J. (1994). Structural Changes in Agriculture: Production Linkages and Agricultural Demand-Led Industrialization. *Oxford Economic Papers, 46*(1), 136–156.

Wade, R. (1990). *Governing the Market: Economic Theory and The role of Government in East Asian Industrialization*. Princeton: Press Princeton University.

Wirth, J. D., & Bresser-Pereira, L. C. (1985). Development and Crisis in Brazil, 1930–1983. *Hispanic American Historical Review, 65*(2), 383.

World Trade Organization. (2011). World Trade Report 2011-The WTO and Preferential Trade Agreements: From Co-existence to Coherence, Geneva, https://www.wto.org/english/res_e/booksp_e/anrep_e/world_trade_report11_e.pdf

Yu, Y. Y. (1988). Characteristics of Agricultural Processing Industry in Singapore, Issue 2. World Agriculture.

Zhang, J. Q. (2018, October 27). China's Reform and Opening Up Influences the World Profoundly: Forum. China.org.cn. http://www.china.org.cn/business/2018-10/27/content_68475172.htm

CHAPTER 2

China's Agricultural Growth, Technological Change and Consumption

2.1 Introduction

China has had sustainable economic growth for a considerable length of time, and there have been different development strategies over different periods. In 1978, China's total agricultural output value was 139.7 billion RMB, a figure that represented an increase of 203% from 1952 (Han 2019). Total agricultural output value increased to 6171.97 billion RMB by 2017 (National Bureau of Statistics of China 2018).Mean annual disposable income for farmers was USD $2288.7 in 2019, while the average monthly income of rural migrant workers was USD $ 566 in 2019 (National Bureau of Statistics of China 2020).

Over the last four decades, China's agricultural sector has grown rapidly. Agricultural output value in real terms has grown at an average rate of 5.4% annually, while annual growth of grain production is 2.1% (Huang and Rozelle 2018). The diversification of agricultural products has been one of key characteristics in the transformation of agricultural production in the past four decades. The value of agricultural products has increased through development of activities and crops such as vegetables, aquaculture and husbandry. In addition, the processing of grain foods with high value has also experienced rapid growth. The diversification of agricultural products is a trend of agricultural development. One of the major drivers is market demand, reflecting the growth in Chinese people's incomes. This has stimulated high demand for high-value agricultural products.

L. Sun, *Economic Growth and Development*, Palgrave Studies in Economic History,
https://doi.org/10.1007/978-3-030-46099-0_2

New forms of agricultural production need new technology and new agribusiness management. Technological change is a key factor in improving agricultural productivity and agricultural growth.

Agricultural gross output value increased rapidly between 1978 and 2000 at a national level, on top of a moderate growth rate between 1952 and 1978, before economic reform. The average annual growth rate of agricultural gross output value was 3.4% between 1952 and 1978, increasing to 5.9% between 1978 and 1984, remaining at 5.9% between 1984 and 2000, slowing slightly to 5.3% between 2000 and 2005, and to 4.8% between 2005 and 2010, and to 4.2% between 2010 and 2016 (Huang and Rozelle 2018).

At the end of the 1970s, a majority of China's population lived in rural areas, and farmers engaged in primarily on grain production. The agricultural sector has always played a very important part in the economic composition of China. It still provides considerable opportunities for employees in rural areas, and most smallholder farmer largely rely on agricultural production for their livelihood. Therefore, a successful agricultural development is vital for poverty reduction and food security, as well as economic development in China. Reducing poverty and inequality are central to the UN's Sustainable Development Goals (SDGs) and the World Bank Group's twin goals for 2030: ending extreme poverty and promoting shared prosperity in every country in a sustainable manner (World Bank 2018). Sustainable crop production and global food security depend on innovation in multiple fields of crop science and technology, including genetics, breeding, agronomy, crop chemistry, grain storage and processing, crop management practices, crop biotechnology, and biomathematics (Xu and Wan 2017). China's rapid economic development and its agricultural growth have helped a majority of extremely poor rural households to lift themselves out of poverty in the past four decades.

Importantly, China's government has adopted different economic development strategies and policies of agricultural and rural development at different development stages, in which technological innovation has been an important factor in increasing agricultural growth over the long term. One major factor of technological changes in China is that new technology, new products and new management has been dedicated to improving agricultural productivity and growth over several decades. The technological changes have improved the China's agricultural productivity. Dynamic development of China's family agribusinesses and rural enterprises has driven the improvement of diversified agricultural products so that new technology has been adopted to match the demands of agricultural production and market competition. China's agricultural growth has improved the livelihoods of a large number of poor small farmers and created ample job opportunities through the successful development of agribusiness and rural enterprises, while its institutions have transformed to meet the conditions of the country's policy and to implement poverty-reduction programs when the development stages of markets were incomplete and deficient in respect of a new economic reform blueprint and the adoption of new technology and the introduction of new products.

This chapter analyzes how technological change contributed to the growth of China's agricultural sector. Section 2.2 analyzes the role of technological innovation in the agricultural growth; Sect. 2.3 analyzes agricultural growth at accumulated development stages; Sect. 2.4 analyzes how technological changes contributed specifically to agricultural growth; Sect. 2.5 analyzes structural changes, growth and market consumption; and Sect. 2.6 presents the summary.

2.2 The Role of Technological Innovation in Agricultural Growth

China's agricultural production has diversified. The improvement of agricultural productivity has been a key factor in the sustainable development of China's agricultural industry. Technological innovation has contributed to the improvement of agricultural productivity and diversification of agricultural products as well as sustainable development in recent decades. In the past three decades, China has accelerated its technological innovation in the cultivation of high-value agricultural products. Most recently, China's policies have also strengthened technological innovation in respect to markets, businesses and environmental sustainability. China's strategic development objective is innovation-driven, holding it to be fundamentally important to further promote scientific and technological agricultural innovation and to guide modern agricultural development towards efficient production, product safety, resource-economical, and environmentally friendly improvement (Xu and Wan 2017). Some scholars have suggested that technological changes contributed into China's agricultural growth since the economic reform of 1978. Huang and Rozelle (1996) concluded that technology adoption was the most important determinant factor in the increase in of rice yield in the period 1978–1990.

Fan (1999) studied the rice sector and suggested that the rate of technological change continued to increase over the whole study period of 1979–1993.

China had improved technological innovation in agricultural production before the economic reform of 1978. For instance, it had improved breeding livestock since 1949 (Han 2019), and China completed hybridization of wheat at an early stage, before the economic reform. Between 1951 and 1954, China extended the cultivation of hybrid wheat, including hybridized new varieties of wheat, throughout China and abroad, an example of innovative cooperation. China's government has also encouraged international cooperation on technical innovation. The innovative hybridization of wheat was shared abroad by China in the 1950s. In 1960, China made breakthroughs in rice breeding, and since the 1970s, China has adopted technological innovation in its grain production, resulting in high output of hybridized rice. China's progress in attaining higher output of cotton included technological application in the processing of cotton raw material into intermediate and final products.

Compared with the pre-reform period, China's technological innovation has accelerated development to enhance development of industrialized agricultural and the supply chain for the food industry. In addition there has been integration of agribusiness and enterprise development since the country adopted a market-oriented economy. Technology and science has played an important role on China's agricultural modernization: the technological system of the modernized agricultural industry is based on the core competence of industrial development in the agricultural sector, and agricultural products are elements of an industry chain. The chain is managed from farm to dining-table, from production to consumption, and from research and development to the market (Han 2019). Industrial development in the agricultural sector is mainly about technological change, and how technological changes impact on strategy, commercial patterns, and enterprises' organization, management of operations and methods. Tidrick and Chen (1987) suggested that China has had one of the world's highest sustained rates of industrial growth during the past 35 years. It has broadened its industrial base to encompass an increasingly wide range of production. Industrial development needs technology changes to improve the output of agricultural products. For instance, technological innovation in the cotton sector has been a key drivers of the industrial development of cotton production in China. China is expected to import 1.6 Mt in 2025 and retains barely its position as the world's largest import market. Its dominant role in the world cotton market will be significantly challenged as other importing countries emerge (OECD-FAO, Agricultural Outlook, 2016–2025).

> Using only 15% of the world's cotton land, China currently produces 30% of the world's cotton. Such a great achievement is largely attributable to adoption of intensive farming technologies and cultural practices, including seedling transplanting, plastic mulching, double cropping, plant pruning, and super-high plant density techniques (Dai and Dong 2014). Compared with direct-seeded cotton after the wheat harvest, the yield from transplanted seedlings was higher by 20–30% (Dai and Dong 2014).

Graph 2.1 shows that China enjoyed rapid growth in the agricultural sector between 1978 and 2016. Economic reform measures resulted in the enhancement of agricultural production. In 2017, total agricultural output value reached 10,933.2 billion RMB, a 236-fold increase over 1952 (Han 2019). Between 1978 and 2016, the mean nominal annual growth rate was 8.8% (Han 2019). The gross output value of agriculture underwent rapid growth over the reform period of 1978 to 2016, which provided the foundation for the successful transformation of the Chinese economy (McMillan and Naughton 1991).

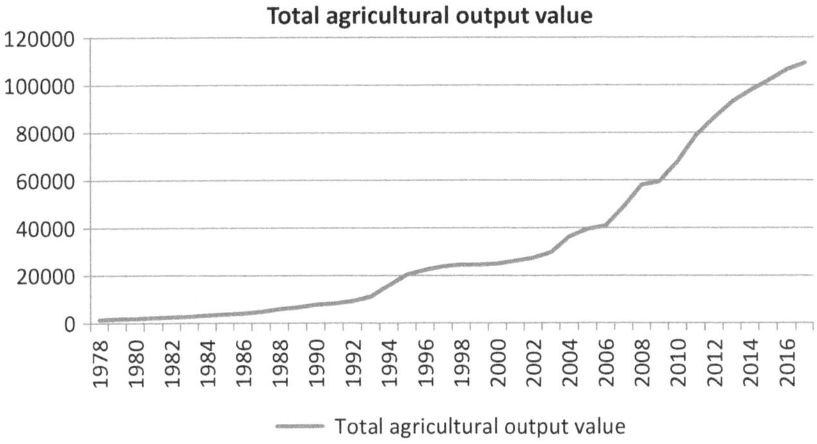

Graph 2.1 China's total agricultural output value 1978–2016 (Unit: 100 million RMB). (Sources: China's statistics data over 60 years; *China's Statistic Yearbook* 2018; Note: agricultural output value is calculated by current year)

2.3 Agricultural Growth at Accumulated Development Stages

China's first long-term development plan—The First Five Year Plan—operated between 1953 and 1957. By the fall of 1954, about 60% of the nation's 110 million peasant households were reported to be engaged in some sort of agricultural cooperative work (Shabad 1955). China's agricultural sector was a major economic component during this period, while the government carried out the economic development plan to implement structural changes to the industrial sector. In the all-out drive for industrialization, China stressed the development of modern mechanized enterprises, as opposed to handicraft workshops, cooperatives and individual artisan work (Shabad 1955).

China's technological progress and industrial development did accomplish agricultural growth during the period between 1952 and 1978. Agricultural total factor productivity (TFP) grew by 35% from the low of 1962 to the peak of 1966, but was still 25% below the peak of 1958 (Cheremukhin et al. 2015). Agricultural transformation and industrial development in the agricultural sector contributed to agricultural growth during this period. China's development polices strengthened industrial cooperative transformation and the transformation of industry and commerce during the period between 1952 and 1978. Cheremukhin et al. (2015) showed that reform yielded a significant growth and structural transformation. The role of China's agriculture in GDP was also important, with more than 70% of value added produced in agriculture in 1952, declining only to 30% in 1977 (ibid).

Since 1952, China's government has carried out Five Year Plans in every five years, which have provided the major economic development strategies at the national level and facilitated China's sustainable economic development. Between 1952 and 1978 total agricultural output increased in China: the growth rate of China's agricultural output was 11.6% in 1970 at the national level (see Table 2.1). Table 2.1 shows that the share of cropping in total agricultural output decreased from 83.1% in 1952 to 76.7% in 1978, and that the share of cropping in total agricultural output continuously decreased from 76.4% in 1979 to 60% in 1991. The growth rate of agricultural output was 8.3% in 1979 and 3.1% in 1991 (see Table 2.1). Lin (1994), from the Asian Development Bank, suggested that the structural change–growth connection is positive and the growth in agriculture since 1978 can be explained partly by structural changes.

Table 2.1 Growth Rates of Agriculture and Structural Change in Chinese Agricultural Production: 1952–1991[a]

Year	*Growth Rates of Agricultural Output (%)*[b]	*Growth Rates of Cropping Output (%)*[b]	*Share of Cropping in Total Agricultural Output(in% total = 100)*[c]
1952	–	–	83.1
1957	5.6	2.9	80.6
1962	6.2	3.2	78.9
1965	8.1	7.8	75.8
1970	11.6	10.6	74.7
1975	3.1	3.0	77.5
1978	8.1	9.4	76.7
1979	8.3	7.2	76.4
1980	4.1	-1.0	72.0
1981	6.5	5.9	71.6
1982	11.3	10.3	71.0
1983	7.8	8.3	71.3
1984	12.3	9.9	69.9
1985	3.4	-2.0	66.2
1986	3.4	0.9	64.6
1987	5.8	5.3	64.3
1988	3.9	-0.2	61.8
1989	3.1	1.8	61.0
1990	7.6	8.6	61.6
1991	3.7	1.0	60.0

[a] Rural output data underwent a revision in 1984, which moved village-and-below small industries from sideline production of the agriculture sector to townships and village enterprises

[b]Annual growth rate in 1952 constant prices. See the *China Statistical Yearbook 1984*, pp. 132–134

[c] The 1991 data were computed using the index of agricultural growth (previous year = 100). See the *Statistical Yearbook of China 1992*, p. 330. The entire period (1952–1991) is divided into before and after the reform periods

Sources: China *Statistical Yearbook 1984*; China *Rural Statistical Yearbook 1991*; Lin 1994, Asian Development Bank

Stone (1993) pointed out that several technological improvements were made prior to 1979 in China.

China's population increased to 1.4 billion in 2019 (National Bureau of Statistics of China 2020) from 0.96 billion in 1978 and 0.5 billion in 1949. More than 70% of the population was still employed in the agricultural sector in 1978, and only 17% in industry (China Statistical Yearbook 2017). This is despite the fact that agriculture only contributed 28% of GDP and industry almost 50% (China Statistical Yearbook 2017). China's agricultural production was mainly the labor-intensive agricultural production system in 1970s. The average annual growth rate of agricultural gross output value was 3.4% between 1952 and 1978 at the pre-reform period, and it was 5.4% between 1978 and 2016 at the reform period in China (Huang and Rozelle 2018). The average annual growth rate of grain sector was 2.5% between 1952 and 1978 and it was 2.1% between 1978 and 2016 in China. The average of annual growth rate of cotton output value was 4.0% in the period of 1952–1978, and it was 3.8% between 1978 and 2016; and the average of annual growth rate was 4.4 % for the output value of pork, beef and mutton between 1952 and 1978, it was 5.9% between 1978 and 2016 at a national level in China (ibid). The agricultural growth played an important role for the taking-off the economic growth at the accumulated development stage in China.

> In the 1950s, China and western scientists were aware that increasing factor intensification was not the only way to enhance the potential growth of agricultural output. They recognised that an even more important factor was technological innovation in agriculture, with its great potential for agricultural productivity growth. After the initiation of the green revolution, a series of breakthrough agricultural initiatives, in areas such as seed and fertiliser development and field management, marked the beginning of a new and transformative phase in the long history of global grain production (Du 2018).

2.4 Technological Changes Contributed to Agricultural Growth

This section analyzes contribution of technological change to agricultural output value. It presents the achievement of agricultural productivity and structural change as a national development trend. It also analyzes the contribution of technological change to agricultural growth based on a survey in Shandong province. The survey data examines relations between technology change and agricultural growth in the periods 1971–1978 and 1971–2001.

The growth of non-farm sectors accelerated after 1978. Also, new technology, new varieties and new management were adopted in the diversification of agricultural production and exploitation of new agricultural products. The structural changes in China's agricultural production featured a shift into high-value products, such as livestock, poultry and fish as well as vegetables and fruit. The structural changes were driven by China's rapid economic development that led to greatly increased market demand. Under the policy of agricultural product diversification, grain production's share of total agricultural output value declined, and the pace of growth of high value-added agricultural products (the non-grain sector) increased faster than the grain sector at the national level. Farming's contribution to China's agricultural output decreased to 80% in 1978, 64.7% in 1990 and 53.1% in 2017 (*Chinese Statistical Yearbook* 2018), whereas the contribution of husbandry output value increased from 11.3% in 1952 to 15% in 1978, 25.7% in 1990, and 26.9% in 2017; fishery output value rose from 1.3% in 1952, to 1.6% in 1978, 5.4% in 1990, and 10.6% in 2017; and forestry output value was 1.5% in 1952, 3.4% in 1978, and 4.6% in 2017 (*Chinese Statistical Yearbook* 2018). The farm sector had the overwhelmingly largest weight of China's agricultural production in 1952, output value accounted for 85.9% of China's total agricultural output value. Structural changes in agricultural production, driven by the market, are reflected in the proportion of high value-added cash crops that help increase farmers' income: their share of agricultural production value increased continuously, from 19.7% in 1978 to 32.8% in 2006, and the national growing area devoted to grain shrank year by year, from 80.3% in 1978 to 67.2% in 2006 (Cheng 2007). Consumption and market demand have stimulated the diversification of Chinese agricultural production, responding to increasing personal disposable income.

The improvement of agricultural productivity is the source of China's agricultural growth. This improvement has had different input sources at different stages of agricultural development: one view is that efficiency contributed to the increase in agricultural output; another is that technological change was the major contributor. Given the fluctuating nature of Chinese agricultural growth, these differing opinions, focused as they are on different periods, may both be correct.

Post-reform Chinese agriculture can be divided into two periods: 1979–1984 and 1985 onwards (Wu and Yang 1999). The average growth rate of gross agricultural output value was 7.7% in the period 1979–84 (Johnson 1990). The general trend of rapid diversification of agricultural production clearly has been influenced by changes in the non-farming sector, which grew much faster than the farming sector. During the period 1978–1984, China's grain production grew by an average of 5% annually in real terms, vegetables by 7.5%, fruits by 7.2%, and cotton by 19.3%; both supply and demand for China's agricultural products have undergone a fundamental change, from long-term shortage to approximate equilibrium or even excess supply in bumper harvest years (Cheng 2007).

2.4.1 *Agricultural Growth: Pre-Reform and Post Reform Compared*

The section uses data of agricultural output value between 1971 and 2001 for Shandong province in China. Shandong province's GDP was China's fourth-highest in 1978 and the third-highest in 2018. Appendix 1 shows growth rate of agricultural output value for selected counties between 1971 and 2001. The data shows that there were fast growth trends in agricultural output values in both pre-reform and post-reform periods. Although growth trends of the agricultural output value for the survey counties fluctuated, there was a general trend of rapid growth even before economic reform. Growth trends of agricultural output value are presented in Graphs 2.2, 2.3, 2.4 and 2.5, covering pre-reform and post-reform periods.

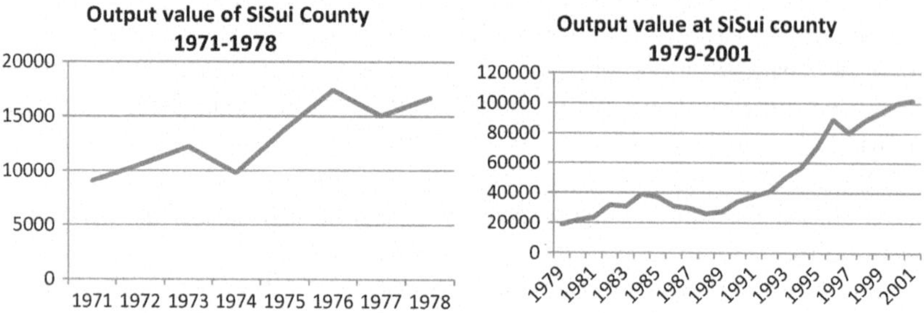

Graph 2.2 Growth trend of agricultural output value in SiSui county in the periods 1971–1978 and 1979–2001

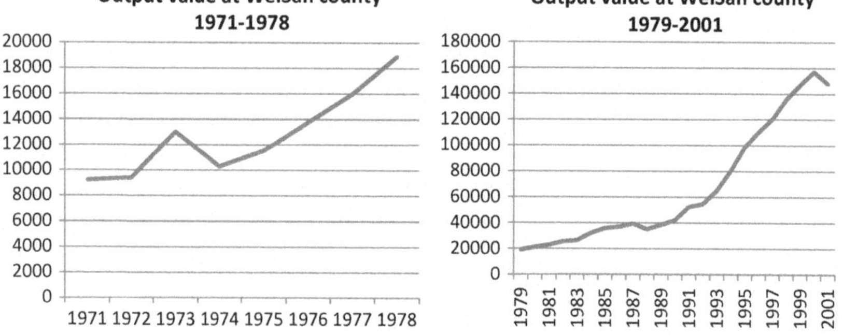

Graph 2.3 Growth trend of agricultural output value in Weishan county in periods 1971–1978 and 1979–2001

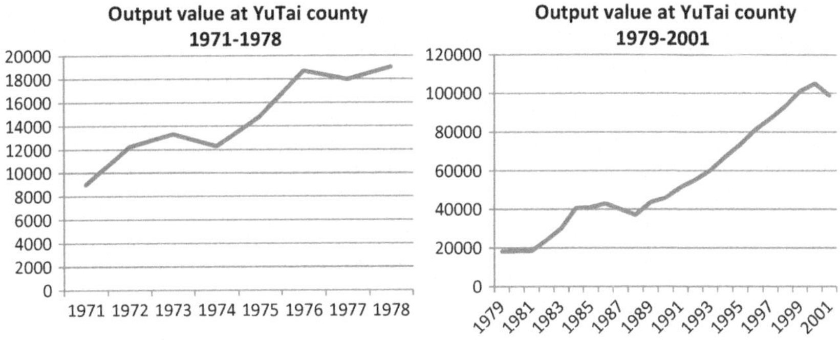

Graph 2.4 Growth trend of agricultural output value at Yutai county 1971–1978 and 1979–2001

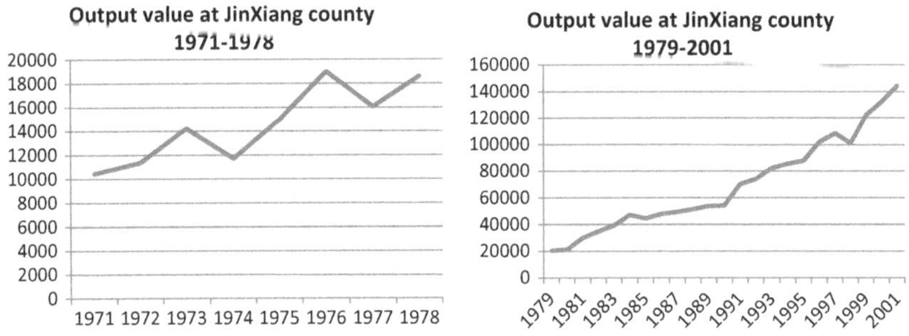

Graph 2.5 Growth trend of agricultural output value at JinXiang county 1971–1978 and 1979–2001

Graph 2.2, for SiSui county, shows that gross agricultural output value increased rapidly in the period 1971–1978, and that rapid growth continued between 1979 and 1984, slowing down from 1985, and then rising sharply from 1990.

Graph 2.3, for Weishan county, shows fast growth of agricultural output value between 1971 and 1973, a slow-down between 1973 and 1974, and a sharp increase between 1974 and 1978 Thereafter, growth was steady between 1979 and 2000, decreasing in 2001.

Graph 2.4 shows that there was rapid growth of agricultural output value in Yutai county between 1971 and 1978, with a fluctuating trend in this period. Output growth has sharply increased between 1979 and 2001.

Graph 2.5 shows that there was rapid growth of agricultural output value in JinXiang county, with a fluctuating trend between 1971 and 1973. Growth rate decreased between 1973 and 1974, then sharply increased between 1974 and 1976. Output growth declined in 1976 but increased in 1978 and increased steadily between 1979 and 2001.

2.4.2 Technological Change Contributed to Agricultural Growth

Technological change has been the main contributor to growth of Chinese agricultural output both in in the pre-reform period (1971–1978) and the post-reform period (1979–2001). I use econometrical methods to analyze correlations between technology change and growth in the agricultural sector in the case of Shandong province. Panel data is used in this study, covering five counties (SiSui county, Zou County, WeiShan county, YuTai county and JinXiang county) in Shandong province for the period of 1971–2001 (in Appendix 1).

Firstly, technological change significantly contributed to agricultural growth in both periods. The survey data reveals (see Appendix 1) that the average growth rate was 8.75% in SiSui county in the period 1971–1978, and 7.86% in the period 1979–2001; the average growth rate was 5.48% in Zou county in the period 1971–1978, and 7.74% in the period 1979–2001; the average growth rate was 10.26% in Weishan county in the period 1971–1978, and 8.94% in the period 1979–2001; the average growth rate was 10.74% in Yutai county in the period 1971–1978, and 7.16% in the period 1979–2001; and the average growth rate was 8.25% in JinXiang county in the period 1971–1978, and 8.91% in the period 1979–2001.

Secondly, the analysis of production functions includes output value growth, and the inputs are labor, land, fertilizer and total power of agricultural machinery in agricultural production for the five counties in the two periods from 1971 to 2001. Technology change significantly contributed to the growth rate for both periods for all five counties.

In addition, increase in land area devoted to agriculture has not contributed to growth (see Appendix 1). The counties implemented diversification and structural changes in agricultural production; non-farm sectors contributed strongly to the growth in areas such as animal husbandry and aquaculture. One key factor is that the sowing area of grain decreased, as was the case at national level. The national sowing area of grain increased from 1.65 billion mu[1] in 1949 to 1.91 billion mu in 1958 but then

[1] Measured united of area of land in China. One mu equals 0.0667 hectare.

decreased to 1.81 billion mu in 1978, 1.69 billion mu in 1984, and 1.64 billion mu in 1994 (Chen and Han 1996). Huge population density and limited land resources are shifting China's comparative advantage from land-intensive economic activities such an agriculture to labor-intensive manufacturing and industrial activities (Anderson 1990). The growth of non-farming sectors has been remarkable, and growth in output of foods such as mutton, pork, beef and poultry as well as fish cannot be attributed to an increase in land devoted to their production.

2.5 Structural Changes, Growth and Market Consumption

Some authorities regard technological change as having become the primary engine of agricultural growth since the completion of the household responsibility system reform in 1984 (Huang and Rozelle 1996; Fan 1999) Technological progress plays an important role in the agricultural growth: R&D needs to be carried out in laboratories and experimental stations, staff are then needed to apply R&D findings and disseminate results. All R&D operations need an external environment and institutional framework. Importantly, the evolution of a technological innovation project needs to measure whether it improves agricultural productivity, and its commercialization and marketization also need to be considered.

2.5.1 Structural Changes at Different Economic Development Stages

China has adopted policies to stimulate structural changes, and developed agribusiness to drive structural changes and technology innovation. There are four stages in regard to economic growth and structural changes (Liu et al. 2018):

- First stage: the contribution of the first industry (the agricultural sector) to the national gross domestic product (GDP) was 32% in 1984. The mean annual growth rate of the first industry was 14.5%, the second industry (industrial sector) was 10%, and the third industry (service industry) was 12.7% between 1978 and 1984.
- Second stage (1985–1992): China's non-agricultural sector develops rapidly. The contribution of third industry to GDP has increased to 34%.

- Third stage (1993–2001): a rapid development of heavy industry, and China's economy accelerates its globalization after accession to the WTO, including transformation of a large number of rural workers, and rapid industrial development.
- Fourth stage (from 2012): China's economic development is largely driven by urbanization and industrialization (Liu et al. 2018). Aquaculture output has increased to 69.01 million tons in 2016 from 4.65 million tons in 1978. China's total output of husbandry has increased to 85.38 million tons in 2016 from 9 million tons in 1978 (see Table 2.2).

Table 2.2 shows that the growth rate of several key agricultural products has not increased after China's access to the WTO. In Table 2.2, the growth rate of agricultural output was slower in the period 1979–2016, compared with the period 2001–2016. In addition, despite grain output value decreasing as a share of total agricultural output value, the total output of grain actually increased to 616.25 million tons in 2016 from more than 304.77 million tons in 1978 (see Table 2.2). The cause for this is that the non-farm sector significantly increased over the period under study.

Table 2.3 shows national average incomes of rural households per head and average per capita disposable incomes of urban and town families in China between 1978 and 2018. Net incomes of rural households per head have increased rapidly since 1978. The disposable per capita incomes of China's urban and town households have also increased significantly between 1978 and 2018. There remains a gap between the per capita income of rural households and that of urban and town families.

Table 2.2 China's Major Agricultural Products: Output and Rate of Increase (1978–2016)

	Total Output (10,000 tons)				*Average growth rate (%)*	
Agricultural Products	*1978*	*2000*	*2015*	*2016*	*1979–2016*	*2001–2016*
Grain	30,476.50	46,217.50	62,143.90	61,625	1.9	1.8
Cotton	216.7	441.7	560.3	529.9	2.4	1.1
Edible oil	521.8	2954.8	3537.0	3629.5	5.2	1.3
Husbandry	943.0	6013.9	8625.0	8537.8	6.0	2.2
Aquaculture	465.4	3706.2	6699.6	6901.3	7.4	4

Source: *China Statistic Yearbook 2018*

Table 2.3 Average per capita income of urban households and rural households in China, 1978 to 2018 (RMB)

Year	*Per capita disposable income of urban and town families (RMB/per annum)*	*Per capita net income of rural households (RMB/per annum)*
1978	343.4	133.6
1983	564.6	309.8
1987	1002.1	462.6
1991	1700.6	708.6
1995	4283.0	1577.7
1999	5854.0	2210.3
2004	9421.6	2936.4
2008	15,780.8	4760.6
2013	26,955.1	8895.9
2018	39,250.8	14,617.0

Sources: China's statistics data over 60 years

In the non-farm sectors, aquaculture and livestock have enjoyed rapid growth in the past three decades, following the structural changes in China's agricultural production. China continues to be the regions' most important livestock producer, especially pork. South and East Asia are projected to continue dominating aquaculture production, with China, India, Indonesia and Viet Nam accounting for the majority of growth over the next decade (OECD-FAO 2016). China's aquaculture and livestock growth meets market demand for high protein and nutrition, a consequence of the improvement of living standards and increase in incomes. There is a large number of middle class consumers in China, a rapidly growing proportion of whom prefer a health and nutritious diet. This trend will strengthen in the future. Therefore, changing consumption patterns have and will continue to effectively drive structural changes in Chinese agriculture. With the country's rapid economic development and increases in the mean income of the population, the demand for aquatic products and livestock products will continue to grow.

The structural changes that have contributed to the agricultural growth had already started before economic reform. China's total agricultural output value was 46.1 billion RMB in 1952, of which grain output value was 39.6 billion RMB, forestry output value was 700 million RMB, animal husbandry output value was 5.2 billion RMB, and fishery output value was 600 million RMB (Han 2019). The grain sector accounted for 85.9% of total agricultural output value in 1952, animal husbandry was 11.3%, the fishery sectors was only 1.3%, and the forestry sector was 1.5% (*ibid*). China's agricultural output value increased between 1952 and 1978, and the share of the grain sector in total agricultural output value decreased from 80% in 1978 to 53.1% in 2017. The ratio of animal husbandry to total agricultural output value increased from 15% in 1978 to 26.9% in 2017, the fishery sector increased from 1.6% in 1978 to 10.6% in 2017, and the forestry sector increased from 3.4% in 1978 to 4.6% in 2017 (Han 2019). Grain production remains the largest component of agricultural output, although its share of total agricultural output value has diminished. Structural changes were made to China's agricultural sector through several strategies and policies of economic development, including the development of agribusiness and rural enterprises, structural changes in consumption patterns, diversification and upgrading of agricultural products through technological innovation, opening up of international markets and implementing institutional reform.

2.5.2 *Consumption, Markets and Technological Innovation*

Several actors have influenced the structural changes and changing patterns in food consumption:

1. Per capita income growth, which adds to the consumption of each person. The main impetus for consumption growth will come from developing countries since their per capita income growth rate is expected to be higher than the global mean (OECD-FAO, *Agricultural Outlook* 2016–2025).
2. Population growth and changing consumer habits.
3. Impact of globalization on China's food consumption.

There are strong correlations between consumption, market demand and supply as well as technological innovation. China's government policy influenced the diversification of food consumption, and changing patterns of income for different agricultural products. China has implemented policies to encourage the diversification of agricultural production and public investment in technological innovation in agricultural production. Market demand for the diverse foods and high-value agricultural products has significantly increased in recent decades, thanks to China's rapid economic development. The impact of economic development has been enormous for the majority of the Chinese population, whose standard of living has improved markedly. The food industry has been pushed by demand and consumption toward a diversified, healthy, nutritious, and safe pattern. Chinese polices have supported the application of science and technological innovation to agricultural development.

2.5.2.1 Market Consumption and Income

Agriculture is facing fundamental change. High population growth, improved incomes and purchasing power will lead to greater demand for food. This will, in turn, increase pressure on the agricultural supply system (World Development Report 2011). Rising income affects diversification of food consumption, and also impacts on the structure of food consumption. Since economic reform started in 1979, China's income distribution is believed to have become more uneven in the course of rapid economic growth. The income elasticity of demand for food differs between different food categories: the effect of rising income on the demand for staple foods has been slight, but far-greater on non staple foods such as fish and livestock products. Processing the diversified foods and technological innovation have resulted the market making increasing demands on crop production.

China's economic growth has contributed an increase of income for urban and rural residents. Compared with the urban residents, rural households spend less on protein. But the rural households have diversified and increased their food consumption. Households in coastal cities and large cities spend more on food than those in in small cities. However, in small cities households have increased expenditure on healthy, safe and diversified food consumption. The price of food has risen significantly in the past 30 years in big cities. Even for the population the big cities, with their higher mean per capita income, food consumption has been large component of expenditure for those on low and middle incomes. High-income urban households have a high expenditure on high-quality food. Table 2.4 shows the different urban income groups' expenditure on different categories of food.

The different level of average annual household food consumption expenditure for urban residents affects the composition of their food basket. Table 2.4's seven groups' average annual food consumption expenditure were as follows: the lowest 1222.76 RMB, low 1594.67 RMB, below-medium 1926.06RMB, medium 2293.98, above-medium

Table 2.4 Comparison of food composition among different income-group households, 2003 (percentages)

Food Category	*Income Group*						
	Lowest	*Low*	*Below-Medium*	*Medium*	*Above Medium*	*High*	*Highest*
Grain	28.5	23.8	21.5	18.9	17	16	14.2
Poultry	47.3	48.7	47.7	47.4	46	45	42.2
Eggs	7.6	7.2	6.9	6.1	6	5	4.5
Aquatic products	10.1	11.4	14.1	15.3	17	20	24.4
Dairy products	6.4	8.8	10.9	12.2	13	14	14.8
	100	100	100	100	100	100	100,0

Source: Chinese Statistic Yearbook 2004

2762.75RMB, high 3337.82RMB, and the highest 4332.62RMB. (*Chinese Statistic Yearbook* 2004). The highest-income group devotes nearly one-quarter of its total annual food expenditure on aquatic products, indicating an increasing demand for aquatic foods as average purchasing power rises. One of key changes in food consumption is that Chinese people are consuming lesson grain, and the food basket has diversified, with a trend to food quality and high nutrition as income has increased over the past several decades. The consumption of poultry took a large share of expenditure for the low-income group and high-income group in 2003. Therefore, rising income has impacted on the structure of food consumption and demand for high-value agricultural products, and hence on the structure of China's agricultural production.

Rural Residents' Consumption in the Transitional Period

As income has increased in both rural and urban areas, so the ratio of food consumption to total annual living expenses in rural households declined too, from 62% in 1980 to 47% in 2002 (*China Yearbook of Rural Household Survey of 2003*). There is disparity of income for rural and urban residents in China and this is reflected in the composition of the farmers' food-basket. In China, rice and wheat are treated as staple foods, and vegetables, fish, and meat as non-staples. Graphs 2.6 and 2.7 show that the consumption of grain has been significantly higher than meat products for rural households.

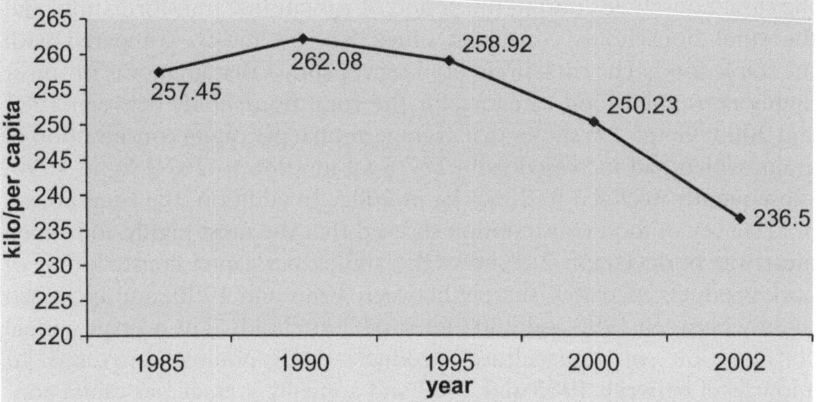

Graph 2.6 Average annual per capita consumption of grain 1985–2002 for rural households at national level. (Source: China Yearbook of Rural Household Survey 2003)

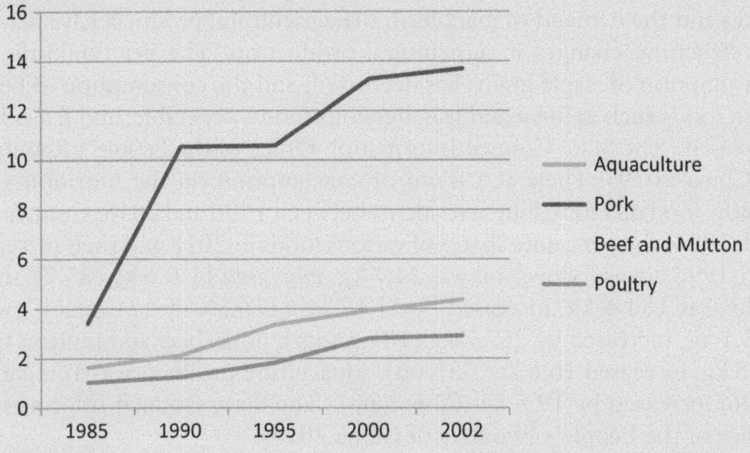

Graph 2.7 Average annual per capita consumption of aquaculture, pork, beef and mutton, and poultry products in rural households 1985–2002 (Unit: kg per capita). (Source: *China Yearbook of Rural Household Survey 2003*)

The staple food remained the key composition of the food basket for the rural households during the period of agricultural transformation, and the rural households consumed much less on meats, compared with the staple food. The rural household survey shows that grain was the most highly consumed food category for the rural households between 1985 and 2002. Graph 2.6 shows that average annual per capita consumption of grain, which had increased from 257.5 kg in 1985 to 262.1 kg in 1990, subsequently declined to 236.5 kg in 2002. In addition, the rural household survey of food consumption showed that the most highly consumed meat was pork. Graph 2.7 shows the annual per capita consumption of pork products increased sharply between 1985 and 1990, and increased slightly between 1990 and 2002 for rural households. The average annual consumption of aquaculture products and poultry increased at a low level between 1985 and 2002 and annually average per capita consumption of beef and mutton was low, falling from 0.8 kg per capita in 1990 to 0.71 kg in 1995, it grew relatively quickly to 1.17 kg in 2002 at rural households with a national level.

The facts indicate that the food consumption of rural households have changed obviously in the past more than two decades. Therefore, the prices and the demand of markets in the agricultural products have driven the structural changes in agricultural production. The per capita direct consumption of staple grains has decreased, and the consumption of non-grain foods such as meat and fish, ligneous foods, vegetable, and fruits has increased (The State Council Information Office of the People's Republic of China 2019). There is a trend of consumption on the nutrition and healthy food diet for Chinese residents between 1996 and 2018. Compared with 1996, the per capita shares of various foods in 2018 and their increase over 1996 are as follows: oil was 24.7 kg, increased by 6.6 kg (35.7% up); fruits was 184.4 kg, increased by 117.7 kg (176.5% up); vegetables was 505.1 kg, increased by 257.7 kg (104.2% up); pork, beef and mutton was 46.8 kg, increased 16.6 kg (55% up); aquaculture products was 46.4 kg in 1996, increased by 19.5 kg (72.5 % up) (The State Council Information Office of the People's Republic of China 2019).

2.5.2.2 Technological Innovation, Consumption and Markets

Technological progress also improved before 1979. Technological changes contributed to growth and structural changes have driven high-value agricultural products, associated with a robust development of agribusiness and rural enterprises. Further, technological change has also been an important driver for agricultural growth during the agricultural transformation since 1979. Technological innovation and market changes are important in the development of agribusiness and rural enterprises, which are big influences on international and domestic demand now present and in the future. There are lucrative business opportunities and a huge market demand for high-standard, and safe and healthy processed agricultural products.

Table 2.5 shows that industrial countries exported higher volumes of processed (final) agricultural products than developing countries in the periods of 1980–81, 1990–91 and 2001–01. Developing middle-income countries exported higher volumes of processed (final) agricultural products than developing low-income countries. Developing countries usually export more raw materials and intermediate products to obtain foreign currencies and partly to support their domestic food supplement. Production of final agricultural products comes by adopting technological innovation. The prices of the final agricultural products normally are higher than raw materials and intermediate agricultural products in all categories of agricultural product.

Therefore, there are opportunities for the developing countries to adopt technological innovation in their food industrial development and so derive more from international markets and agribusiness through technological innovation of agricultural product processing. The agricultural innovation lab (Ag-LabCx) has been designed to reach out to partners and promote innovation in the food systems arena, to explore new mechanisms for funding working with private-sector partners and start-ups in reshaping food systems (FAO 2017).

Agricultural sciences and technological innovation are crucially important for development opportunities for China's rural enterprises and

Table 2.5 Agricultural Final Products' Share of Exports, 1980–81 to 2000–01 (%)

Years	*World*	*Developing Countries*	*Developing Low-Income Countries*	*Developing Middle-Income Countries*[a]	*Industrial Countries*
1980–81	27.3	15.5	6.6	17.4	33.8
1990–91	33.2	19.1	7	21.2	39.8
2000–01	38.3	24.8	10.4	27.8	45.6

Source: *Global Agricultural Trade and Developing Countries, the World Bank* (2005)

[a]Includes China and India

agribusiness firms. Food consumption will be driven by market demand that promotes healthy food processing management and production of final agricultural products to safety standards appealing to the global value chain. Agricultural technology transformation and promotion capacity has enhanced the development of farm mechanization services across China. Conditions for structural change and innovation at the farm level in China could be further improved by securing the long-term stability of land rights as well as reducing transaction costs (OECD 2018). Development of small-scale family farms and diverse farm management units are key organizational innovation to enhance agricultural productivity and profitability in China.

Global market and technology innovation have impacted on China's food consumption and dynamic changes of markets. Overseas firms such as Nestle and Cargill have played an important role in China's agricultural processing development. International companies have impacted on China's food consumption pattern and on the application of technology in the processing of agricultural products.

2.6 Summary

China has experienced fast agricultural growth, and structural changes have resulted in a faster increase in the non-farming sectors, such as husbandry and aquaculture. China's policies carried out effective strategies and practices to support technological innovation in the pre-reform period and post-reform periods. Agricultural growth was rapid at the accumulated economic development stages, and technological changes made a great contribution to that growth. China's government has accelerated its policies supporting markets' development and agribusiness development both domestic and international. Consumption and market demand have driven technological innovation in the past three decades, and technological change has contributed to the improvement of agricultural output value in the period of agricultural transformation.

The rising incomes of the Chinese population have driven consumption and market demand for high-value agricultural products, which have contributed to structural changes in agricultural production. Rapid economic growth has increased the number of middle-class consumers. The market has driven the fast growth of high-value and diversified agricultural products. Technological change and agricultural sciences are very important for agricultural growth in the future. Compared with the developing countries, industrial countries have a high proportion of exports in processed (final) agricultural products. China has accelerated its industrial development in the past four decades, and is a large consumer and producer of many agricultural products in the international markets. Therefore, there is still great potential for rapid agricultural growth. Technological change and agricultural sciences are key drivers for growth in China's agricultural industry. Technological changes include inventing new machineries, fertilizers, and high-yielding crop varieties, and introducing new approaches to managing production.

Appendix 1

Growth accounting and technology change to agricultural growth for five counties in Shandong province 1971–1978 and 1979–2001.

	SiSui County	*Zou County*	*WeiShan County*	*YuTai County*	*JinXiang County*
GLY_output value	8.07%	7.21%	9.25%	8.00%	8.75%
GLX1_labour	0.13%	0.09%	0.15%	0.16%	0.16%
GLX2_land	-0.16%	-0.21%	-0.17%	-0.14%	-0.15%
GLX3_fertilizer	1.03%	1.13%	1.40%	0.79%	2.07%
GLX4_Total power machinery	0.40%	0.41%	0.43%	0.43%	0.41%
Technology	6.67%	5.80%	7.44%	6.76%	6.27%
Fix effect	6.67%	5.80%	7.44%	6.76%	6.27%
Growth rate 1971–78	8.75%	5.48%	10.26%	10.74%	8.25%
Growth rate 1979–2001	7.86%	7.74%	8.94%	7.16%	8.91%

Sources: Statistic Bureaux of Counties at Shandong province 1971–2001

References

Andersen, K. (1990). *Changing Comparative Advantages in China: Effects on Food, Feed and Fibre Markets* (Development Centre Studies). Paris: OECD.

Chen, J. Y., & Han, J. (1996). *China's Agricultural Growth with Large Population Country*. ShangHai: Shanghai Far East Publishers.

Cheng, G.Q. (2007). *China's Agriculture Within the World Trading System*. China Agricultural Trade: Issues and Prospects Symposium, No. 55022. Beijing: International Agricultural Trade Research Consortium.

Cheremukhin, A., Golosov, M., Guriev, S., & Tsyvinski, A. (2015). *The Economy of People's Republic of China from 1953.* (NBER Working Paper No. 21397, Issued in July 2015). Cambridge, MA: The National Bureau of Economic Research).

China Yearbook of Rural Household Survey (2003). Beijing: China Statistics Press.

China Statistical Yearbook (2017). National Bureau of Statistics of China, Beijing: China Statistics Press.

China Statistical Yearbook (2018). National Bureau of Statistics of China, China Statistics Press.

Dai, J. L. and Dong, H. Z. (2014). Intensive Cotton Farming Technologies in China: Achievements, Challenges and Countermeasures, *Field Crops Research, 155*, 99–110.

Du, J. (2018). *Agricultural Transition in China–Domestic and International Perspectives on Technology and Institutional Change.* Cham: Palgrave Macmillan.

Fan, S.G. (1999). *Technological Change, Technical and Allocative Efficiency in Chinese Agriculture: The Case of Rice Production in Jiansu.* Environment and Production Technology Division International Food Policy Research Institute, Working paper, January.

Food and Agriculture Organization of the United Nations. (2017). Harvest Day of Innovation on Food Technology. Accessed 8 Dec 2017.

Han, C. F. (2019). *New China's Agricultural Development with 70 Years-Policies Achievement Volume.* Beijing: China's Agricultural Publisher.

Huang, J. K., & Rozelle, S. (1996). Technological Change: Rediscovery of the Engine of Productivity Growth in China's Rural Economy. *Journal of Development Economics, 49*, 337–369.

Huang, J. K. & Rozelle, S. (2018). *China's 40 Years of Agricultural Development and Reform*, In R. Garnaut, L. Song and C. Fang (2018) *China's 40 Years of Reform and Development 1978–2018*, Acton: Austrialian National University Press.

Johnson, D. G. (1990). *The People's Republic of China: 1978–1990.* San Francisco, California: ICS Press.

Lin, B.Q. (1994). Rural Reforms, Structural Change and Agricultural Growth in the People's Republic of China. Asian Development Bank, Report No. 62.

Liu, X. H., Zhang, P., & Zhang, P. (2018). *Economic Growth and Structural Transformation in China's Reform Period.* Shanghai: Gezhi Press & Shanghai People's Publishing House.

McMillan, J., & Naughton, B. (1991). How to Reform a Planned Economy: Lessons from China. *Oxford Review of Economic Policy, 8*(1), 130–144.

National Bureau of Statistics of China. (2018). The World Bank (2018) 'Poverty and Inequality.' http://datatopics.worldbank.org/world-development-indicators/themes/poverty-and-inequality.html. Accessed 1 Oct 2018.

National Bureau of Statistics of China. (2020). The China's National Economy and Social Development Statistical Bulletin in 2019. http://www.stats.gov.cn/tjsj/zxfb/202002/t20200228_1728913.html. Accessed 28 Feb 2020.

OECD (2018). Innovation, Agricultural Productivity and Sustainability in China, OECD Food and Agricultural Reviews, Paris: Organization for Economic Cooperation and Development.

OECD/FAO (2016). OECD-FAO Agricultural Outlook 2016–2025, Paris: OECD Publishing, http://dx.doi.org/10.1787/agr_outlook-2016-en

Shabad, T. (1955). Communist China's Five Year Plan. *Far Eastern Survey, 24*(12), 189–191.

Stone, B. (1993). Basic Agricultural Technology under Reform. In Y. Y. Kueh & R. F. Ash (Eds.), *Economic Trends in Chinese Agriculture: The Impact of Post-Mao Reforms*. New York: Oxford University Press.

The State Council Information Office of the People's Republic of China. (2019). Food Security in China. www.scio.gov.cn. Accessed 14 Oct 2019.

Tidrick, G., & Chen, J. Y. (1987). *China's Industrial Reform*. New York: Oxford University Press.

Wen, G. Z. (1993). Total Factor Productivity Change in China's Farming Sector: 1952–1989. *Economic Development and Cultural Changes, 42*(1), 1–41.

World Bank. (2010). *World Development Report 2011: Food Security and Conflict*. Washington, DC: Agriculture and Rural Development Department, World Bank.

World Bank (2018). Poverty and Inequality-Overview, https://datatopics.worldbank.org/world-development-indicators/themes/poverty-and-inequality.html

Wu, Y. R., & Yang, H. (1999). Productivity and Growth in China: A Review. In K. P. Kalirajan & Y. R. Wu (Eds.), *Productivity and Growth in Chinese Agriculture*. Basingstoke: Macmillan.

Xu, Y. B., & Wan, J. M. (2017). Agriculture and Crop Science in China: Innovation and Sustainability. *The Crop Journal, 5*(2), 95–99.

CHAPTER 3

The Role of Property Rights in Allocation Efficiency and Inclusive Economic Growth

3.1 Introduction

This chapter analyzes the relations between allocation efficiency and inclusive economic growth in the agricultural sector in developing countries and transitional economies. It considers the role of property rights in inclusive economic growth and the way in which property rights can help to solve the development dilemma in some developing countries and transitional economies. Over the past three decades, some developing countries have had economic growth, but agricultural transformation has slowed. One key development challenge is finding a way to improve allocation efficiency in agricultural transformation in developing countries and transitional economies, where the majority of farmers are smallholder producers.

Farming land is important an important source of growth for agricultural production in both developing and developed countries. It has become clear that the property rights of farming land are also important to progress to industrial development from traditional agricultural production, to commercialize and industrialize agricultural transformation in developing countries and transitional economies. Smallholder farmers are unable to change the local policies in localities at many developing countries, because of institutional barriers. Governments can carry out policies to help smallholder farmers through incentive property rights of farming lands. Incentive property rights and contracts made under the law's

L. Sun, *Economic Growth and Development*, Palgrave Studies in Economic History,
https://doi.org/10.1007/978-3-030-46099-0_3

protection can secure profits for smallholder farmers. The incentive property rights of land in many developing countries are heavily distorted: smallholder farmers own little or no land. In Brazil, 15% of landowners own 90% of the land; in all Latin America, 1% of landowners own roughly 70% of the land (Thirlwall and Pacheco-López 2017).

When land is held and worked in the form of large estates, it is frequently under-utilized and farmed inefficiently by peasants who may have no security of tenure and may have to relinquish to the landowner a large fraction of their output (Thirlwall and Pacheco-López 2017).

This chapter sheds light on the role of property rights in China's farming lands and the way that it helps efficiency, inclusive growth in the agricultural sector and industrial development. The agricultural sector and the industrial sector need to be complementarily developed, and the large numbers of surplus rural workers allocated efficiently. China's small rural households have the leasing rights of small cultivated lands rights. In addition, there are rural lands in non-grain sectors which have adopted a contract system. The property rights of farming lands in China are allocation-efficient. This chapter will measure the role of allocation efficiency in agricultural production at different development stages. It addresses the importance of allocation efficiency in facilitating inclusive growth.

Allocation efficiency has contributed significantly to the China's agricultural growth. This efficiency has been an essential factor in the improvement in the country's agricultural productivity in recent decades. China's market-oriented economic reform and reform of property rights have contributed to the improvement of agricultural productivity. There are different methods for analyzing productivity growth and efficiency measurement in agriculture, but this chapter uses case studies to analyze the way in which property rights in farming land facilitates allocation efficiency, and helps agricultural transformation and industrial development.

3.2 China's Property Rights of Farming Land and Allocation Efficiency

Section 3.2.1 defines the classification of China's property rights of farming land; Sect. 3.2.2 analyzes economic efficiency and China's agricultural growth; Sect. 3.3 looks at property rights and allocation efficiency in agricultural transformation and industrial development;

Sect. 3.3.1 addresses the role of property rights in allocation efficiency in agricultural transformation; Sect. 3.3.2 is a synthesis of case studies on allocation efficiency and property rights; Sect. 3.3.3 analyzes the role of property rights in industrial development; and Sect. 3.4 summarizes the chapter.

China's rapid industrial development has significantly improved agricultural productivity and technological progress, which has helped a large number of surplus rural workers to be released from traditional agricultural production methods in recent decades. A key economic development phenomenon in China has been the improvement in agricultural productivity and the large numbers of rural workers transferred to the industrial sector or to work in rural enterprises. Large numbers of rural workers have come to work in urban areas. In 2019, the total number of rural workers was 290.77 million, of whom 116.52 million worked in local villages, and 174.25 million worked outside of the local villages (National Bureau of Statistics of China 2020). This economic phenomenon demonstrates that allocation efficiency has significantly contributed to a long-term agricultural growth, with fewer rural workers engaged in agricultural production. That is, while the number of rural workers has significantly during the agricultural transformation, agricultural output value has increased. Based on this fact, it is reasonable to surmise that allocation efficiency has contributed to long-term agricultural growth.

3.2.1 The Classification of China's Property Rights of Farming Land

The property rights of rural farmlands in China are rooted in collective ownership. Farmers are members of a "village collective cooperative." Before the market-oriented economic reform, a People's Commune had a leading social and economic function, directing a village's collective economic organization. Since economic reform, village committees have similar social and economic functions in rural areas, playing the key role as a village's collective economic organization. The Land Administration Law of the People's Republic of China decrees that "Land owned by peasant collectives that belongs lawfully to peasant collectives of a village shall be operated and managed by collective economic organizations of the village or by villagers' committees; land already owned by a peasant collective of a township (town) shall be operated and managed by the rural collective economic organization of the township (town)."

A village collective cooperative organizes individual farmers into a team in respect to work, socializing, culture and communication and learning. Although the ownership of rural lands are collective property rights vested in the village committees, farmers have leaseholder rights. China's property rights of farming land have helped the agricultural transformation and industrial development, and facilitated inclusive growth.

The classification of China's rural land property rights has three important characteristics to do with ownership, leasing rights and management rights. Li et al. (2020) analyzed the central government proposal for the "trifurcation of farmland rights" intended to improve land-use efficiency on the basis of secured land rights of farmers.

1. Ownership is collective, vested in the village committees of rural China. The village committee is the primary non-governmental organization. China has officially five layers of governmental structures, i.e. central government, provincial government, prefecture government, county government and township administrative level. Village committees do not belong to the official five layers. Heads of villages have been elected by farmers since the 1980s. In the context of the household contracting system, the reform of property rights has played an important role to the management of family agribusinesses. The full implementation of the Household Responsibility System in rural China since the beginning of the 1980s, and the consequent individualization of the right to contract and manage (agricultural) land facilitated the (mostly temporary) moves of rural people, especially with the recognition and permission of (contracted) land transfer in central policies since 1984 (Li et al. 2020). The organizational and institutional changes seem to be two main factors responsible for the improved efficiency of Chinese agriculture (Perkins and Yusuf 1984).
2. Farmers have leaseholder rights. The length of leaseholder rights of cultivated land areas was initially 30 years. China's polices have implemented another 30 years of the leaseholder rights.
3. There are also management rights of farming lands. Farmers are able to sign contracts of land use with local rural enterprises or the Farmers Specialization Cooperation. The enterprises then hold the

right of management of farmland after the contract becomes operative. By the end of 2018, there were 2.17 million small farms in partnership with the Farmers Specialization Cooperation and 600,000 family farms (National Bureau of Statistics of China 2019). The development of the Farmers Specialization Cooperation, and family farms as well as large-scale rural enterprises helped economic scale development. China is currently implementing the "separating three property rights" (STPR) reform to consolidate rural land. This reform divides rural land property rights into three components: non-tradable ownership, non-tradable contractual rights and tradable land use rights (Li et al. 2018).

China has implemented a diversified management system of property rights. This has facilitated growth that fits with different perspectives of development. Household responsibility systems adopted grain production at early development stages in the 1980s. Joint-venture contracting systems and household contracting systems have also operated in the non-grain sectors for the smallholder farmers since middle of the 1980s. Further, the Farmer's Cooperative has also been gradually introduced into the farmers' working. Land circulation in various forms can bring about economy of scale and makes for the development of modern agriculture (National Bureau of Statistics of China 2019).

Efficient organization entails the establishment of institutional arrangements and property rights that create an incentive to channel individual economic effort into activities that bring the private rate of return close to the social rate of return (North and Thomas 1973). Incentive property rights encourage secure private profits for firms. The companies pursue low transaction costs and maximum profits. Efficiency can help companies to gain more profits. Eggertsson (1990) defined transaction costs as: "the cost that arise when individuals exchange ownership rights to economic assets and enforce their exclusive rights" that is, transaction costs include the costs that parties to a deal pay during the process of the transaction, including information and measurement costs, negotiating costs and enforcement costs. The transaction cost approach regards the transaction as the basic unit of analysis and holds that understanding of transaction cost economizing is central to the study of organizations through assessing how their governance structures serve to economize on these transaction costs (Williamson 1981).

3.2.2 *Economic Efficiency and China's Agricultural Growth*

Productivity is commonly defined as a ratio of a volume measure of output to a volume measure of input (OECD 2001). Improvement in productivity has traditionally been regarded as one of the main features of economic growth and production capacity, an important parameter in measuring a country's degree of economic development. Improvement in agricultural productivity is an essential part of the growth of the agricultural sector.

Technical efficiency is the ratio of actual or observed output to maximum possible output. Maximum technical efficiency is a state when a farm achieves the maximum attainable output given a fixed level of inputs and the available technology (Farrell 1957).

Economic efficiency has two elements: technical efficiency and allocative efficiency. The notion of allocative efficiency captures the fact that not every form of technical efficiency makes economic sense, which implies profit-maximizing behavior by a firm (OECD 2001). For a firm, productive efficiency combines technical efficiency and the ability to combine inputs and outputs in optimal proportions, given their respective prices (Yang 2004). Efficiency improvement can be decomposed into optimizing technical and allocative efficiency (Fan 2000). Allocative efficiency is the ability to produce a commodity using the combination of inputs which corresponds to the minimum cost of production, it is the ability to produce a given level of output by using the optimum combination of inputs (Rathnayake and Amaratunge 2016). Allocative efficiency in input selection involves selecting the mix of inputs (e.g., labor and capital) which produces the desired quantity of output at minimum cost (given the prevailing input prices); allocative inefficiency arises when the input mix is not consistent with cost minimization (Coelli et al. 1998).

Technical inefficiency arises when actual or observed output from a given input mix is less than the maximum possible (Fan 2000). Fan (2000) estimated a stochastic frontier shadow cost function for Chinese agriculture using a flexible functional form. Both technical and allocative efficiency have reached a plateau: 0.75 for allocative efficiency and 0.91 for technical efficiency.

Institutions provide a precondition, an environment for social and economic development in which individual farmers can pursue their profits through hard work and operation of their small agricultural businesses in rural China. China implemented a market system grafted on to a planned system, a mixed system of private property rights and domestic firms owned by local government (Dutraive 2009). Institutions were supplemented by features like private property rights and markets, all of which stimulate economic growth (Rodrik 2005).

Agricultural output grew rapidly in the years following reform, and there is a growing body of evidence that resource use has become more efficient in Chinese agriculture (Dollar 1990). Agricultural productivity gains in China have come from efficiency gains, and most of the efficiency gains have been attributed to the institutional reform called the "Household Responsibility System" that operated in the period 1979–84 (Lin 1987). Nolan (1988) described that China's rural economy from the 1950s to the 1980s was inhibited by serious shortcomings of the collective farms—they were not the most suitable institutional form for rural economic development in poor countries (Nolan 1988). The household responsibility system, a much more flexible system for farmers, contributed to agricultural growth by providing greater incentive for farmers by giving the rights to use land as they saw fit, linking rewards closely with their performance.

China had already implemented inclusive agricultural production in the pre-economic reform periods. After the formation of higher Agricultural Producers' Cooperatives (APCs), a further enlargement of the scale of rural organization into People's Communes took place to enable better coordination of rural construction projects and provide an even larger economic base for financing rural development (Stavis 1974). China's institutional development supported agricultural growth in the pre-economic reform period. If economies of scale exist, then collective farming may have advantages, and work incentives under the systems of group farming were operative between 1955 and the early 1980s, the time of adoption of agricultural reform (*baogan daohu*) (Putterman 1988).

In 1958, China launched a large scale agricultural cooperative movement; rural people's communes were established in large numbers by siphoning manpower, funds and materials from brigades and teams originally engaged in sideline production and by annexing more than 30,000 handicraft cooperatives that had previously operated in small towns (Byrd and Lin 1990).

The Chinese People's Commune is a unique organization. It should not be identified with the Russian collective farm (*kolkhoz*). While the latter concerns itself only with agricultural production, the Chinese People's Commune is an inclusive organization, running agricultural, industrial, cultural, political and military activities (Gluckstein 1960). The inclusive agricultural production management was organized by local governments, which directed farmers to agricultural production in work teams. Between 1956 and 1958, local government organized higher-level APCs in which the land previously privately owned by the peasants, their tools and other production means were all transferred to the collective (Ye 2015).

The agricultural cooperatives production system improved technical efficiency. Gong et al. (2019) used survey data from 2015 for China's "family farms plus cooperatives" as the preferred mode of organization in agriculture, and they investigated technical efficiency in crop production comparing family farms that were members of cooperatives with farms that were not. Non-member farms showed lower technical efficiency and a wide gap between observed and potential production. By contrast, core members of cooperatives showed the highest technical efficiency and a narrow gap between observed and potential production.

Some cross-country evidences are provided to measure the allocative efficiency of farmers in Nigeria, Greece, Bangladesh and China (Laha and Kuri 2011). In the process of transformation, a proper modification and replacement of existing institutions are assumed to take place especially for those inefficient institutions which put an obstacle in the allocation of resources (Laha and Kuri 2011).

3.3 Property Rights and Allocation Efficiency in Agricultural Transformation and Industrial Development

Reform of property rights, combined with collective and private management, played a critically important role in China's agricultural transformation and industrial development. During the economic transformation periods, as Table 3.1 shows, agriculture's share of total GDP decreased from 40% in 1970 to 10.3% in 2009. The industrial share of total GDP was 46% in 1970 and 46.3% in 2009. And the share of services in total GDP was 13% in 1970 which increased to 43% in 1970. Although the proportionate contribution of the industrial sector to GDP was similar in 1970 and in 2009, the increase in GDP meant that the scale of the sector had increased significantly by 2009. During this period, agricultural output increased rapidly, although its share of GDP declined.

Industrial development includes the level of industrialized agricultural production, the industrial chain in the agricultural sector and rural enterprise development. The services sector and industrial sector also impacted

Table 3.1 Shares of Agriculture, Industry and Services to China's GDP (%) 1970–2009

Year	*1970*	*1980*	*1985*	*1990*	*1995*	*2000*	*2005*	*2009*
Agriculture	40	30	28	27	20	15	12	10.3
Industry	46	49	43	41	47	46	47	46.3
Services	13	21	29	32	33	39	41	43.4

Source: Huang (2011)

on industrial development in the agricultural sector. For instance, some industrial products operate in agricultural production. Industrial development also refers to cluster and agglomeration of agro-industrialized development. Some service sectors are integrated with urban development.

Private and collective features of farmlands and farmers' property rights have helped to secure smallholder farmer's private profits, and the private and collective features of property rights helped the diversification of the agricultural products during agricultural transformation. Further, these features of farming property rights helped industrial development, and the combined business pattern of rural enterprises and smallholder farmers.

This section analyzes the role of property rights in maintaining and improving the allocation efficiency of the agricultural transformation and the industrial development of the agricultural sector. China's economic reform is radically changing property rights and the efficiency of resource utilization. The key to long-term economic growth is state protection of an efficient property rights system (Zhou 2009). Property rights have helped smallholder farmers to reduce their transaction costs. The incentives arising from improved property rights have transformed allocation efficiency, contributing to agricultural growth. The property rights of farming and farmland have private and collective features which jointly have accelerated inclusive growth during the transitional period: China upgraded the level of industrial development of its agricultural sector within a few decades and improved the sector's allocation efficiency.

3.3.1 Role of Property Rights in Allocation Efficiency in Agricultural Transformation

With China's reform of property rights, transaction costs are lower for smallholder agricultural producers and family agribusiness and cooperative management. Increases in land rental activity and in aggregate output and productivity are consistent with the hypothesis that the reduction of transaction costs associated with leasing land increases aggregate output by allowing for a more efficient allocation of factors across producers (Chari et al. 2017).

1. China's property rights and allocation efficiency have contributed to structural changes in agricultural transformation. China has implemented two different features of rural land property rights in allocation of local resources. Market-based economic reform has impacted on property rights in China's rural lands. Property rights there are affected indirectly by prices and market forces in the grain sector. Further, the Chinese government implemented the Household Responsibility System (HRS) for China's crop production at the beginning of the 1980s. Under this system, each household that takes responsibility for a field also assumes a tax burden: a portion of the former team's quota of grain sales, at a price fixed by the government (Kung and Liu 1997). The Household Responsibility System allocates small-scale areas of cultivated land to rural households according to the number of households in a village. Every household has the same area allocated to it. In the non-grain sector, the household contracting system does not demand that land be equally allocated by rural village committees. There are different strategies of China's marketization of farming land. Prices determine leasing rights of non-grain producing land, such as that devoted to aquaculture and livestock, allocation reflecting limited efficiency in markets.

Traditionally, grain is the staple food for Chinese people. For grain production, every rural household has an equal plot of cultivated lands areas allocated to it within their home village area. In past decades, agricultural transformation and enterprise development have also impacted on the property rights of farming lands. The change from land-intensive production to labor-intensive production has been driven by agricultural commercialization, consumption and markets. Land-intensive products include grain, oil seeds and cotton, whereas labor-intensive products include live animals, dairy products, coffee and tea.

High-value agricultural products have increased significantly during the period from 1952 to 2018. In 1952, the output value of the grain sector was 85.9% of national agricultural output value; the shares of forestry, livestock, and fisheries sectors were 1.6%, 11.2% and 1.3% respectively of total agricultural output values. By 2018, the output value of the grain sector was 57.1% of the national agricultural output value, the shares of forestry was 5.0%, livestock was 26.6%, and fisheries were 11.3% (National Bureau of Statistics of China 2019). Structural changes in agricultural production and market development as well as rural enterprise development have increased the prices of agricultural products, which has helped farmers' profits. Allocation efficiency is one of the key factors in the development of high-value agricultural production, because the smallholder farmers gain profits, hence property rights can be seen to be incentives to secure profits.

In parallel with these changes, structural changes in high-value agricultural production has been driven by transformation of agricultural management patterns linked to commercialization and marketization. Property rights have played a very important role in the structural changes directed toward high-value product development. Following up the reform of its property rights, China's small-scale family agribusinesses have been a key feature in the country's agricultural development. Rural workers now often work in processing primary agricultural products and have witnessed improved technical capacity in agricultural processing factories and agricultural production. Labor allocation has increased efficiency.

2. Allocation efficiency of property rights impacts on the diversification of agricultural production. Since the reform, grain production's share of total agricultural output has declined from 78% in 1979 to 50% in 2003 (*Chinese Statistic Year Book* 2004). At the same time, high-value products such as fisheries and livestock have contributed markedly to the income of small household producers. Considerable structural adjustments have also been observed as a result of changes in demand and consumption patterns. Consequently, the livestock and fishery sectors have expanded rapidly. The shares of these two sectors increased from 16(14 + 2)% in 1970 to 44 (34 + 10)% in 2009 (Huang et al. 2011). China's aquaculture has come to play an overwhelming role in world aquaculture production: from 29.8% in 1970, China's share of world aquaculture was 62.3% of the world total in 2008 (FAO, *The State of World Fisheries and Aquaculture* 2010). According to the FAO, China accounted for 67% of the global production of 51.7 million tonnes and 49% of the global value of $78.8 billion in 2006 (FAO 2006).

Household pond culture accounted for 70% of China's output of farmed fish in 2009 (*Chinese Fishery Statistic Yearbook* 2009). Property rights of aquaculture ponds follow different economic policies than apply to grain sectors. The different approaches have played an important role in agriculture's rapid structural changes and transformation. A welfare system operates in the grain sector. The leaseholder rights of cultivated land have adopted the Household Responsibility System allocating the same area of cultivated land to all households within a village. The leaseholder rights of aquaculture ponds have been allocated by price, and market competitions has played the key role in their allocation.

3. Property rights of non-grain sector e.g. fish pond management of rural household is incentive. The leasing rights of the household fish pond have been allocated through local market mechanism within the villages. Since the reform, fishery and livestock sectors have significantly increased their output values. as grain production's share of total agricultural output has declined, meaning that high-value products have come to contribute more and more to the income of small household producers. The income of fishery farmers is significantly higher than grain income: farmers' average income in the fishery sector was 19,885 RMB annually in 2018 (China Fishery Association 2019).

China has gradually and experimentally implemented the household contracting system in different regions since the early 1980s. In addition, China's non-grain sectors have implemented commercialization and the marketization since the earliest stages of its agricultural transformation. The market-directed economy is an incentive mechanism. Meanwhile, with the adoption of contracting systems of non-grain sector lands areas, China's fishery production management has been privatized and marketization has been adopted.

China adopted the household contracting system in its non-grain sectors, such as fish ponds. For instance, by 1981, at Nanshui Brigade in Zhujiang Delta 70% of fish pond area had been contracted to individual households (Ruddle and Zhong 1988). The household contracting system differs from the household responsibility system. The household contracting system is management of farming areas for commercialized agricultural production, which are not equally allocated to every rural households. Leasing rights are allocated by market price. The production management of non-grain agriculture has been highly developed by family agribusinesses and rural enterprises.

Land use reform and an open-door policy greatly stimulated farmers' enthusiasm and productivity (Li et al. 2013). The commune system was replaced gradually by a household contracting mechanism, shifting land stewardship from collectively managed farms to individually chartered small plots, and decision making on farmland management was transferred from commune leaders or government officials to smallholder farmers themselves (Li et al. 2013).

3.3.2 *Case Studies: Allocation Efficiency and Property Rights*

A synthesis of case studies follows that analyze allocation efficiency. They examine the allocation efficiency of property rights in facilitating smallholder farmers' increase of income and move on to analyze the impacts of property rights on the industrial development of combinations of enterprises and smallholder farmers.

A 2013 survey of Weisan county in Shandong province sampled 100 rural households. The survey showed that more than 90% of households in the sample engaged in aquaculture production as well as producing crops. Every rural household was allocated a small plot of cultivated land by its village committee. In addition, farmers could lease fish ponds for aquaculture through market allocation.

1, The change in property rights improved efficiency allocation in smallholder agricultural production. The allocation of labor resources was more intensive in the individual farming households that adopted aquaculture. We find that aquaculture and crops typically follow a complementary production pattern. Small-scale pond aquaculture production can play an important complementary role in farmers' household economy. The incomes of farmers who produced fish were significantly higher than the farmers who produced only grain. Small-scale household pond aquaculture production has improved intensification of allocation of labor in the small-scale household peasant economy. In order to gain higher profits, the farmers improved allocation efficiency.

(2) The property rights of the ponds are different from those of cultivated land. The property rights of the land areas belong to village collectives, but the ponds are allocated through public bidding for a lease. The length of lease is important. The freshwater pond fish farmers are the leaseholders, and village committee have the freehold and act as agents that organize and coordinate the public bidding for the leaseholder rights to ponds. The freshwater ponds are complementary assets for the fish

farmers, as they also own leaseholder rights to cultivated land. Associated with the market mechanism, in the later reform period market behavior has driven the reform of property rights toward more privatization compared with the earlier stage.

The fish farmers signed contracts with their village committee, and paid their rental to the village. The length of contract was later extended to 30 years from the original 1 or 5, then 10 years, in the early stage of the reforms. Long-term contracts of 30 years offered more assurance for freshwater pond fish farmers.

Since 1985, heads of villages and members of the village committee in the counties have been elected by farmers and local residents. Within the tenure property rights fixed by contract, with the exception of selling their ponds, the fish farmers have full control of the ponds, including subcontracting or selling the lease, transfer and rent. The leaseholder rights of ponds are allocated through open market and there are four copies of the contracts for the management of ponds during the period of lease: the notarization office, the contractor (fish farmer), the judicature office and the village committee each hold a copy.

The survey shows that there were three different stages of pond property rights reform. In the first stage there was a joint-venture contracting system: several farmers contracted jointly for pond production. In the second stage, the Household Contracting System came into play. Compared with the joint-venture contracting system, the household contracting system improved allocation efficiency, because individual agribusiness can make and retain more private profits and improve output value. Under the long-term contract system, fish farmers are entitled with the possession's rights to use the fish ponds' land areas for the families' business investment. Moreover, compared with the grain sector in China, the property rights of the fish ponds' land areas have different characteristics. The leasing rights of fish ponds' land areas are determined by the price of market mechanism. The allocative efficiency can improve the farmers income.

The public and private features of property rights have helped to reduce transaction costs. Farmers' transaction costs include transportation by truck (driver, petrol), living expenses, information costs (how and where to find suppliers), and a communication costs (phone calls). These costs will exceed revenue for most small-scale family agribusinesses. Under "incomplete property rights" coordination by local government can help transaction small-scale household aquaculture producers to have sustainable development. Coordination by local government is also important in the introduction and evaluation of new species, for instance, with regard to fees for information dissemination and R&D projects. In the 2013 household survey, 15% of the sampled farmers reported producing fish improved in quality through the application of bio-technology.

The property rights of China's collectively owned land is helpful in implementing technological progress with smallholder farmers and small-scale rural entrepreneurs. Technological innovation is normally beyond the capability of individual farmers, but local governments have an obligations to foster local economic development, and they are supportive of R&D projects. The funding of R&D projects will also be supported and coordinated within local governments, including township governments. Complementary economic function offices are located at the township level, for instance, fiscal stations and scientific & technological stations. Implementation of R&D projects and information dissemination can be coordinated by local officials at grassroots level.

Property rights over land have contributed to rapidly improving agricultural productivity, helping family agribusinesses to engage in non-farming sectors. A farm formerly called Integrated Enterprise General Company operated under the Production Responsibility System. It entered into contracts with branch companies in specific spheres of activity and with production teams in the case of fish breeding. The township entered into contracts with the integrated enterprises which in turn fixed quotas for branch companies and teams (Mohanty 2017).

China's institutions play an important role and the government facilitates the operation of the market (McMillan et al. 1989). Since the reform, independent rural households have managed their small plots of land and agricultural production. The advantages of the household management of agricultural production include incentivization and flexibility as well as ease of management. The disadvantages are that the smallholder farmers alone find it difficult to progress their industrial development and to improve their scaled economies. In particular, smallholder farmers found it difficult to make a profit in underdeveloped and developing countries.

3.3.3 Role of Property Rights in Industrial Development

The property rights of collective ownership have helped development priorities at different stages, following China's polices and economic plan. The collective ownership of property rights helped to develop the industrial and scale economies. In recent decades, the local rural economy has developed rapidly in the field of industrial development. Farmers and collective economic cooperation nurtured industrial development. Rural enterprises have also developed the stakeholder business system to organize local smallholder farmers in engaging with local agro-industrial development.

Farming land areas are collectively owned by village committees that have the features of a farmers' association and are organized by local farmers. Starting in 2014, the rural land ownership reform allows farmers to retain the contract rights but to transfer the management rights (Sun et al. 2018). The rural land circulation system is associated with the rural land ownership reform. Land rights confirmation that started with a nationwide pilot implementation in 2011 for the first time issued certificates for contracted land for rural households based on field management, laying a foundation for property rights for large-scale rural land circulation. By the end of 2016 approximately 31.3 million hectares of agricultural land, accounting for 35.1% of the overall contracted land in China, had been transferred in various forms (Sun et al. 2018). The rural land circulation system could boost the scale of development of agricultural sector in China. Additionally, families' private rural firms have partly adopted the approach of rural cooperative agricultural management.

China's husbandry industry started the development of agribusiness and firms in the husbandry industry in the 1970s and 1980s. Market demand has driven the dynamic development of the husbandry industry, following on from productivity improvement of cash grain supply and rising living standards.

China's government has implemented targeted poverty reduction, requiring local governments to work out an effective strategy to tackle local poverty reduction. Targeted poverty reduction aims to work out a development plan for poor individual rural households, seeking to motivate them to participate in the process of alleviating poverty.

Poverty reduction projects need to be planned. The government provides financial aid to support them and China's growth and economic development, as well as government policies have helped the majority of poor people to improve their living standards. Farmers, too, have made efforts to increase their income and make profits through their family agribusiness. There are still some poor people, mainly living in mountain and high-altitude areas where there are severe disadvantages for agricultural production. These areas often have natural advantages in developing special agricultural products, including fruits, tea and herbs, oil of seeds and so on. Central government carried out an overall deployment solution: "Development of Special Industries to Target Poverty Reduction."

Kang Bao county is the key exemplar county for government implementation of its poverty reduction plan. The county is located around Zhang Jia Kou city in Hebei province, and is very dry land, not suitable to be sown for grain farming. The county includes 15 towns, and HanXin Husbandry Enterprise (Han Xin Mu Ye) has ten farm plants. The enterprise rented land for a 50-year term to build up farming plant and enterprises (Liu and Yu 2017).

The industrial development of livestock has driven the development of the agribusiness value chain, notably chicken production, which includes production, R&D, processing of chicken, cold storage and logistics, transportation and supply chain. The integrated industrial development of agribusiness has helped local farmers to increase their income. The Industrial Development Fund of the state's poverty regions has provided 70 million RMB to develop the agribusiness with the firm as stakeholder (Liu and Yu 2017). The enterprises' and cooperatives' shareholders have accepted agreements with 115 local poor farmers for three years, and state fiscal funds for poverty reduction have supplied 690,000 RMB to invest in the development of chicken agribusiness. These farmers are able to share 12% fixed profits (Liu and Yu 2017).[1] The poor rural households can sign the agreements again for further cooperation. Family agribusinesses can be stakeholders involved in the value chain with local large-scale rural enterprises, a key development trend to enrich small family agribusinesses. The farmers have the right to contract out their land to the mangers of large-scale rural enterprises, and because they are the leaseholders of the lands they can share the profits from the large-scale rural enterprises as stakeholders in the value chain of agribusiness.

3.4 Summary

Different developing countries and transitional economies have different economic growth paths to solve the challenges of development. One country's successful path may not work for another. However, there is a

[1] "One Poor County's Cooperation with One Rural Enterprise," *China Farmers Daily*, June 23, 2017.

principle factor in the economic growth: efficiency needs incentive property rights for improvement of agricultural productivity. The surveyed cases have shown that China's changed property rights have improved the allocation efficiency of its agricultural production and management. China's rapid agricultural growth has played a very important role in the rapid economic growth in recent decades.

The property rights of rural land have significantly improved allocation efficiency in agricultural production and agribusiness management. Firstly, new property rights have secured private profits to help smallholder farmers' agricultural production and management. The incentive property rights for cultivated lands and non-grain farming lands have improved allocative efficiency for smallholders' agricultural production. In particular, farmers have leasing rights for cultivated land areas, which is an incentive for smallholder farmers to improve their agricultural output. Smallholder farmers have invested the minimum costs of agricultural production and worked hard to increase output, because agricultural production and management have connected with their own private profit.

Secondly, property rights for cultivated land areas and non-grain sector land have helped smallholder farmers to reduce transaction costs. Cultivated land areas have been equally allocated to rural households. Rural village committee control property rights, and local households can lease non-grain sector lands areas for agricultural production.

The property rights of farming lands have secured private profit return. Farmers have management rights over farming land. Smallholder farmers have rights to assign land to farmers' cooperatives, which helps inclusive growth. In many developing countries, there are challenges to agricultural transformation and industrial development. Collective ownership and private leaseholder property rights have helped to bring about structural changes and industrial development in China. the country has carried out a process of diversified and flexible management of the property rights of rural farming land. The property rights of farming land have contributed to inclusive growth in China, and the government has gradually carried out policies to reform property rights toward a secure and legal protection to property rights. Local rural village committees hold property ownership rights of local farming land. Rural villages are "non-governmental organizations," and the management committees of rural village committees are elected by local farmers; the director of the village committee is elected by local farmers too, and he or she needs to re-elected by the local farmers. The length of leases of farming lands has tended to increase, and farmers have leasing and management rights. Amended property rights have contributed to agricultural growth and helped to improve allocation efficiency.

However, many enterprises have contracted with smallholder farmers in respect to land management. These enterprises can help economic scale development and improve industrial development. Further, local farmers' cooperatives have increased agricultural cooperation between smallholder farmers. Agribusiness cooperation and enterprises' investment in farming lands have involved smallholder farmers. The marketization of farming lands has also caused introduced new risks to smallholder farmers. Law improvements affecting contracts on farming lands are necessary to avoid rent-seeking behavior and inefficiency.

References

Byrd, W. A., & Lin, Q. S. (1990). Entrepreneurship, Capital, and Ownership. In W. A. Byrd & Q. S. Lin (Eds.), *China's Rural Industry: Structure, Development and Reform*. New York: Oxford University Press for A World Bank Research Publication.

Chari, A. V., Liu, E. M., Wang, S. Y., & Wang, Y. X. (2017). *Property Rights, Land Misallocation and Agricultural Efficiency in China*. NBER Working Paper No. 24099, National Bureau of Economic Research, Inc.

China Fishery Association. (2019). 2018 China's National Fishery Economic Statistic Bulletin. http://www.china-cfa.org/xwzx/xydt/2019/0605/141.html. Accessed 5 Jun 2019.

Coelli, T., Rao, D. S. P., & Battese, G. E. (1998). *An Introduction to Efficiency and Productivity Analysis*. Boston: Springer.

Dollar, D. (1990). Economic Reform and Allocative Efficiency in China's State-Owned Industry. *Economic Development and Cultural Change, 39*(1), 89–105.

Dutraive, V. (2009). Economic Development and Institutions. Revue de la Régulation – Capitalisme, institutions, pouvoirs, Association Recherche et Régulation, vol. 6.

Eggertsson, T. (1990). The Role of Transaction Costs and Property Rights in Economic Analysis. *European Economic Review, 34*(2–3), 450–457.

Fan, G. S. (2000). Technological Change, Technical and Allocative Efficiency in Chinese Agriculture: The Case of Rice Production in Jiangsu. *Journal of International Development, 12*(1), 1–12.

Farrell, M. J. (1957). The Measurement of Productivity Efficiency. *Journal of the Royal Statistical Society, Series A (General), 120*(3), 253–290.

Gluckstein, Y. (1960). The Chinese People's Communes. *International Socialism, 1*, 20–28.

Gong, T. C., Battese, G. E., & Villano, R. A. (2019). Family Farms Plus Cooperative in China: Technical Efficiency in Crop Production. *Journal of Asian Economics, 64*, 1–12.

Huang, J., Yang, J., & Rozelle, S. (2011). Changing Food Consumption Pattern and Demand for Agri-based Industrial Products in China: Implications for Southeast Asia's Agricultural Trade. In P. S. Intal Jr., S. Oum, & M. J. O. Simorangkir (Eds.), *Agricultural Development, Trade & Regional Cooperation in Developing East Asia* (pp. 162–210). Jakarta: ERIA.

Kung, J., Kai-sing and Liu, S. Y. (1997). Farmers' Preferences Regarding Ownership and Land Tenure in Post-Mao China: Unexpected Evidence from Eight Countries, The China Journal Published by: the University of Chicago Press, No 38: 33–63, https://www.jstor.org/stable/2950334

Laha, A. and Kuri, P. K. (2011). Measurement of Allocative Efficiency in Agriculture and its Determinants: Evidence from Rural West Best Bengal, India. *International Journal of Agricultural Research*, 6: 377–388.

Li, A., Wu, J. G., Zhang, X. Y., Xue, J. G., Liu, Z. F., Han, X. G., & Huang, J. H. (2018). China's New Rural "Separating Three Property Rights" Land Reform Results in Grassland Degradation: Evidence from Inner Mongolia. *Journal of Land Use Policy, 71*, 170–182.

Li, Y. X., Zhang, W. F., Ma, L., Wu, L., Shen, J. B., Davies, W. J., Oenema, O., Zhang, F. S., & Dou, Z. X. (2013). An Analysis of China's Grain Production: Looking Back and Looking Forward. *Food and Energy Security, 3*(1), 19–32.

Li, L. L., Tan, R., & Wu, C. F. (2020). Reconstruction of China's Farmland Rgiths System Based on the 'Trifurcation of Land Rights' Reform. *Land, 9*(2), 51.

Lin, J. Y. (1987). The Household Responsibility System Reform in China: A Peasant's Institutional Choice. *American Journal of Agricultural Economics, 69*(2), 410–415.

Liu, B., & Yu, X. D. (2017, June 23). One Poor County's Cooperation with One Rural Enterprise. *Journal of China's Farmers Daily.*

McMillan, J., Whalley, J., & Zhu, L. (1989). The Impact of China's Economic Reforms on Agricultural Productivity Growth. *Journal of Political Economy, 97*, 781–807.

Mohanty, M. (2017). *China's Transformation: The Success Story and The Success Trap*. New Delhi: Sage.

National Bureau of Statistics of China. (2019). 'Rural Economic Sustainable Development and Rural Revitalization Stride – 13th Series Report of China's Achievement for Economic and Social Development with 70 Years', (Beijing: National Bureau of Statistics of China), 7th August 2019, http://www.stats.gov.cn/tjsj/zxfb/201908/t20190807_1689636.html

National Bureau of Statistics of China. (2020). National Economic and Social Development Statistic Bulletin in 2019 (Beijing: National Bureau of Statistics of China), 28th February 2020, http://www.stats.gov.cn/tjsj/zxfb/202002/t20200228_1728913.html

Nolan, P. (1988). *The Political Economy of Collective Farms: An Analysis of China's Post Mao Rural Reform*. Cambridge: Polity Press.

North, D. C., & Thomas, R. P. (1973). *The Rise of the Western World. A New Economic History*. Cambridge: Cambridge University Press.

Organization for Economic Co-Operation and Development. (2001). *Measuring Productivity-Measurement of Aggregate and Industry-Level Productivity Growth*. Paris: OECD.

Perkins, D., & Yusuf, S. (1984). *Rural Development in China*. Baltimore: The Johns Hopkins University Press.

Putterman, L. (1988). Group Farming and Work Incentives in Collective-Era China. *Modern China, 14*(4), 419–450.

Rathnayake, R. M. A. K., & Amaratunge, S. P. P. (2016). An Analysis of the Technical and Allocative Efficiency of Paddy Farming: the Case of Mahaweli System H. *Sri Lanka Journal of Economic Research Volume, 4*(1), 35–57.

Rodrik, D. (2005). Growth Strategies. In A. Philippe & D. Steven (Eds.), *Handbook of Economic Growth* (Vol. 1, 1st ed., pp. 967–1014). Amsterdam: Elsevier.

Ruddle, K., & Zhong, G. F. (1988). *Integrated Agriculture-Aquaculture in South China, The Dike-Pond System of the Zhujiang Delta*. New York: Cambridge University Press.

Stavis, B. (1974). *People's Communes and Rural Development in China*. Ithaca: Cornell University Rural Development Committee.

Sun, Z. L., You, L. Z. and Müller, D. (2018). Synthesis of Agricultural Land System Change in China Over the Past 40 Years, *Journal of Land Use Science, 13*(5), 473–479.

Thirlwall, A. P., & Pacheco-López, P. (2017). *Economics of Development*. London: Macmillan Education Palgrave.

Yang, Q. G. (2004). *Has China's Economic Reform Improved Enterprise Performance? A DEA Evaluation of China's Large and Medium Enterprises*. ESRC Centre for Business Research, Working Paper No. 287, University of Cambridge.

Ye, J. Z. (2015). Land Transfer and the Pursuit of Agricultural Modernization in China. *Journal of Agrarian Change, 15*(3), 314–337.

Williamson, O. E. (1981). The Economics of Organization: The Transaction Cost Approach. *American Journal of Sociology, 87*, 548–577.

Zhou, Q. R. (2009). Reform in China's Rural Areas: The Changes in the Relationship between the State and Land Ownership-A Retrospect on the Changes in Economic Institutions. *China's Economy*, 337–404.

CHAPTER 4

Inclusive Growth of Rural Enterprises and the Role of Institutions

4.1 Introduction

China's inclusive growth has helped a large numbers of poor farmers to reduce poverty and increased their incomes in recent decades. The scale of the market, driven by supply and demand, has rapidly developed; prices of agricultural products, also affected by supply and demand have simultaneously increased. Farmers make bigger profits from high prices of agricultural products. When large numbers of farmers are poor, production costs of agricultural products are low as are the prices of agricultural products. There is a common economic phenomenon that the majority of the population of developing countries live in rural areas and earn their livelihood through agricultural production. The average income of rural residents was below the poverty line, in terms of the World Bank's standard of poverty in 1979. The declining trend of poverty incidence, if measured by the international standard—$1 a day per capita in 1985 PPP$—is very clear. It dropped from about 60% in 1978 to less than 40% in 1985 (Zhang 1993).

The development of rural enterprises has been an accelerator in China's rural industrialization. China started to develop its small rural industrial enterprises in the 1970s. Sigurdson (1975) used two field visits to China in 1971 and 1973, and recorded that rural areas in most provinces were dotted with hundreds of thousands of small rural industrial enterprises most of which served very limited local markets. At the same time, rural industry was playing an important role in the social transformation of the

L. Sun, *Economic Growth and Development*, Palgrave Studies in Economic History,
https://doi.org/10.1007/978-3-030-46099-0_4

Chinese countryside and was contributing considerably to rectifying the imbalance between urban and rural areas (Sigurdson 1975). Markets have expanded rapidly since the 1980s. During this time, rural enterprises and small family agribusinesses have driven the development of markets in agricultural products, a high-value food processing industry and the service and industrial sectors.

China's institutions' have contributed to the rapid development of rural enterprises and inclusive growth during the era of economic transformation. China's collectively owned rural enterprises (i.e. the town and village enterprises) developed dramatically between the 1980s and 1990s. During this period, private rural enterprises gradually developed during the 1990s, then increased rapidly in 2000s. Institutions have fostered the diversified development of rural enterprises.

The development of rural enterprises has mitigated the disparities between rural areas, and facilitated rural and urban integration in the past three decades. During this period, consumption of and market demand for high-value agricultural products and high-protein food have increased. The diversification of consumption is a consequence of rising incomes—large numbers of rural and urban residents have increased their income, and more work opportunities have been created by the dynamic development of agribusiness and rural enterprises in China. The development of agribusiness enterprises has been important in integrating agricultural commercialization and rural industrialization, which jointly upgrade the value of agricultural products, so stimulating agricultural industrialization. In China, supporting specialty farmers' cooperatives and leading enterprises have enhanced agriculture, to the benefit of farmers' income, rural development and modernized agriculture (Chen et al. 2009).

This chapter analyzes how China's inclusive growth of agribusiness and town and village enterprises has contributed to growth, and helped to absorb surplus rural labor. China's agricultural transformation has been combined with commercialization, rural industrialization and rural–urban integration. The development of China's agribusinesses and rural enterprises is an effective development approach to accomplish agricultural modernization, commercialization and rural industrialization.

Some developing countries have been undertaking rapid progress in urbanization, but urban poverty and urban slums are challenging. There are large numbers of surplus rural workers in rural areas in developing and underdeveloped countries. Inclusive growth is a concept that advances equitable opportunities for participants during economic growth, with benefits incurred by every section of society. For growth to be sustainable and effective in reducing poverty, it needs to be inclusive (Andrew and Ostry 2011).

The increase in inclusiveness in Brazil, Mexico, Malaysia and Thailand has come from growth as well as improvement in equity, but growth has not been fast enough to benefit the entire population in the way that it has in China (Anand et al. 2013). China has undergone a rapid economic transformation, with the movement of large numbers of rural migrants from rural to urban areas, but the development of rural enterprises has helped to create many work opportunities for potential rural migrants.

Inclusive growth in developing and underdeveloped countries needs national government to implement effective policies to foster markets and rural enterprises development. Wade (1990) directed attention to the way allocation decisions were divided between markets and public administration and the synergy between them. Institutions can facilitate inclusive growth. The policy underpinnings of sustained, high growth create an environment for high levels of investment, job creation, competition, mobility of resources, social protection, equity and inclusiveness (Anand et al. 2013). The role of China's institutions has been to promote the rapid development of rural enterprises. China is a regionally decentralized developmental state, where government plays a major role in development (Chen et al. 2019). Coordinated urban-rural development has been national policy since 2003, and China began to experiment with integrated urban–rural development in 2006 (Chen et al. 2019).

The agricultural sector is the economic backbone of many countries: the majority of their populations live in rural areas. These rural households depend on traditional agricultural production to make their living before the countries progress towards industrialized economies, as in India, Brazil, China and African countries. Smallholder farmers in many developing countries often lack funding to start agribusinesses and to adopt new technology; where pro-poor policies are absent, there is no effective support for loans or financial aid for smallholder farmers. A World Bank survey in 1994 reported that 92% of employees of collectively owned or state-owned farms did not want to become private farmers. The main reasons were difficulties with the purchase of farm inputs (60% of respondents) and insufficient capital (74%) (Brooks et al. 1996). The institutional role is important to develop inclusive growth, which is crucial for smallholder farmers in the developing countries.

This chapter is structured as follows: Sect. 4.2, Inclusive Growth of China's Town and Village Enterprises; Sect. 4.3, The Role of Institutions in Inclusive Growth of Rural Enterprises; Sect. 4.3.1, Local Government's Role in the Inclusive Growth of Agribusiness Enterprises; Sect. 4.4, The Role of Rural Enterprises in Inclusive Growth; Sect. 4.5, Inclusive Rural Enterprises in Rural and Urban Integration; Sect. 4.6, The Role of Institutions in Inclusive Growth of Agribusiness; Sect. 4.6 is a summary.

4.2 Inclusive Growth of China's Town and Village Enterprises

China's town and village enterprises illustrate the features of local social enterprise organization and inclusive development entrepreneurship (Sun 2015). One of the objectives for inclusive growth is to improve living conditions and increase the food consumption of poor people. Under the relative definition, growth is pro-poor if and only if the incomes of poor people grow faster than those of the population as a whole; that is, inequality declines (Dollar and Kraay 2002). The challenge for policy is to combine growth-promoting reforms with the right policies to assure that the poor can participate fully in the opportunities unleashed, and so contribute to that growth (Ravallion 2004).

The development pattern of town and village enterprises have features of inclusive growth. Firstly, the people of the town or the village set up town and village enterprises and own the firm collectively during its early development stage (this was the normal process in the 1980s) while collective ownership management dominated across the country. Town and village enterprises are characterized by inclusive development entrepreneurship. The characters of China's town and village enterprises are different from China's private firms, owned by individuals, and state-owned enterprises. Town and village enterprises refer to the typically rural industrial business unit that belongs to all the residents of a rural community, where it is also usually located (Che and Qian 1998). From 1985 to 1996, the share of town and village enterprises in gross industrial output expanded from 14.6% to 27.8%, whereas that of state-owned enterprises (SOEs) shrank from 65% to 28.5% (Jefferson and Rawski 1999). In 1984, the central government of China began to explicitly encourage the making and development of town and village enterprises; in the following decade,

6.06 million town and village enterprises, employing 105.8 million people, were founded (Yang 2016).

The inclusive growth framework allows for the analysis of growth, poverty and inequality in a coherent manner. Each of the three mentioned components can be quantified in terms of their impact on growth inclusiveness (Kireyev and Chen 2017). China had a large number of farmers who suffered poverty in 1980s, when the central government accelerated rural industrialization. The industrial department of local government could help to support local farmers to increase their income but it could hardly create enough work opportunities to solve the massive poverty directly. Rural enterprises and markets could create more work opportunities and increase the income of farmers to reduce pervasive poverty. Town and village enterprises stem from local government's sector of rural industry at grass-root level. They implemented the collective economic system operated by local governments at its infant development stage in 1980s. In the process of decollectivization, the partial transformation from people's commune to household–collective organization offered the opportunity to develop collective enterprises under the jurisdiction of the recently established towns, townships and villages, which later evolved into the well-known township and village enterprises (Yang 2016).

The collective management of local rural enterprises has advantages in the sources of growth, including collective land areas, workers and markets when economic transformation was at its early development phase. The advantages of local collective enterprises include low production costs, collective lands areas, large rural surpluses of labor and local resources during the early development phase.

Employment grew from 28 million in 1978 (7% of the workforce) to 140 million (25% of the workforce) in 2005 (Dowling 2008). In addition, low production costs helped the local development of towns and village enterprises in the early stage of the economic transformation. Despite the three-cornered conflict of interest between peasants, village cadres and the township governments in the implementation of rural reform, the new configuration of authority in villages, as embodied by the emergence of private entrepreneurs as village leaders, seems to present a positive-sum game in which all principal players get what they want (Yang 2016).

Secondly, market-driven agribusiness development is one of the key features that fosters inclusive development entrepreneurship in China's rural areas. Farmers and local officials are stakeholders in the management of rural enterprises. On the one hand, farmers have management rights over rural land, assured by binding legal contracts. And the farmers are also members of the collective economic corporation. As the leaseholders of the land, the farmers share the profits of business from town and village enterprises. On the other hand, the village communities, as collective economic organizations, have obligations to manage town and village enterprises as well. The heads of village communities often played the role of managers of town and village enterprises in the 1980s.

Thirdly, the ownership rights belong to all residents of the community, instead of the managers of town and village enterprises or the community government. The ownership of the town and village enterprises is defined by the Regulation on Township and Village Collective Enterprises of the People's Republic of China, (Che and Qian 1998). China's town and village enterprises played an important role in creation of employment opportunities for the enormous numbers of rural surplus workers and mitigated the income inequality gap between rural and urban residents.

> Assets of the town and the village enterprises are owned collectively by the whole of rural residents of the township or village who run the enterprise; the ownership rights over the enterprise assets shall be exercised by the rural residents meeting (or congress) or a collective economic organization that represents the whole of rural residents of the township or village. (Che and Qian 1998)

Town and village enterprises had many more rights of autonomous decision-making. A part of the charges they levied were used to support the running costs of the community government, the rest supported communal social welfare programs and infrastructure projects, which benefited the ownership-village residents (Chang and Wang 1994).

Fourthly, market prices are affected by demand and supply. And market forces turn up commercial opportunities and competition, in which technological innovation has become an important factor in China's agribusiness. Markets are not efficient in that allocation of resources by price does not reduce inequality of inclusive growth. China's institutional role facilitates inclusive growth in mitigating inequality and helps development and poverty reduction in the early development stage when the markets are at the initial development stage.

The rapid development of local rural enterprises has contributed to the value chain and industrial development during China's economic transformation. Town and village enterprises contributed more than 55% of industrial output, more than 30% of GDP and more than 50% of exports (Dowling 2008). China's town and village enterprises have helped smallholder farmers to upgrade their value chain, and they mitigated inequality through collective business management when the majority of smallholder farmers were producing low-value agricultural products and many farmers were in poverty in the1980s and 1990s.

There were only small numbers of private enterprises in rural areas. Town and village enterprises proved to be efficient allocators of land, labor and agricultural resources in the initial markets for the new commercialized products at the early stage of economic transition in China.

The Regulation on Township and Village Collective Enterprises also stipulates rules for the distribution of after-tax profits of town and village enterprises (TVEs): "The part retained by the enterprise should be no less than 60% of the total and should be arranged under the enterprise's autonomous decision (Che and Qian 1998)".

The remarkable development of China's town and village enterprises is widely recognized, and rural industry is the most dynamic sector and the main engine of growth. Rural enterprises formed the most dynamic segment of the non-state sector, accounting for 36% of the national industrial output in 1993, up from 9% in 1978. Within the rural sector, town and village enterprises account for about three-quarters of rural industrial output (Che and Qian 1998).

4.3 The Role of Institutions in the Inclusive Growth of Rural Enterprises

China's institutions have contributed to inclusive growth. This section analyzes the role of institutions in the inclusive growth of agribusinesses and rural enterprises. Rural enterprises are important sources of China's inclusive growth in the past four decades. Recognizing that smallholder farmers lack resources and competitive strength in markets, local government facilitated the inclusive growth of agribusiness enterprises and the rapid development of China's town and village enterprises. The institutional role was to foster inclusive growth's factors, and the local collectivized enterprises have benefitted from local government intervention. China's private rural enterprises have gradually developed the predominant position the hold at this later development stage. The majority of collective town and village enterprises have changed to rural private enterprises, a transition helped by local government.

It is important to highlight that market forces have played a crucial role in town and village enterprises' success. Neoclassical economics focuses on the economic exchange process itself, driven by "sovereign" consumers and producers. There is a strong reliance on the market as self-equilibrating, and it is assumed that the collective action of self-interested economic agents will produce a socially beneficial outcome for all (Coase 1992). Getting prices rights is an essential part of the analysis of institutions, and thus the evolution of institutions is a direct result of relative price changes. The market acts to coordinate the behavior of individual agents through the price mechanism, i.e. prices are set so as to bring demand and supply into equilibrium within each market. China has carried out policies to support rural industrialization and upgrade its industrial chain as well enable structural changes in its agricultural sector.

4.3.1 Local Government's Role in Inclusive Growth of Agribusiness Enterprises

Inclusive agribusiness development has been associated with the features of national-scale collective management and industrial development. Because "collective ownership" integrates local government activities and agribusiness activities, local government may better serve the interests of the national government, and thus collective ownership may have advantage in utility of local public goods provision through coordination of local resources. Local government has facilitated the establishment of property rights in the rural transitional economy, being substantially involved in their reform.

In China, there are five administrative hierarchies at central, provincial, prefecture, county and township levels. In addition, village committee structure lies below the township level. While it does not belong to the formal administrative hierarchy, the village committee actively participates in all decision-making on public services and economic matters at grass-root level.

In China, the decentralization of state organizations allows local officials operate at the grass-root level, very close to local farmers. Decentralized government structure is a precondition for agribusiness and rural enterprise management. Central government departments pass down policies to local governmental departments, though each region or layer is self-sufficient and autonomous in coordinating economic departments at local levels. All economic sectors can be coordinated within the township, and complementary tasks along specialized function lines are coordinated across departments within each township. For instance, the government departments of finance, justice, agriculture and so on all exist in township level. In addition, the village committee structure falls below the township level. Township governments have played an important role in the development of the town and village enterprises.

Local economic development has been significantly driven by rapid development of local rural enterprises. Local governments can exert considerable influence on financial institutions at the local level. A key function of county governments is to coordinate economic development between prefecture government and township governments. County governments are responsible for coordinating the relationship along specialized functional lines within their region. Town governments maintain different economic departments, including agriculture, commerce and industry, rural construction, general affairs, documents and statistics, finance, justice, family planning, civil administration, education and health, and village peoples' committees. Ferris and Gawande (1998) reported the importance of coordinated government policy from their studies of cases when emerging countries are stuck in a low-wage equilibrium because of a coordination failure.

Nevertheless, China's town and village enterprises carry out the functions of social enterprises whereas local government have been regarded as business corporations (Oi 1999). The role of local governments was even more important in the early development stage between the 1980s and the early 1990s, when markets were not functioning well and private enterprises in rural China were less developed. Chinese local governments have powers to coordinate economic development and allocation of resources through collective town and village enterprises, particularly at the infant stage of market economy reform. Leaders and managers of rural communities had a clear social mission through the development of village cooperatives as collectively-owned enterprises (Zhu et al. 2015).

The rapid growth of TVEs demonstrates that institutions have contributed to their success as part of China's economic transformation. The market acts to coordinate the actions of individual agents through the price mechanism, and prices are set so as to bring demand and supply into equilibrium in each market. In the earlier period of reform, TVEs were mainly producers of consumer goods, and price was an important factor in their rapid growth.

Success in remedying a severe shortage of consumer goods at a high profit rate of industrial products contributed to the prosperity of TVEs. An important factor of market economic reform on the prices of commodities was the dual-track price system in the early economic transition from a planned economic system in China. One of achievements was the dual-track price system to speed up the structural changes in the economic transformation and allocation of market in resources. The dual or two-track price system allows the commodities of the same type to be sold at two different prices, a national command price for planned output and a market price for the commodities. The dual-track price system helped the development of TVEs when two different prices were co-existent for the same type of commodities in the same period. The puzzle of TVEs efficiency as well as the paradox of local corporatism was embodied in a government–business partnership with both a positive function of public alliance for wealth creation and a negative function of private collusion for wealth transfer. The key to both the puzzle of TVEs and the paradox of local corporatism lay in China's dual-track reform paradigm (i.e. enterprises which fulfilled their planned production were allowed to sell surplus output at market prices, although their planned production was sold at prices set by the state) (Li 2015).

Local officials of villages communities were members of collective organizations, and they helped to manage TVEs before they were restructured to private rural enterprises. Since 1985, the private sector has been the most dynamic source of industrial output growth. In recent decades, private enterprises have outpaced the state-owned sector and the collectively owned TVEs. The persistent growth differential has translated into a significant shift in the composition of industrial output by ownership type.

4.4 The Role of Rural Enterprises in Inclusive Growth

Many economists contend that agriculture is a means of contributing to the development of industrialization. The key role of agriculture is that surplus capital and labor are transferred from agriculture to industry to support capital accumulation for industrialization. Thus, economic growth needs to transfer surplus capital from the agricultural to the non-agricultural sector. Population growth creates surplus labor in developing countries, mostly in rural areas; China's agricultural sector maintained hundreds of millions of surplus workers. According to Lewis (1954), a dual economy consists of two sectors: a backward, predominantly rural sector, and an advanced, well-developed capitalist sector where the market operates reasonably well and exchange takes place. In the past several decades, many developing countries have made the attempt to transform their agricultural sector to an industrial sector. In China, the population grew from 575 million in 1952 to 963 million in 1978, of which the rural population accounted for 81% (Putterman 1993). The large number of surplus rural workers had been employed in traditional agricultural methods, but industrial development needed skilled rural workers to transfer into the industrial sector.

A dual economy of rural and urban development was the key problem for economic transformation during the process of urbanization and industrialization in the 1980s in China. Town and village enterprises provided an effective way to help to solve the dilemma of the dual economic structure. The TVES helped to absorb the enormous number of rural migrant workers and to increase farmers' income during the process of rural transformation and urbanization.

Agricultural development itself is crucial in improving living standards and economic development. Investment in agribusiness can improve agricultural productivity and plays an important role in promoting the transformation of a traditional to an industrialized (modernized) agriculture. Lyu et al. (2019) analyzed rural migration over a 30-year period and found a clear link with unemployment, not with better income in urban areas or poor rainfall. Thus, policy interventions needed to support the generation of employment opportunities in rural areas to reduce migration flow to urban areas.

There is an assumption that poor rural workers are unable to invest in agribusiness when low wages or severe poverty severely are present in the local rural society. Under this postulate, consumption and market demand for high-value agricultural products is very low. The profit of agribusiness would be marginal, although there are some private agribusinesses in less-developed rural areas. The value chain of agribusiness and industrial development can help farmers to make more profits, but upgrading the value chain of agricultural and agricultural industrialization needs to be accomplished at a national scale during the initial development stage in developing countries.

China's economic development has progressed through economic growth factors toward its industrialized economy at a national scale.

Table 4.1 Production growth in agriculture, industry and TVEs (%)

	1970–78	*1979–84*	*1985–95*	*1996–2000*	*2001–05*
GDP growth	4.9	8.5	9.7	8.2	9.5
Agriculture	2.7	7.1	4.0	3.4	3.9
Industry	6.8	8.2	12.8	9.6	10.7
Non-farm rural enterprises (TVEs)	n.a.	12.3	24.1	14.0	

Source: Dowling (2008)

Table 4.1 shows that town and village enterprises had a higher growth rate than the agricultural and industrial sectors between 1970 and 2005.

It is predicted that the largest urban population growth will be China, India and Nigeria by 2050, and India is projected to add 404 million urban dwellers, China 292 million and Nigeria 212 million (the United Nations 2014). China's development strategy of rural and urban integration has helped nearly 30% of China's farmers move out of rural areas into cities or towns, but also has significantly absorbed surplus laborers. The development of rural and urban integration continues to be a main driver of Chinese urbanization; steering small towns' and cities' development toward economic and environmental sustainability has become a key development priority in the country. These smaller urban settlements will become the key areas to absorb rural immigrants.

Table 4.2 shows that the development of rural industry created abundant work opportunities for the massive number of rural migrant workers, particularly in the 1990s. Rural enterprises created ever-increasing numbers of opportunities in the 1990s during the acceleration of China's rural industrialization. The number of employees of private rural enterprises increased from 16.04 million in 1990 to 41.22million in 1997. The numbers of employees of TVEs increased from 92.65 million in 1990 to 91.58 million in 1997. Like other developing countries, a dual economy of rural and urban development was the key development dilemma for economic transformation and progressing industrialization. China's town and village enterprises provided an effective way to mitigate the development dilemma of the dual economic structure. In particular, the TVEs helped to absorb the enormous number of rural migrant workers and to increase farmers' income during the economic transformation.

Importantly, inclusive growth has increased the work opportunities through the development of rural enterprises. The small-scale family agribusinesses lacked both funding and technology for kick-starting the

Table 4.2 Growth in rural enterprise employment

	Total TVEs and private & individual enterprises			*TVEs*	*Private & individual enterprises*
	Number of employees(Millions)	*Share of rural labor force(%)*	*Annual growth(%)*	*Number of employees(Millions)*	*Number of employees(Millions)*
1990	108.69	23.0	—	92.65	16.04
1991	113.41	23.7	4.3	96.09	17.32
1992	124.87	25.9	10.1	106.25	18.62
1993	145.42	29.8	16.5	123.45	21.97
1994	148.84	30.5	2.4	120.17	28.67
1995	163.87	33.5	10.1	128.62	35.25
1996	173.67	35.4	6.0	135.08	38.59
1997[a]	132.80	26.9	—	91.58	41.22

[a]Prior to 1997 the official data overstated employment in TVEs and so the 1997 figures are not fully comparable with those for early years

growth of small agribusinesses in the 1980s, especially in less developed and landlocked areas, where there were poor conditions in terms of infrastructure, social services and information technology. However, small-scale family agribusinesses have gradually developed in 1990s. At present, the family agribusiness enterprises play a dominant role in China's rural enterprises. Further, the inclusive growth of business cooperation has developed a stakeholder system, in which smallholder farmers have more opportunities to increase their incomes. These privately owned agribusiness enterprises have adopted new business cooperation with local farmers. Local farmers can lease their lands to become employees of large-scale private agribusiness enterprises.

4.5 Inclusive Growth of Enterprises in Rural and Urban Integration

China has undertaken urbanization on an unprecedented scale: the proportion of the population in towns and cities has increased to 58.52% in 2017 from 10.64% in 1949 (National Bureau of Statistics of China 2018). In 1949, when the People's Republic of China was founded, 89% of the population lived in rural areas. By 2017 more than 800 million people lived in cities and towns 2017 (National Bureau of Statistics of China 2018). China has adopted a development pattern of rural and urban integration. Rural and urban integration has created enormous work opportunities to rural migrant labor during the process of urbanization. In addition, rural and urban integration has mitigated the level of inequality between rural and urban areas; inclusive growth has created incomes for rural migrants.

China's agribusiness and rural enterprises have played important role in China's inclusive growth. The successful development of agribusiness enterprises has helped China's agricultural transformation and has facilitated the reduction of inequality between rural and urban areas.

Rural and urban integration highlights the sustainable development that aims to coordinate development of big, medium and small cities and towns, and new rural communities. The core of this rural and urban integration is ensuring that the development should not be at the expense of agriculture, food production and the environment. The strategy acknowledges farmers and rural areas as crucial participants in the integration, and there is equal development of urban and rural areas in terms of infrastructure and public services, such as water irrigation, water sanitation, road and transportation, energy, information and the communications network.

China's unprecedented scale of urbanization over the past three decades has followed an inclusive development pattern in cities and towns. This development strategy has reduced poverty. Town and village enterprises have provided a linkage of industrial and services sectors. Although the enterprises created large numbers of surplus rural workers over the period of 30 years, the inclusive development of towns has provided opportunities of increased income for rural workers and helped to solve poverty. Inclusive development of rural and urban integration develops rural communities, township enterprises, rural labor and urban development.

The benign process of urbanization has been of fundamental importance in improving the livelihood of Chinese farmers. China has implemented rural–urban integration in the course of its urbanization. China's urbanization is defined terms of "*cheng*" (cities) and "*zhen*" (towns). The town is the link between rural and city areas. China's urbanization has gradually accelerated since 1990. The proportion of the population in towns and cities increased from 17.9% in 1978 to 52.6% in 2012 (National Bureau Statistic of China 2013). Between 1980 and 1990, the phenomenon of "the tide of migrant workers" has been driven by the dynamic development of TVEs in China that pushed the expansion of urbanization and accelerated its progress of industrialization.

The main challenge of the next decade was how to effectively absorb mobilized rural migrant workers moving into urban China, and how to generate higher income and better living conditions for the increased number of urban residents. In the context of sustainable development of the economy, the development approach was one of equality, aiming to mitigate income disparity between urban and rural areas. China had worked out its industrial development to create more work opportunities in the context of a development pattern of rural and urban integration. Income disparity between these two areas declined: the ratio of urban to rural income was reduced from 2.4 to 1.7. After 1985, the ratio started to rise and by 1994 the income of urban residents was 2.6 times that of the peasants, which represented the widest gap since 1978 (Zhang 1993).

China's urbanization was clearly indicated by the scale of rural workers migrating to cities from rural areas during this period. There were about 269 million rural migrants in 2013. And more than 166 million rural migrant laborers worked away from their home villages or provinces, of whom 79% were mobile rural migrants (National Bureau of Statistics of China 2014). The development of small cities and towns has enabled rural migrant laborers to return to the agricultural sector and their farmland if they are unable to find a suitable urban job.

Over the past two decades, this mobility of rural labor has become a feature of China's urbanization. The development of small towns has played a vital role in rural and urban integration in the process of urbanization as well. Importantly, TVEs have contributed to rural and urban integration through the development of rural industrialization and urban enterprises (Sun 2015).

4.6 Summary

This inclusive growth has helped China's to solve its development dilemma in the era of economic transformation. China was facing a huge challenge of economic transformation at the start of the 1980s when approximately 80% of the rural population was working in grain production: how to absorb a very large rural labor surplus displaced by agricultural transformation. The development of town and village enterprises successfully promoted large-scale rural industrialization, which enabled farmers to transform into skilled rural laborers specialized in processing agricultural products and working in local agricultural industrialization firms. China's TVEs have played a crucially important role in rural industrialization and state institutions have helped the growth and transformation of agribusiness enterprises based in collective rural enterprises to privately dominated agribusiness enterprises.

However, there are information asymmetry problems, which lead to inefficient management of TVEs. This information asymmetry affects market development in the long term. China's rural enterprises are considered to be an integral part of its rural industrialization. The inclusive development of TVEs provides a linkage between rural and city areas, where enormous enterprises and factories have been founded during economic transformation. This pattern of inclusive development has mitigated the inequality between rural and urban areas. China had one of the largest number of rural residents and farmers among the developing countries four decades ago; the development pattern of China's town and village enterprises has successfully helped to provide an effective solution to the problems of dual-structural economic growth.

The market has been a key driver in the development of agribusiness enterprises. Marketization and privatization have driven the dynamic development of China's TVEs, which have become an important engine of economic growth and has played a vital role in China's economic transformation. China's inclusive development of rural collective businesses management has helped farmers to build up their small-scale agribusinesses when primary agricultural production was dominated by the farming sector and the value chain of agricultural products was not well-established or effective.

Moreover, China carried out institutional reform that provided incentives for farmers' production and the growth of agribusiness enterprises, including family agribusiness management, collective rural enterprises and private enterprises, as well as joint-venture enterprises development over different stages of development.

References

Anand, R., Mishra, S., & Peiris, S. J. (2013). *Inclusive Growth Revisited: Measurement and Determinants.* The World Bank, Number 122. https://www.worldbank.org/content/dam/Worldbank/document/Poverty%20documents/EconomicPremise_July2013_No22.pdf. Accessed Jul 2013.

Andrew, B., & Ostry, J. D. (2011). Inequality and Unsustainable Growth: Two Sides of the Same Coin?. IMF Staff Discussion Note 11/08. Washington, DC.

Brooks, K., Krylatykh, E., Lerman, Z., Petrikov, A., & Uzun, V. (1996). *Agricultural Reform in Russia: A View from the Farm Level.* World Bank Discussion Paper No. 327, Washington, DC.

Chang, C., & Wang, Y. J. (1994). The Nature of the Township-Village Enterprises. *Journal of Comparative Economics, Elsevier, 19*(3), 434–452.

Che, J. H., & Qian, Y. Y. (1998). Institutional Environment, Community Government, and Corporate Governance: Understanding China's Township-Village Enterprises. *Journal of Law, Economic and Organization, 14*(1), 1–23.

Chen, W. H., Ruide, Z., & Liu, G. (2009). Development Model of Rural Industrialization in China. *Asian Agricultural Research, 01*(07), 8–12.

Chen, C., LeGates, R., & Fang, C. H. (2019). From Coordinated to Integrated Urban and Rural Development in China's Megacity Regions. *Journal of Urban Affairs, 41*(2), 150–169.

China's Statistic Yearbook. (2018). Beijing: China's Statistic Press.

Coase, R. H. (1992). The Institutional Structure of Production. *American Economic Review, American Economic Association, 82*(4), 713–719.

Dollar, D., & Kraay, A. (2002). Growth Is Good for the Poor. *Journal of Economic Growth, 7*(3), 195–225.

Dowling, J. M. (2008). *Future Perspectives on the Economic Development of Asia* (Advanced Research in Asian Economic Studies) (Vol. 5). Singapore: World Scientific Publishing.

Ferris, S., & Gawande, K. (1998). Coordination Failures and Government Policy: Evidence from Emerging Countries. *Carleton Economic Papers* 98–03. Carleton University, Department of Economics.

Jefferson, G. H., & Rawski, T. (1999). Ownership Change in Chinese Industry. In G. H. Jefferson & I. Singh (Eds.), *Enterprise Reform in China: Ownership, Transition, and Performance* (pp. 23–42). New York: Oxford University Press.

Kireyev, A., & Chen, J. (2017). Inclusive Growth Framework. In *International Monetary Fund, WP/17/127.* Washington, DC: IMF.

Lewis, W. A. (1954). Economic Development with Unlimited Supply of Labour. *The Manchester School, 22*(2), 115–227.

Li, P. P. (2015). The Puzzle of China's Township-Village Enterprises the Paradox of Local Corporatism in a Dual-Track Economic Transition. *Management and Organization Review, 1*(2), 197–224.

Lyu, H. Y., Dong, Z. C., Roobavannan, M., Kandasamy, J., & Pande, S. (2019). Rural Unemployment Pushes Migrants to Urban Areas in Jiangsu Province, China. *Palgrave Commun, 5,* 92. https://doi.org/10.1057/s41599-019-0302-1.

National Bureau Statistic of China. (2013). Statistical Bulletin of National Economic and Social Development in China in 2012, Beijing: National Bureau Statistic of China, February, 22th 2013.

National Bureau of Statistics of China. (2014). Statistical Bulletin of National Economic and Social Development in China in 2013, Beijing: National Bureau Statistic of China, http://www.stats.gov.cn/tjsj/zxfb/201402/t20140224_514970.html

Oi, J. (1999). Rural China Takes Off: Institutional Foundations of Economic Reform. Berkeley: University of California Press.

Putterman, L. (1993). Continuity and Change in China's Rural Development: Collective and Reform eras in perspective. Oxford: Oxford University Press.

Ravallion, M. (2004, March). Pro-Poor Growth: A Primer. *World Bank Policy Research Working Paper 3242.*

Sigurdson, J. (1975). Rural Industrialization in China: Approaches and Result. *World Development, 3*(7–8), 527–538.

Sun, L. H. (2015). China's Town and Village Enterprises and Its Implications for Sub-Saharan Africa. *International Journal of Technology and Globalization, 8*(1), 29–50.

The United Nations. (2014). 2014 Revision of the World Urbanization Prospects, New York: the United Nations, https://www.un.org/development/desa/publications/2014-revision-world-urbanization-prospects.html

Wade, R. (1990). *Governing the Market: Economic Theory and the Role of Government in East Asian Industrialization.* Princeton: Princeton University Press.

Yang, D. L. (2016). Designing China's Rural Transformation. In C. C. M. Lee (Ed.), *Common Frameworks: Rethinking the Developmental City in China.* Cambridge: MA: Harvard University Press.

Zhang, A. (1993). Poverty Alleviation in China: Commitment, Policies and Expenditures. *The Human Development Report.* http://hdr.undp.org/en/content/poverty-alleviation-china

Zhu, Y., Lan, H., Ness, D. A., Xing, K., Schneider, K., Lee, S.-H., & Ge, J. (2015). Rural Community Development and the Role of Social Entrepreneurs. In *Transforming Rural Communities in China and Beyond-Community Entrepreneurship and Enterprises, Infrastructure Development and Investment Modes.* Cham: Springer International Publishing.

CHAPTER 5

Application of the Combination Development Approach to Economic Development

5.1 Introduction

This chapter analyzes the application of combination development approach to international development in the case of China. China has upgraded from a developing country to an emerging economy through long-term economic growth and development over several decades. China has carried out a pattern of opening up economic development, and accelerated integration with a policy of development linked to the global economic system. China's international development has been strengthened by an approach to development featuring cooperation with international development organizations, developed countries and developing countries as well as underdeveloped countries. China started its economic cooperation with Western countries and the market economy in the early 1970s. China provided development assistance to underdeveloped countries in the 1950s, notably African and South Asian countries. China's government began to emphasize its economic development plans for an opening-up pattern of development from the moment that the New China was founded in 1949. China started to commercialize agriculture based on the collective system, and industrial development on stated-owned enterprises in the 1950s, following the first Five Years Economic Plan over the period 1952–1957. China's economic growth has solved some key development dilemmas at different economic development stages: agricultural and rural transformation was integrated with the development blueprint at every stage.

L. Sun, *Economic Growth and Development*, Palgrave Studies in Economic History,
https://doi.org/10.1007/978-3-030-46099-0_5

The subjects of international development include analysis of economic growth, and polices for development. Objectives of international development include adopting effective and practical approaches to problems of economic development. The United Nations concedes that the Sustainable Development Goals (eradicate extreme poverty and hunger by 2030) are challenging in many developing countries. In particular, some countries in Africa and South Asia face serious problems in reducing poverty in rural areas. Some developing countries and underdeveloped countries have maintained economic growth in recent years, but the transformation has been slow. China had similar development experiences during its economic transformation before its take-off in economic growth, which helped to solve some key development dilemmas in 1990s and 2000s. During this take-off economic growth stage, the majority, extremely poor, rural population improved their livelihood through agricultural development. China's rural enterprises laid the foundation of the country's rapid economic growth and achieved massive poverty reduction on a national scale in this period. China has carried out the greatest project of poverty reduction in a short period in human history. It is among the earliest countries to have achieved the Millennium Development Goals (MDGs). China's economic growth and poverty reduction demonstrates that growth in the agricultural sector is more effective in poverty alleviation than growth in any other sector, because the majority of the extremely poor lived in rural areas between 1970s and 2015. The development of rural enterprises and rural industrialization has contributed significantly to China's sustainable economic development and growth, which is to say its economic transformation, between 2000 and 2015.

China's rural population as a proportion of the total population declined from 82% in 1978 to 71% in 1995 (China's *Statistic Yearbooks*). There was a similar proportion of rural population to total population in India and some South Asian countries as well as in many countries of the African continent around 20 years ago. For instance, there was a 750 million population in rural India, and the rural population accounted for 72% of the total population between 1997 and 1999 (Wang and Ren 2007). Therefore, there have been some similar development challenges in in developing countries and transitional economies.

How can economic growth solve key development challenges in a sustainable way in developing economies? One major development dilemma is that large numbers of poor people live in rural areas and they depend on the agricultural production for their livelihood before any national-scale economic transformation on a national scale. Agricultural commercialization is not well developed, and the majority of smallholder farmers are unable to make profits through accessing global value chains. The improvement of agricultural productivity is not only related to conventional production inputs and technological progress; it also needs commercialization and market prices to be an incentive for agricultural producers.

China had a similar economic problem in that a majority of the population lived in its rural areas before the acceleration of industrialization and urbanization. Successful development needed effective practical approaches at the grass-root level, with feasible polices of economic development implemented at the national and local levels.

This chapter analyzes why the combination development approach of agribusiness and rural enterprises are practically effective development strategies that lead to take-off of economic growth in developing and transitional economies. Existing literature lacks analysis of China's combination development of agribusinesses and rural enterprises from the perspectives of international development. The combination development approach tends to accelerate industrial development in agricultural transformation and rural industrialization. China's combination development approach facilitated its rapid economic growth, and it may show the way to upgrade developing economies to become emerging economies in a short transitional period.

Section 5.2 introduces a definition of combination development approach, agribusinesses and rural enterprises, indicators of combination development contribution to take-off economic growth, and the indicators of economic growth and development for a combination development approach during the sustainable economic development phase. Section 5.3 analyzes methods of development and investment in poverty reduction, as well as methods of participatory rural appraisal applied to the combination development approach in China. Section 5.4 introduces China's development cooperation in agricultural development. Section 5.5 presents a summary.

5.2 The Combination Development Approach and Agribusiness and Rural Enterprises

International development covers a range of subjects: economic growth, alleviating poverty and development issues, and it adopts approaches of practice, research and policy to find solutions to problems of social and economic development. Economic development is central to development, and agricultural growth is a priority in tackling the problems of economic development in many developing countries. Agriculture makes four major contributions to the process of economic development: a product, a factor, a market and a foreign exchange contribution (Thirlwall and Pacheco-López 2017). Currently, a majority of the poor population in developing countries will usually be farmers and rural residents. Therefore, it is important to examine how agribusiness and rural enterprises improve the livelihood of the rural poor and increase their income in a sustainable way.

Food insecurity, hunger and poverty remain major pressures in developing countries, and sub-Saharan Africa is the region worst affected by poverty and hunger, with the highest incidence of rural poverty (IFAD *Rural Poverty Report* 2011). From 1973 to 2009, the agricultural orientation index of official development assistance (ODA) for sub-Saharan Africa was lower than that of the developing world as a whole (Lowder and Carisma 2011). The World Development Report Agriculture for Development's (World Bank 2017) main message was that agriculture-based countries should invest more in agriculture in order to fully capture agricultural potential for growth and poverty reduction (2020) (de Janvry and Sadoulet 2020).

Ending extreme poverty is at the heart of the Sustainable Development Goals agenda. More than a third of the world lived in extreme poverty 30 years ago, and even now almost 10% of people live on $1.90 a day or less (Barne and Wadhwa 2019). However, there are different routes to progress on poverty reduction being carried out in different regions of the world. Africa remains the biggest challenge in eradication of hunger, reduction of rural poverty and improvement of livelihood for small householders. There are various levels of progress in development and change in the continent. Economic growth and poverty reduction have improved in some countries in North Africa and West Africa, where some countries have also undertaken economic transformation. In particular, the challenges of creating an increased number of suitable work opportunities for rural youth are severe. Despite a decline in the extreme poverty rate in sub-Saharan Africa, to 41%, population growth means that almost 400 million people were still living on less than $1.90 a day in 2013, over 100 million more than in 1990. Half the world's people in extreme poverty are in sub-Saharan Africa (World Development Indicator 2017). There are also widely differing achievements on economic growth and development in South Asia, although the World Development Indicator (2017) showed that in South Asia the extreme poverty rate fell sharply, from 45% to 15.

In plain terms, even with substantial progress, considerable challenges remain.

There were 736 million extreme poor in the world in 2015 (Katayama and Wadhwa 2019). The world's population has grown, and though the regional distribution of extreme poverty changes over time, sub-Saharan Africa and South Asia together accounted for 85% (629 million) of the world's poor in 2015 (Katayama and Wadhwa 2019).

Many developing countries have had a moderate level of economic growth and decreased the number of extremely poor since the 1990s. However, few developing countries have upgraded from low income countries into upper middle level income countries over that period. This chapter analyzes development approaches and economic growth at different stages. We will find economic take-offs are rare in the data, limited to a few Asian success stories. Even then, take-off does not appear to be strongly associated with aid or investment in the way the standard narrative would imply (Easterly 2005).

Removing barriers to development needs inclusive growth. Smallholder farmers need help to invest and to handle the risks associated with investment. And small family-based agribusiness enterprises in less developed regions face barriers in their access to international markets. But, to achieve economic take-off strategies of development have to include policies with a national range. Economic growth empowers development when it is based on industries that the largest group of poor population are engaged in at the start of economic transformation. Easterly (2005) pointed out that the classic narrative of economic development—poor countries are caught in a poverty trap, to escape from which they need a Big Push involving increased aid and investment, leading to a take-off in per capita income—has been very influential in development economics since the 1950s.

Often, the barrier to development in developing countries exists because the majority of farmers are small-scale producers, and vulnerable and fringe farmers in landlocked and underdeveloped areas are a big proportion of this group. The possibility of smallholder farmers making a profit through a local agribusiness is much higher than through directly accessing a global value chain. Many developing countries have a similar economic structure in that the agricultural sector is their economic backbone, and the majority of their population live in rural areas with irregular incomes or subsistence wages. In these circumstances, growth of agribusiness cannot help but increase the income of large numbers of smallholder farmers. For example, a developing countries has 80% of its population living in rural areas; the farmers have land to grow their agricultural products. The food for consumption and agricultural products to gain profits mostly will be the work of the 80% farmers, as they have enough land to produce their self-sufficient products. Assuming 10% of this rural population has very low output and fails to produce self-sufficient amounts of food then the remaining 70% draw on their own farmland, and the possibility of creating a large number of work opportunities from that farmland are extremely low.

5.2.1 *Assessments of Combination Development Approaches*

Assessments of indicators of economic growth consider the upgrade from developing to emerging economies. The first approach to economic growth is the take-off development approach. The second is the sustainable development approach. A combination development approach with agribusiness and rural enterprises is important for take-off economic development in developing countries. Consideration of approach is also necessary when measuring relations between economic growth and economic transformation in developing countries and transitional economies.

There are two assumptions of restrictive conditions that detain or slow down rural industrialization. In the case of China, around 80% of the population lived in rural areas in the 1970s, meaning that the rural population was than 700 million. The first assumption is that cooperative agribusiness enterprises could only create work opportunities for 20 million surplus rural workers. Farmers cannot make a profit and price their output to market level, if their agribusinesses depend exclusively on local demand, because the local rural households have their own farmland to produce agricultural products. The second assumptions is that aggregate consumption of rural households cannot significantly affect market prices, because every rural household has its own cultivated lands and the farmers are self-sufficient in food. Moreover, urban consumption of agricultural products and high-value products is limited because the majority of the population has remained in rural areas. Under these two assumptions, the great majority of farmers and rural workers hardly increase their incomes. Prices of agricultural products are not significantly affected by market demand.

5.2.1.1 *Indicators of Combination Development Approach at Take-off of Economic Growth*

Indicators of the combination development approach are the following:

(1) Most smallholder farmers engage in agribusiness. The large-scale commercialization of agricultural products is not well developed. The development of high-value agricultural products is not only related to agricultural input improvement and technology changes, but is also affected by increased consumption of commercialized agricultural products. The majority of the rural population has low or irregular income, and much of the rural population endures extremely poor living conditions. In these circumstances, diversification of agricultural production and production of high-value products can only take place when supported by state funding and development aid. The majority of farmers cannot increase their income through sale of agricultural commodities, because consumption of high-value food products needs a large group of consumers with regular incomes, and there is no such group in most rural areas. In China, the rural population accounted for around 80%, and the urban population proportion only 20%, of the total population before the acceleration of urbanization. So, even though urban residents tended to consume high-value agricultural products, their relatively small numbers could hardly drive large-scale agricultural commercialization and rapid development of agribusiness firms. So, the majority smallholder farmers can hardly drive rapid development of agribusiness at a large scale, and this development barrier obstructs agribusiness and rural industrial development.

There is a development barrier in some developing countries: the import of agricultural products has increased in the past 20 years; economic growth increased but economic transformation has been slow. The number of poor rural farmers has increased. One reason is that consumption and higher prices in markets could not impel domestic agribusiness in the national scale economy.

Diversification and structural change in agricultural production should be driven by consumer and market demand in a long term. But the majority of farmers lack the access to markets that would facilitate growing their smallholder agribusiness. A 70% rural population of smallholder farmers in developing and underdeveloped countries in a pre-industrial society means that the majority of farmers are producing their agricultural products in a traditional agricultural system.

Therefore, development needs dynamic change and agricultural transformation. Agricultural transformation is needed to create more work opportunities in non-agricultural business and industrial development based in rural areas, which could help some farmers to transform into skilled workers in rural enterprises. Further, agricultural commercialization is low in pre-industrial society, and the majority of farmers have no preference to consume competitively priced food. As a result, this development barrier directly obstructs improvement of agricultural productivity, because the new agriculture and new products demand adoption of new technology. New agricultural products and agricultural diversification call for new markets to drive agricultural output value. Technological change and diversification of agricultural products are associated with structural changes. Therefore, the improvement of agricultural productivity needs domestic policy and state institutions to develop rural industrialization and agricultural commercialization as well as creation of ample work opportunities for surplus rural labor.

Dollar and Pritchett (1998) suggested that:

> research into aid, growth, and poverty reduction provides important evidence about making aid more effective. The positive coefficient on the interactive term also means that policy improvements are more potent if a country is receiving aid. Finally, note that government consumption has no significant relationship with growth—important because aid often finances government.

(2) Rural industrialization needs to be integrated with development of rural enterprises. In order to increase the prices of agricultural products, the rural proportion of the population needs to decrease. Reduction of surplus rural labor in poor conditions will decrease the numbers of extremely poverty in rural areas. Suppose there are approximately three-quarters of a 70% rural population engaged in agricultural production, and this 52% proportion engage in agricultural production for 20 years; then rural industrialization becomes important for the surplus rural labor. If 20% of the population becomes surplus rural labor and migrates into urban areas, most of them will have difficulty in finding fitting work lacking as they do appropriate education and skills. Development needs time. Efficient economic transformation needs rural enterprises to be developed to accelerate rural industrialization. Development of rural enterprises can create a large number of work opportunities for surplus rural labor in rural areas.

The question is "How does economic growth help to deal with the surplus rural labor in the run up to the take-off economic development stage?"

(3) Heterogeneity in specification of production can increase prices of agricultural products. For instance, the rural enterprises include a textile industry and manufacturing sector. At the same time, the development of rural enterprises is an effective method of moving to industrial development with a scaled economy. Farmers can transform rural workers into skilled industrial workers in local rural enterprises, as employees.

The assumption of agricultural growth is that the conditions of agricultural production do not change over time; only the number of farmers declines; all the conditions of agricultural inputs do not change for production of same agricultural products, application of technology to agricultural production is also the same, the weather condition is unchanged, and cultivated land areas do not change. Under this assumption, the possibility of increasing prices of agricultural products will be higher, because the supply of agricultural products with 40% farmers should be lower than the supply of grain produced by 52% farmers. Therefore, there are 12% surplus rural workers realized.

In addition, if there are work opportunities for the 12% surplus rural workers in non-agricultural sectors, as employees in industrial development in the local rural areas, allocation efficiency of labor could be improved to increase the output value of agricultural production. Simultaneously, if they are employees of local rural enterprises the surplus rural workers are now consumers of agricultural products. As a result, they increase consumption and contribute to the level of agricultural commercialization in a sustainable way.

(4) Development of agribusiness and rural enterprises with scale economy is important for successful take-off of economic growth. The large numbers of surplus rural workers are employed in rural enterprises and can increase consumption of diversified agricultural products. Importantly, take-off economic growth only can happen when the development blueprint can be put into practice nationally.

In China's case rapid economic growth and development was needed to sustain agricultural and rural transformation and to alleviate massive poverty. Development of inclusive agribusiness enterprises and rural enterprises needed government policies and an active role for a take-off of economic growth to approach a national scale. This is an important note for a successful agricultural transformation and rural industrialization, because small-scale household agricultural production system and family agribusinesses remain the norm in developing countries. Economic transformation needs industrial development to balance agribusiness and rural enterprise development. Rural enterprise development requires 30% of the enterprises to be in non-agricultural sectors in the take-off phase of rural industrial development. These rural enterprises can locate in non-farming areas and the areas linking rural and urban areas, which are not cultivated land. The development of rural enterprises can create large numbers of jobs if a developing country can generate large-scale nationwide industrial development of rural enterprises. Some rural workers are employed in rural enterprises, which can drive local consumption; the increased consumption helps smallholder farmers to increase profits from agricultural production. In addition, agricultural production has seasonal labor features and rural workers can work on their own agricultural production as well as at rural enterprises offering flexible work times, thereby increasing their incomes.

Importantly, domestic policies and institutions are important for the take-off of rural industrial development. In the initial development of rural enterprises, an active local government is important for the development of scale economy. National policies foster market development and incentivize institutions to drive take-off development of rural enterprises at grass-root level nationwide.

Development challenges include the enormous numbers of surplus rural workers being unable to find suitable work in rural areas in the short term. Large numbers of rural workers then move into urban areas, where some of them suffer poverty if they fail to find work. Urban development cannot absorb the enormous number of rural workers when they move into urban areas in a very short term synchronously. The extremely poor rural migrants will cause instability in social development, for as long as their large numbers challenge the transitional economy.

Therefore, the take-off economic stages need to enhance the combination development approach of agribusiness and rural enterprises. In this stage, a large number of rural workers can increase their incomes. One-third of them can increase their income from employment in grass-root local rural enterprises with a national range. Economic growth and the chosen development approach impact on the pace of economic transformation. The combination development approach of agribusiness and rural enterprises helps take-off of economic growth and rural industrialization.

5.2.1.2 Combination Development Approach in the Sustainable Economic Development Phase

Indicators of economic development may suggest transition towards the sustainable stage of economic growth. The indicators include the following:

(1) Agricultural transformation is well commercialized. Cooperation and scale economy drive industrial development in association with smallholder farmers. Enterprises' management can help to upgrade their value chain for both domestic and international markets. Industrial development needs to enhance structural changes in agricultural markets to upgrade value and quality from the global chain.
(2) In rural transformation, social development indicators are important for rural development. Rural transformation needs comprehensive change to education, skills, social welfare and culture. But industrial development cannot substitute for agricultural development at the sustainable development stage, so social development is important in rural transformation. Social development focuses on the need to "put people first" in development processes. Poverty is more than low income—it is also about vulnerability, exclusion, unaccountable institutions, powerlessness and exposure to violence (World Bank 2019). Empirical evidence and operational experience show that social development promotes economic growth and leads to better interventions and a higher quality of life (World Bank 2019).
(3) Combination development approach with rural transformation and urbanization helps integration of rural and urban development, and also mitigates urban poverty and decreases disparity between rural and urban development. Acceleration of industrialization is an indispensable development at the sustainable economic development phase. The agricultural role in economic development is fundamentally important at every development stages. Rising industrialization cannot substitute for the importance of the agricultural sector in economic development. Relations between the

agricultural and industrial sectors need complementary, proportionate development at the sustainable economic growth phase.

(4) Environmental indicators are important factors that should be improved at the sustainable economic development phase. Living standards and food quality demand change dynamically. Environmental indicators include improvement of food safety, improvement of environmental infrastructure and agricultural production and a secure, hygienic living environment.

5.3 Methods of Development and Investment on Poverty Reduction

There is a consensus among development institutes at both international and national levels, as well as among academic and policy makers that public investment and financial aid will contribute to agricultural growth and help poverty reduction (World Investment Report 2009). If the Sustainable Development Goals are to be met by 2030, while the majority of the world's very poor live in rural areas and live by agriculture, development in agriculture is critical.

Developing countries like Kenya, having become highly dependent on foreign aid, face huge foreign debts and cry out for debt relief-and more aid (Njeru 2003). In the past in Kenya, development aid management was carried out by central government. Under this regime, most funding was directed at big projects, meaning it easily caused corruption, while only a small amount of funding was allocated to local rural areas, and that aid did not always reach poor smallholder farmers in a timely manner. Poverty reduction and eradication of hunger in Kenya has made significant progress since the introduction of governmental decentralization, since development aid is allocated by local governments into local rural development, which is helpful to development of smallholder farmers. Asuna (2014) suggested that it is important to create more work opportunities through enhancing private firms and business development in Kenya:

> The overarching challenge Kenya is facing today is to generate economic growth that is more inclusive in order to more effectively reduce poverty

> across the country. To achieve this, it is necessary to stimulate private-sector activity through the creation of an enabling business environment, while enhancing the skills of Kenya's workforce to respond to the demands of the emerging labour market of a transforming economy. (Asuna 2014)

There are uncertainties in assessing whether development aid can be equally and efficiently allocated into extremely poor rural households. Government in developing countries uses some development aid to R&D and the introduction of new technology in agricultural development in rural areas. Further, the introduction of public investment in implementing new technology and R&D into innovative agricultural projects demands local government coordination, and this increases the difficulty of measuring whether and how much development aid flows is being allocated by national governments to appropriate recipients. Development aid alone cannot effectively reduce poverty and hunger in most developing countries. Dollar and Pritchett (1998) assessed foreign aid's impact on poverty reduction and suggested that when properly managed it can make a big contribution toward improvement in people's lives, but recipient countries must move toward sound policies and development agencies must shift away from total disbursements and the narrow evaluation of implementation, and instead create high-impact assistance.

The standard technique for assessing ex-ante the merits of a proposed public investment project is cost–benefit analysis (CBA). It involves identifying all the people likely to be affected by a public project, and then measuring the net impact of the project on each person—the benefits minus the costs in terms of current money income. Using CBA to assess poverty impacts, an appropriate weighting system would be one which places zero weight on net benefits going to households above a poverty line, and a weight of one on net benefits going to households below that line. In this case, the CBA would show the impact of the project on the welfare of the poor, measured in money terms, which would correspond closely to the change in the poverty gap measure of income poverty (assuming the CBA was carried out reliably).

Government can implement a combination development approach to using development aid effectively. It can use development aid to support projects of agricultural development and investment in infrastructure in rural areas and impoverished regions. National government carries out big plans to target poverty reduction, in which the combination development approach gives priority to sustainable development and economic growth, and local governments implement development initiatives at the grassroots. The combination development approach emphasizes government policies to reach take-off in its economic growth through development of agribusiness and rural enterprises to alleviate poverty; that is, it aims to achieve the goals of economic development at micro and macro levels. Combination development is not only intended to tackle poverty reduction at a micro level; its development theme addresses upgrading economic transformation at macro level. Economic development creates suitable work opportunities and increases farmers' income in developing countries and transitional economies at a micro level. Combination development supports economic growth and development to upgrade the national economy of low-income countries to upper-middle income at a macro level. Therefore, it is important to address challenges of development and strategies of domestic development in which the role of government is to implement policies effectively at macro and micro levels.

The research consortium consists of the international academic community and policy decision-making institutes devote to conducting a trans-national inventory and comparative research into agricultural sectors, and national policies on or related to the role of agriculture in achieving the Sustainable Development Goals and poverty reduction. Importantly, understanding the needs of agricultural growth and priorities of poverty reduction should be based on the local context through participation of local government and private sectors.

The World Bank's Development Prospects Group has developed a tool for economy-wide, country-level analysis of medium- and long-run development policies, including strategies for reducing poverty and achieving the Millennium Development Goals (MDGs). A target-based approach related to the achievement of the MDGs has been developed by the World Bank, and goes under the name of Maquette for MDG Simulation (MAMS). The MAMS model is

> a dynamic Computable General Equilibrium (CGE) model that has been extended to cover the generation of outcomes in terms of growth, MDGs, and the educational make-up of the labor force, as well as the interaction of these outcomes with other aspects of economic performance (World Bank 2010).

It combines micro and macro elements, with the goal of developing an economy-wide, model that captures the combined effects of many of the key MDG-related policies and required foreign aid flows that a low-income country can utilize to achieve the MDGs. It analyzes strategies for achieving the MDGs and, more broadly, strategies for growth and poverty reduction in developing countries.

The Chinese take-off economic growth and reducing poverty is a valuable case to apply the combination development approach in analysis of the important role played by the development of agribusiness and rural enterprises. For instance, it is worth considering how China significantly improved the livelihood for a majority of poor farmers and created enormous work opportunities through a series of innovative programs while its institutions were transformed to meet the conditions of the country's policy and to implement an innovative program when markets and market access were imperfect. Institutions and policies determine the economic and political environment within which individuals accumulate skills, and firms accumulate capital and produce output (Besley and Burgess 2003). Hence, institutions and policies should take center stage. However, institutional conditions are also major obstacles for small households' farming production in many developing countries. Therefore, government's role is important in implementing development policies and projects for poverty reduction effectively at local levels. Local governments will necessarily focus on identifying policy and institutional changes that can directly reduce poverty or can improve the mapping of growth onto poverty.

5.3.1 Methods of Participatory Rural Appraisal Applied to the Combination Development Approach in the Case of China

This section introduces the methods of participatory rural appraisal (PRA) as applied to the combination development approach. Combination development involves agribusiness (agricultural commercialization) and development of rural enterprises. The practical implication of participatory rural appraisal (PRA) is to enhance people's participation in rural development. PRA describes a growing family of approaches and methods to enable local people to share, enhance and analyze their knowledge of life and conditions, to plan and to act. It is intended to enable local people to conduct their own analysis, and often to plan and take action (Chambers 1994). PRA enhances local learning, management capacity and skills. It provides timely, reliable information for management decision-making. It involves systematic consultation with the local project beneficiaries and other stakeholders to identify and design development initiatives, signal constraints to participation, and provide feedback to improve services and activities. The purposes of PRA are to identify and trouble-shoot problems and to evaluate a project, program or policy and to provide knowledge and skills to empower poor people during implementation by learning about local conditions and local people's perspectives and priorities to design more responsive and sustainable interventions.

The PRA methods used to analyze combination development in the case of China are:

(1) Family agribusinesses in forest development aim to increase incomes of local rural households. The target group is actively involved in the forest project. The analysis of family forest development through adoption of PRA methods includes preparing and implementing development plans at the village level. Professional farmer associations were created to represent both crop-specific and common interests of producers of crops with good market potential. Farmer associations benefit from markets. Project investments in non-timber forestry production increase the profitability of the related credit packages, while simultaneously reducing environmental hazards by planting perennial trees on some of the most erosion-prone land, in order to replace low-yielding land used for food crops. The development projects strengthen crop-extension and animal-health services, in which the poor and women increase incomes. In addition, the development project carried out numerous small demonstrations of recommended packages on the fields of poor farmers, particularly those of women.
(2) Development of rural enterprises helped the take-off of economic growth at a national level between the 1990s and 2000s in China. PRA was adopted as a methodology in the assessment on combination development approach when international organizations and China's government collaborated on the project of development and poverty reduction to enhance the development of rural enterprises in poor areas to tackle poverty reduction and increase farmer's income in the 1990s. In the1990s, some private rural enterprises had started to develop, and cooperative rural enterprises abruptly developed compared with private rural enterprises. China's town and villages enterprises (TVEs) are typical developments of cooperative rural enterprises located at villages or towns areas in rural areas of China between the 1980s and 2000s. In landlocked regions and mountainous regions, the development of TVEs was slow compared with rural areas in inland regions or in villages and towns near coastal cities and well-developed regions. China's TVEs refer to the typically industrial business unit that belongs to all the resi-

> dents of a rural community where it is also usually located (Che and Qian 1998). Township and a village are the lowest levels of government in China (Che and Qian 1998) and rural village communities and township governments participated in the dynamic development of rural enterprises. The rapid development of rural enterprises changed the landscape of China's industries. It is widely recognized that rural industry is the most dynamic sector and the main engine of growth. In 1978, State-owned Enterprises (SOEs) were 78% of the national industrial sector. By 1993, that percentage had shrunk to 43%, with non-state enterprises providing 57% of total production. Rural enterprises formed the most dynamic segment of the non-state sector, accounting for 36% of national industrial output in 1993, up from 9% in 1978. Within the rural sector, TVEs accounted for about three-quarters of rural industrial output (Che and Qian 1998).

Box 5.1 states the case of development and poverty reduction in impoverished rural areas in China. This development project was a collaboration between the Leading Group for Poverty Reduction of China, the World Bank and the United Nations Development Program in 2001. Labor mobility has been a key feature of Chinese economic development during the transitional period to industrial development

Box 5.1 World Bank Projects on Poverty Reduction in China
Available evidence indicates that the majority of China's absolute poor are increasingly concentrated in remote and mountainous townships and villages in the western provinces in 1990s. China's National Poverty Reduction Plan has been associated with sustained and significant reductions in the numbers of the extremely poor during the 1990s, will conclude at the end of 2000. The primary purposes of this report are to assess the state of poverty in China at the end of the 1990s, and to contribute to the determination of the most effective and efficiency means of overcoming remaining absolute poverty in the new decade.

Source: *China Overcoming Rural Poverty, A World Bank Country Study* (2001)

at a national level. The World Bank and China's governments implemented the South West China Poverty Reduction Project. The report of the project suggested that agriculture's potential to provide employment has been greatest in cultivation of high-value, labor-intensive crops, horticulture, and livestock production (World Bank 2001). During the 1990s, off-farm employment has also been an important source of new employment, with migration and private and individual enterprises playing a growing part in generating jobs. Poverty programs should recognize these trends and assist the poor in gaining access to migrant jobs and participating in private business either as entrepreneurs or employees (World Bank 2001).

The development projects that attempted to foster enterprise development in poor areas through direct funding have had mixed results. The collaborative project of the World Bank and China's Leading Group for Poverty Reduction aimed to increase farmers' income and reduce poverty as well as creating work opportunities for the surplus rural workers who were living below the poverty line. Box 5.2 shows that the World Bank and Chinese government implemented development projects for rural enterprises and agricultural development in underdeveloped rural regions in the 1990s. This cooperative project was supported by development aid, and the project was community-driven. Local people participated effectively in the project.

Box 5.2 The World Bank's Rural Enterprises Development on Poverty Reduction in China

The World Bank collaborated with China's governments on rural enterprise development in rural areas in north western and northern China in the 1990s.

Fostering Rural Enterprise and Agricultural Development in Poor Areas Small-scale private enterprise (PE) appears to be best suited to the underdeveloped markets of the poor areas. Government initiatives to augment the development and poverty alleviation impact of rural enterprise in poor areas have included the introduction of appropriate technologies, the subcontracting of simple manufacturing or production activities to poor households and villages, and the provision of subsidized credit to enterprises which agree to employ a

(*continued*)

Box 5.2 (continued)

specified minimum number of poor. The recently enacted Regulations on Rural Collective Enterprises, which seek to limit local government's excessive extractions from collective enterprises and protect the rights and interests of such enterprise, are also of particular importance in creating a favorable environment for poor area rural enterprise development.

Source: World Bank (1992)

In Guangxi autonomous region, rural enterprise development in the 1990s created large numbers of work opportunities for surplus rural workers, thus reducing poverty. The development of rural enterprises was mainly directed toward labor-intensive industries. Rural workers had access to low-cost housing in the villages and towns where the rural enterprises were based. Agribusinesses developed included the processing of agricultural products and tree plantation schemes.

China's combination development approach, featuring agribusinesses and rural enterprises, improved incomes for farmers and created off-farm job opportunities through innovative programs. Jin and Qian (1998) suggested that because there are costs and restrictions on labor migration, towns and village enterprises could contribute to raising per capita income through increased local employment opportunities. If mobility were low-cost and without constraints, a local increase in demand for labor would have little effect on per capita income because it would provide employment for persons who otherwise would have migrated.

5.4 China's Development Cooperation in Agricultural Development

Development cooperation activity that aims explicitly to support national or international development priorities is not driven by profit, discriminates in favor of developing countries, and is based on cooperative relationships that seek to enhance developing countries ownership (Alonso and Glennie 2015). Official Development Assistance (ODA) is defined by the OECD Development Assistance Committee (DAC) as government aid that promotes and specifically targets the economic development and welfare of developing countries.

China has enhanced its development cooperation. It comprises ODA, trade, and partnership in development initiatives as well as enterprise development. China has developed technological exchange and training projects on agriculture through South–South Cooperative Development and other intergovernmental agreements on agricultural development with developing countries.

China's has increased its ODA in recent years and has increasing impact on development cooperation with international organizational, and regional development initiative partnerships, such as South–South Cooperative Development and other intergovernmental agreements. Among emerging economies China is the largest development aid provider to some sub-Saharan African countries, and is actively participating in development practices for international poverty reduction.

China started its technical and economic development assistance to some countries in Asia, Africa and Latin America in 1950. Between 1950 and 1977, China experienced primary development stages in technical and economic development assistance to some developing countries in these regions. These agricultural development projects included advice and introduction of new technologies of plant breeding and management. China has had extensive experience in both traditional and modern agricultural technology, and its agricultural technologies, such as hybrid rice, are advanced and have contributed significantly to the country's agricultural growth. One such example is Guinea-Bissau, where China State Farm and Agribusiness Corporation collaborated with the China Hybrid Rice Engineering Research Centre in introducing high-yielding hybrid rice. In 2009 the construction of Chinese-aided agricultural technology demonstration centers commenced in Benin, Cameroon, Ethiopia, Liberia, Mozambique, Sudan, Tanzania and Uganda. Chinese development assistance includes training, production and administrative facilities.

The importance of South–South and triangular in international development cooperation has grown significantly (UNESCAP 2018). South–South cooperation is one of the important drivers of the regional cooperation in Asia and the Pacific and has resulted in increased volumes of South-South trade, foreign direct investment flows and transfer of technology (ibid).[1] Furthermore, emerging economies could provide appropriate technologies that will help to develop agricultural production in developing countries. South–South cooperation largely involves capacity development

[1] "Technological Transfer and South–South Cooperation Key to Food Security in Asia Pacific", UNESCAP, 25 August, 2009, http://www.unescap.org/unis/press/2009/aug/g58.asp

Table 5.1 Gross concessional flows for development co-operation (current $Millions)

Country	*2007*	*2008*	*2009*	*2010*	*2011*
Brazil	291.9	336.8	362.2	482.1	n.a.
China	1466.2	1807	1946.5	2011.2	2470
India	392.6	609.5	488	639.1	730.7
South Africa	108	108.5	99.6	106	146.6

Source: OECD. Development Co-operation Report 2013

Notes: Figures for India and South Africa are based on their fiscal years

Not all information is accessible through the web, so parts of the development co-operation program might not be reflected in these figures

to bridge knowledge or technology gaps, through sustainably enhancing capacities at a number of different level (FAO 2015).[2]

China has been the largest contributor of ODA among emerging economies. The launch of the New Partnership for African Development (NEPAD) and debt-relief initiatives for poor countries have helped in poverty reduction and solving hunger in Africa. China is the largest provider of development aid to Africa among key actors of NEPAD, which has been increasing its impact on African agricultural development.

Table 5.1 shows the estimated gross concessional flows for development cooperation from key partners 2007–2011 (Source: OECD 2013).

Development aid will not work alone, without dynamic economic development. For sustainable development, FDI, trade and business investment can impact on economic growth, which will facilitate poverty reduction through creation of more employment opportunities and increased farmers' income. OECD (2019) states the following:

> Since the start of the aid for Trade Initiative in 2006, donors have disbursed USD 409 billion in ODA to help developing countries build trade capacities. South–South providers contributed USD 9 billion according to OECD estimates. Empirical studies and programme evaluations find that this support is helping developing countries improve their competitiveness, expand and diversify their trade, attract foreign direct investment, and create employment.

[2] "Supporting Programmes for Food Security-South South Cooperation", http://www.fao.org/spfs/south-south-spfs/ssc-spfs/en/

China was the largest provider of development aid to Africa among the South–South cooperation countries between 2005 and 2010. Most official flows are given on concessionary terms and are referred to as Official Development Assistance (ODA). To quality as such, the concessional (or grant) element of the flow must be at least 25%. Only the concessional element of international financial flows really qualifies for the term "aid" (Thirlwall and Pacheco-López 2017). Compared with the OECD countries, China's development assistance to Africa, especially that component aimed at the agricultural sector, has different development assistance aims and has undergone dynamic changes in the past 20 years or more.

Financial assistance/ investment is multi-factorial in approach, and includes investment, trade and enterprise investment in the agricultural sector, which has undergone dynamic changes over the years. China's international development initiative is a combined approach of trade, enterprise investment and foreign direct investment.

(1) China has accelerated its international development initiatives through combination approach with trade in recent decades. Currently, China is already the largest importer of several agricultural raw materials and agricultural-resource products in the world. Free trade is highly prized as a route to peace and prosperity (FAO 2002). In developing countries, particularly in the least developed economies, freer trade in agriculture can raise incomes greatly, be an important source of foreign exchange and act as a catalyst for overall development (ibid).[3] For most countries, food imports are already an important source of supply and will continue to contribute to food security.

China has followed a quota system in international trade since 1985 (Han et al. 2019). China's government founded entity companies which had permission to transact international trade and business around the end of the 1980s and the early 1990s. During this period, there were quotas for the import and export of agricultural products, which the government used to forge international markets for domestic products.

(2) China's enterprise investment and multinational corporations have been involved as a part of the country's development strategies in association with development assistance during its later development stage in development assistance. China's overseas farming investments include private and joint-venture, shareholder cooperation and state-owned enterprises. Originally Chinese state-owned enterprises were the dominant

[3] *World Agriculture: Towards 2015/2030, summary report*, FAO, 2002.

suppliers of agricultural business aid to developing countries. Since the mid-1990s, these have been joined by many private agricultural enterprises, most of which are small and medium-sized. China has carried out a series of supporting policies to expand agribusiness in both domestic and international markets in recent decades.

Under its tenth Five-Year Plan for National Economic and Social Development (2001–2005), China adopted a strategy of international cooperation to strengthen its outward economic development, referred to as its international business cooperation strategy. It has carried out a series of policies encouraging well-established Chinese enterprises and private companies to undertake agricultural investment and development projects abroad in developing countries.

The big-scale companies are leaders in their respective sectors, as they have advantages in R&D, technology and resources both human and capital. The share of state-owned enterprises (SOEs) in the total outward of FDI stock has declined, and it will continue to decrease in the future. Private companies are becoming a major force in outward FDI as they are facing increasing pressures of production costs and profits in domestic markets. More and more private enterprises have developed into large multinational companies in international agribusiness and agroindustry. In addition, private small-and middle enterprises (SMEs) are also increasing their interest in overseas investment.

5.5 Summary

The industrialization process in developing countries cannot be carried out in the absence of agricultural development. Industrialization should increase work opportunities for surplus rural labor at the stage of accelerating agricultural and rural transformation in developing countries and transitional economies.

The solution of the development dilemma is to give priority to rural industrialization at the take-off stage of economic development in developing countries where the majority of the population lives in rural areas. The combination development approach with agribusiness and rural enterprises can help economic growth in developing countries. Agribusiness is very important for agricultural commercialization, and market demand and consumption can drive agricultural commercialization. Transforming large numbers of rural workers into employees in non-agricultural rural enterprises locally can improve allocation efficiency of labor. It can also stimulate consumption of high-value agricultural products, and improve agricultural commercialization at grass-root level. Domestic policies and an active government role are important to the take-off of economic growth at a national level.

Agribusiness is associated with agricultural commercialization, which can increase profit for farmers, and agribusiness can improve technology and agricultural productivity. The development of rural enterprises is an accelerator to industrial development. The development of rural enterprises at a national scale can absorb surplus rural labor. When rural workers increase their income they will be able to spend more on consumption of high-priced agricultural products, hence diversification of agricultural production will increase.

Many developing countries fail to take-off their economic growth. The combination development approach with agribusiness and rural enterprises needs to be implemented at grass-roots for simultaneous national transformation. Policies of economic development should implement domestic industrial development in the early stage of progress toward an industrialized economy. The development of agribusiness and rural enterprises at a national scale can accelerate sustainable rural and overall industrialization.

As the world's second-largest economy and its largest trader, China will play an increasingly important role in investing in agricultural development projects. Agribusiness enterprises and trade will be increasing their role in poverty reduction in developing countries. Since its accession to the WTO, the Chinese economy's integration into the world market has created an interactive network and development agenda of economic activity between China and the rest of the world.

Agricultural growth is critically important to achieving Sustainable Development Goals. Successfully agricultural development is essential to overall economic development and to meeting the ambitious targets for poverty reduction put forward in the Sustainable Development Goals. Agriculture is central to the provision of food and the eradication of poverty and hunger. In the context of international development, agricultural cooperation and agribusiness enterprises as well as agricultural trade will strengthen development practice and research. Official development aid needs to be implemented effectively. Government can play a role in investing in rural enterprises projects to help create work opportunities in rural areas.

Importantly, poverty-reducing development or constraints today control the chances of poorer people to catch up. Previously, official development aid was the major resource for poverty reduction and the eradication of hunger. Now we know that agricultural growth needs commercial investment. Development is not just poverty reduction. Development is the creation of more employment opportunities and increased incomes for rural workers and farmers.

References

Alonso, J. A., & Glennie, J. (2015). What Is Development Cooperation? *Economic and Social Council, ECOSOC Development Cooperation Forum.* https://www.un.org/en/ecosoc/newfunct/pdf15/2016_dcf_policy_brief_no.1.pdf

Asuna, M. (2014). Country Policy Brief-Country: Kenya, Global Partnership for Effective Development Co-operation. http://effectivecooperation.org/wp-content/uploads/2015/12/Kenya-Country-Brief-English-October-2014.pdf. Accessed Oct 2014.

Barne, D., & Wadhwa, D. (2019). *Year in Review: 2019 in 14 Charts.* Washington: The World Bank. Accessed 20 Dec 2019.

Besley, T., & Burgess, R. (2003). Halving Global Poverty. *Journal of Economic Perspectives, 17*(3), 3–22.

Chambers, R. (1994). The Origins and Practice of Participatory Rural Appraisal. *World Development, 22*(7), 953–969.

Che, J. H., & Qian, Y. Y. (1998). Institutional Environment, Community Government, and Corporate Governance: Understanding China's Township-Village Enterprises. *Journal of Law, Economics and Organization, 14*(1), 1–23.

de Janvry, A., & Sadoulet, E. (2020). Using Agriculture for Development: Support- and Demand-side Approaches. A Development Review paper for World Development. *World Development, 133*, 1–31.

Dollar, D., & Pritchett, L. (1998). *Assessing Aid – What Works, What Doesn't, and Why (English).* World Bank policy research report. New York: Oxford University Press Published for The World Bank. http://documents.worldbank.org/curated/en/612481468764422935/Assessing-aid-what-works-what-doesnt-and-why

Easterly, W. (2005). Relieving the 50s: The Big Push, Poverty Traps, and Takeoffs in Economic Development. Assessed 28 Jul 2005.

FAO. (2002). *World Agriculture: Towards 2015/2030 Summary Report.* Rome: Food and Agriculture Organization of the United Nations. http://www.fao.org/3/Y3557E/y3557e00.htm#TopOfPage

FAO. (2015). *FAO's Quick Guide to South-South Cooperation: Fostering Partnerships among the Global South.* Rome: Food and Agriculture Organization of the United Nations.

Han, C. F., et al. (2019). New China's Agricultural Development with 70 Years-Policies Achievement Volume (Beijing: China's Agricultural Publisher).

Jin, H. H., & Qian, Y. Y. (1998). Public Vs. Private Ownership of Firms: Evidence From Rural China. *The Quarterly Journal of Economics, 113*(3), 773–808.

Katayama, R., & Wadhwa, D. (2019). Half of the World's Poor Live in Just 5 Counties. *The World Bank Data Blog*. Accessed 9 Jan 2019.

Lowder, S. K., & Carisma, B. (2011, December). Financial Resource Flows to Agriculture: A Review of Data on Government Spending, Official Development Assistance and Foreign Direct Investment. *Food and Agriculture Organization of the United Nations Working Paper* No. 11–19. Roma: Food and Agriculture Organization of the United Nations.

Njeru, J. (2003). Impact of Foreign Aid on Public Expenditure: The Case of Kenya. In *AERC Research Paper 135*. Nairobi: African Economic Research Consortium.

Organization of Economic and Co-operation Development. (2013). *Development Co-operation Report 2013: Ending Poverty*. Paris: Organization of Economic and Co-operation Development. http://www.oecd.org/dac/dcr2013.htm

OECD (Organization for Economic Co-operation and Development). 2019. 'Multilingual Summaries Aid for Trade at a Glance 2019 Economic Diversification and Empowerment' (Paris: OECD Publishing). https://doi.org/10.1787/18ea27d8-en.

IFAD (The International Fund for Agricultural Development). (2011). Rural Poverty Report. Roma: International Fund for Agricultural Development. https://www.ifad.org/en/web/knowledge/publication/asset/39176373. Accessed Nov 2010.

Thirlwall, A. P., & Pacheco-López, P. (2017). Economics of Development. London: Palgrave Macmillan.

UNESCAP. (2018). *South-South Cooperation in Asia and the Pacific – A brief overview*. Bangkok: United Nations for Economic and Social Commission for Asia and the Pacific. https://www.unescap.org/sites/default/files/SSC_Paper_v04_20180621_FINAL_formatted.pdf

Wang, W. J., & Ren, R. (2007). Indian Healthy System Performance and the Lessons to China. *Health Economics Research*, 2007 (1). Accessed http://xueshu.baidu.com/usercenter/paper/show?paperid=1cdb79819c1ed9e6bf16f1e21ecc8212&site=xueshu_se

World Bank. (1992). *Governance and Development*. Washington, DC: The World Bank. http://documents.worldbank.org/curated/en/604951468739447676/Governance-and-development

World Bank. (2001). *China Overcoming Rural Poverty*. Washington, DC: World Bank.

World Bank. (2010). *MAMS: A Tool for Country Strategy Analysis*. Washington, DC: World Bank.

World Bank. (2017). *The World Development Indicators 2017*. Washington, DC: The World Bank.

World Bank. (2019). *Poverty Continues to Decline, but Pace of Poverty Reduction is Slowing in Central Asia, Infographic: Poverty in Central Asia*. Washington, DC: World Bank.

CHAPTER 6

International Development and Inclusive Development of Enterprises

6.1 Introduction

China has carried out social and economic policies, leading to economic and institutional reforms in the past several decades. The country has achieved a rapid and sustainable economic growth over more than four decades. China is the first developing country to meet the Millennium Development Goals (MDGs) target of reducing the population living in poverty by half ahead of the 2015 deadline. Since China began to open up and reform its economy in 1978, GDP growth rate has been very high. More than 850 million people have been lifted out of poverty (*China Overview*, World Bank 2020).

China has upgraded to an upper middle-income country from the low income country in the past four decades. But its per capita income is still only about a quarter of that of high-income countries, and about 373 million Chinese are living below the upper-middle-income poverty line of US$ 5.50 a day (*China Overview*, World Bank 2020). Large numbers of the Chinese population suffered poverty and food insecurity in 1970s. In 1979, China's per capita income was only US$182, less than one-third of the average in African countries at the time (Lin 2013). China's per capita income was approximately US$9313 annually in 2018 (The National Bureau of Statistics of China 2019). The annual per capita income was calculated from data in China's National Economy and Social Development Statistic Bulletin in 2018 and the foreign exchange rate in 2018. China is

L. Sun, *Economic Growth and Development*, Palgrave Studies in Economic History,
https://doi.org/10.1007/978-3-030-46099-0_6

an upper-middle-income country, in terms of the World Bank's incomes categorization. Farmers' net average income increased to 14617.0 RMB Yuan in 2018 from was 133.6 RMB Yuan in 1978 (Han et al. 2019).

China has accelerated its industrial development during a period of agricultural and rural transformation. The dynamic development of agribusiness and rural enterprises has played a pivotal role in its remarkable progress in agricultural and rural transformation. The development of agribusinesses and rural enterprises has had an enormously positive impact on wages, productivity, wealth generation, social mobility and standard of living in China. It is important to analyze the role of China's agribusiness and rural enterprises in its inclusive growth and economic development. China's unprecedented progresses of industrialization are rooted in its rural industrialization. The development of agribusiness and rural enterprises has been a central part of its rural industrialization. As of 2014, at a national level, approximately 60% of total rural migrant labor had worked in town and village enterprises (TVEs) near their home (Sun 2015).

The development of agribusiness and rural enterprises has largely solved the problem of rural surplus labor and increased income for farmers. China's rural industrialization has driven and been driven by rural transformation and the development of rural enterprises, and by application of industrial development and technological changes in agricultural production.

This chapter analyzes the development of agribusiness and rural enterprises for the inclusive growth model. It recommends the role of inclusive growth of agribusiness and rural enterprises role in international development. There is an obvious feature that a majority of population engaged in agricultural production and lived in rural areas in many developing countries before industrialization and urbanization, for example, China, India, Brazil and many nations in Africa.

China has experienced rapid economic growth and economic transformation. The agricultural and rural transformation has paved the foundation for its overall economic transformation. Given its size, China is a growing market-driven development cooperation with developing countries through trade and investment. It has cumulatively played an important role in agribusiness and enterprises development as well as trade in the developing countries, such as in the regions of South Asia and Africa.

Section 6.2 presents a study of global governance and inclusive development enterprises. Section 6.3 analyzes inclusive growth of agribusiness and industrial development in developing countries. Section 6.4 presents perspectives on theories of development economics. Section 6.5 analyzes governance and bottom-up development approach on China's agribusiness, and Sect. 6.6 presents conclusion.

6.2 Global Governance and Inclusive Development of Enterprises

Chinese inclusive development of agribusiness and rural enterprises has been fundamentally important in increasing the majority of farmers' income and changing these farmers in the rural labor force into participants in industrial development. China's economic growth has significantly contributed to poverty reduction in the past three decades. UNDP states that China has made great leaps in reducing poverty and reaching the benchmarks laid out in the Sustainable Development Goals (SDGs). China has lifted more than 750 million people out of poverty over the last three decades, accounting for four-fifths of all people lifted out of extreme poverty globally (Trankmann, UNDP 2019).

6.2.1 Development and Poverty Reduction in Developing Countries

The number of people living in extreme poverty around the world has declined rapidly. The most widely held and understood definition of extreme poverty, established by the World Bank, defines poverty in strictly economic terms—earning less than $1.90 a day, set by the World Bank in 2015. Globally, 1 person in 10 is undernourished, without enough food to meet his or her dietary needs. Undernourishment is most widespread in sub-Saharan Africa, South Asia, and East Asia and the Pacific (*Atlas of Sustainable Development Goals* 2018: World Development Indicators). To reduce extreme poverty globally, it is crucial to accelerate progress in the countries with large numbers of extremely poor. These countries are mainly in South Asia and sub-Saharan Africa, home to 85% (629 million) of the world's extreme poor (Katayama and Wadhwa 2019).

The world attained the first Millennium Development Goal target—to cut the 1990 poverty rate in half by 2015 (*Understanding Poverty*, the World Bank 2019c). Two regions, East Asia and Pacific (47 million extreme poor) and Europe and Central Asia (7 million) have reduced extreme poverty below 3%, achieving the 2030 target (*Understanding Poverty*, World Bank 2019c).

The world's most populous countries are China and India. In 1990s, these two countries together had the largest group of extremely poor, mainly living in rural areas. As a result of progress in China, the extreme poverty rate in Eastern Asia has dropped from 61% in 1990 to only 4% in 2015 (the United Nations 2015: the Millennium Development Goals Report 2015). Southern Asia's progress is almost as impressive—a decline from 52% to 17% for the same period—and its rate of reduction has accelerated since 2008 (ibid).

China has one of the fastest economic growth rates in East Asia: GDP grew on average by 9.8% per annum between 1979 and 2012 (Lin 2013). During this period, farmers' per capita net income increased on average by 7.5% per annum at a national wide range (China Business News 2013). The average per capita disposable income of rural residents was $2308.50 annually in 2019 (The National Bureau of Statistics of China 2020a). China has carried out national economic development policies to mitigate disparities of rural and urban areas, including rural and urban integration development plans. The increasing rate of income of rural residents was 1.7% higher than the urban residents in 2019 at a national level (National Bureau of Statistics of China 2020a).

China's economic reform started from agricultural sector, which has led to a rapidly agricultural growth. China presents a successful case, showing that inclusive growth and development of agribusiness enterprises can significantly reduce poverty and improve the living standards for a majority of rural workers and smallholder farmers during its economic transformation. A report from UNDP indicates that development can be inclusive—and reduce poverty—only if all groups of people contribute to creating opportunities, share the benefits of development and participate in decision-making (UNDP 2020).

China is a valuable case study on poverty reduction and inclusive growth in respect of studies in international development. Although poverty rates in Central Asia continue to decline overall, the pace of poverty reduction is slowing, according to new data released by the World Bank. High levels of poverty remain in pockets of rural and remote areas, which also suffer from lack of employment opportunities. Rekindling inclusive growth should therefore be among the region's most urgent priorities (Infographic: Poverty in Central Asia, World Bank 2019a).

China has adopted inclusive growth and development policies to tackle poverty reduction in its less-developed rural areas in recent years. It has carried out policies to reduce poverty, especially in impoverished rural areas. These policies aim to improve the income of extremely poor rural residents; their total incomes include wage income and metastatic funds. China's rural residents per capita annual income was US$1652.40 in 2019 the impoverished rural areas, an increase of 8.6% over the previous year (The National Bureau of Statistics of China 2020b). The per capita annual income of rural residents is lower in the impoverished rural areas than the per capita annual income of rural residents at the rural areas that are not identified as the impoverished rural areas in China.

6.2.2 *Global Governance and China's International Development*

It is important to analyze the role of global governance in inclusive development of agribusiness and rural enterprises in developing countries. The United Nations development agenda underscores a global consensus and a shared vision of inclusive development, based on the three pillars of sustainable development: economic, social and environmental (United Nations, Committee for Development Policy 2014).

Intergovernmental cooperation is at the center of the global partnership for development (United Nations, Committee for Development Policy 2014). The development path of a developing country is strongly dependent on the specific resources, institutions, economic structure and political ideologies and social and cultural fabric of individual countries. The kind of foreign direct investment activity it might attract (or wish to attract), too, at different stages of development, varies widely (Narula and Dunning 2000).

Firstly, global governance on development highlights sustainable development, which is often defined as "meeting the needs of the present without compromising the ability of future generations to meet their own needs." The three main pillars of sustainability are social, environmental and economic, which are often referred to informally as "people, planet and profits" (De Feis 2018).

The heterogeneity of economic structural differences in upper middle-income countries may result in different market demand for agricultural products that can help low-income countries to export agricultural products. The changing trade landscape will also demand innovative ways to improve market access and address non-tariff barriers, particularly as trade in services expands. Also, it will be crucial to strengthen the integration of developing countries into the multilateral trade system, as measured by their trade diversification and share in value added (the United Nations 2015, The Millennium Development Goals Report 2015).

Many developing countries have undertaken economic transformation and agricultural transformation. Large numbers of rural communities are facing serious challenges to build up the industrial development that can link agribusiness and efficient technologies for creation of suitable work opportunities in the local rural communities. Sustainable and inclusive business opportunities are important for developing countries to upgrade their economy at a national level. Box 6.1 shows that indicators of sustainable development from the World Development Indicators (2016) of the World Bank. The development indicators include comprehensive indicators of people, and the sustainable development indicators also include economic development and environmental sustainability. Poverty and shared prosperity are indicators that measure progress toward the World Bank Group's twin goals of ending extreme poverty by 2030 and promoting shared prosperity in every country. Box 6.1 shows highlights in tackling progress toward the Sustainable Development Goals from the World Bank.

Box 6.1 Progress Toward the Sustainable Development Goals

1. People presents indicators covering education, health, jobs, social protection, and gender. Together with the indicators in world view, such as population, poverty, and shared prosperity, they provide a multidimensional portrait of societal progress across the world.
2. Environment, presents indicators to measure the use of resources and the way human activities affect both the natural and the built environment. They include measures of environmental goods (forest, water, cultivable land) and various measures of environmental degradation, including pollution, deforestation, loss of habitat, and loss of biodiversity, which must be considered in shaping development strategies.
3. Economy section provides a picture of the global economy and the economic activity of the more than 200 countries and territories. It includes measures of macroeconomic performance and stability as well as broader measures of income and savings adjusted for pollution, depreciation, and resource depletion.

(*continued*)

Box 6.1 (continued)

4. States and market sencompass indicators on private investment and performance, the quality and availability of infrastructure essential for growth, and the role of the public sector in nurturing investment and growth. These indicators measure the business environment, government functions, financial system development, infrastructure, information and communication technology, science and technology, government and policy performance, and conditions in fragile countries with weak institutions.
5. Global links presents the world economy is bound together by trade in goods and services, financial flows, and movements of people. The indicators in Global links measure the size and direction of these flows and document the effects of policy interventions, such as tariffs, trade facilitation, and aid flows, on the development of the world economy

Source: World Bank, *World Development Indicators 2016*.

Market and prices are key factors to sustain international cooperation of agribusiness and rural enterprises in developing countries. Some small and medium-sized enterprises as well as large scale agribusiness enterprises face higher production costs in upper middle-income than low-income countries. These agribusiness enterprises are increasing their investment and business cooperation in low-income countries. Small and medium-sized enterprises (SMEs) make up more than 90% of businesses and more than 50% of employment worldwide, and there are some 500 million smallholder farms worldwide with more than 2 billion people that depend on them for their livelihoods. These small farms produce about 80% of the food consumed in Asia and sub-Saharan Africa. Therefore, fostering enterprise creation and nurturing SMEs in developing countries, and linking agriculture and processing capacity, is crucial for job creation and enhanced prosperity (United Nations Industrial Development Organization 2017).

Secondly, China is increasing its development cooperation with developing countries. In 2018, China's total value of imports and exports from Africa was US$ 204.2 billion, an increase of 19.7% over the previous year. China has become Africa's largest trade partner. China has set up more 3700 enterprises. China is also accelerating its agribusiness cooperation with South Asian countries. China is Burma's largest trade partner and investor. China is a large market, and the country is the largest importer of several agricultural products. China is an important development partner to some developing countries. It is the largest development aid supporter in inter-governmental and economic development cooperation such as South–South cooperation and the Asian Infrastructure Investment Bank. China and African countries set up the Forum on China and Africa Cooperation two decades ago, and the forum has supported knowledge-sharing and communication on challenges and opportunities of development and poverty reduction. Further, the national development projects of agribusiness and private rural enterprises have increased.

International development practitioners and scholars have provided valuable suggestions on lessons from China for Africa in the context of agricultural and rural development against poverty reduction. Li et al. (2013) stated that China and Africa have developed their agricultural sectors under different historical conditions; this chapter proposes that China's poverty-reduction and smallholder-based agricultural policies can provide a useful model for African countries to develop their own strategies in agrarian change. Ravallion (2009) suggests that China's farmers responded dramatically to market incentives when institutional reforms gave them the chance to do so. African farmers are not likely to be any different in this respect. Dollar (2008) suggests that one important lesson is China's careful attention to agriculture and rural development, complemented by rural–urban migration. Fan et al. (2010) remark that lessons from China's development experiences and policies in the areas of agricultural and rural development could reduce poverty for sub-Saharan Africa, but a combination of clear public policies and institutional reforms are needed for this to happen. Juma (2011) suggests that lessons for Africa from China are detailed: sustained focus on smallholder farmers by unleashing their potential and meeting their needs can lead to growth and poverty reduction, even when the basic agricultural conditions are unfavorable. But, again, a combination of clear public policies and institutional reforms are needed for this to happen.

Thirdly, the global governance of the United Nations implements relevant policies that are related to international firms' cooperation in the context of environmentally sustainability (See Box 6.2). International agribusiness has increased rapidly in the perspectives of international development in developing countries. The agricultural industry is a crucially important for developing countries: over 800 million people suffer from hunger; of these, 70% live in rural areas of developing countries (United Nations Industrial Development Organization 2017).

Box 6.2 Global Governance Impacts on Environmentally Sustainable International Agribusiness Corporations

1. The principles of inclusiveness, transparency, and accountability imply that the recognition of the linkages between environmental and human well-being leads to acknowledgement that the fundamental rights to a healthy environment is a human right.
2. International environmental governance also impacts other areas of global governance besides the environment, such as international trade. Outside the treaty realm, institutions have voluntarily developed mechanisms such as environmental and quality standards of international organizations for standardization and codes of conduct for corporate social responsibility developed by various corporations.
3. Environmental sustainability requires deeper changes in current production and consumption patterns-changes that constitute important threats and challenges for the way international corporations operate in the energy, mining and chemical sectors, among others.

Sources: Global Governance and Global Rules for Development in the Post-2015 era, United Nations 2014

Industrial development is important for agricultural productivity and profits in some developed countries. Some transitional economies have also accelerated their industrial development, such as China. China stresses the importance of an industrial development pattern in its agriculture-based products as it moves toward environmentally sustainable development. Environmentally sustainable development can impact on prices of agriculture-based industrial products in both domestic and international markets. Domestically, products of industrial development and environmental protection have higher prices than agricultural products produced in polluted farming areas. For instance, organic agricultural products and famous brand food products have high prices. These organic agricultural products are associated with agri-environmental awareness. Internationally, agriculture-based industrial products account for half of all exports from developing countries, yet only 30% of those exports involve processed goods, compared to a figure of 98% in the developed world (United

Nations Industrial Development Organization 2020). When environmental polices negatively affect the production of agricultural products, the consequence can be a significant decrease in EU agricultural exports. Therefore, the essential question for these products is whether or not environmental policies will result in a decrease in agricultural production (Blom 2018).

Developing-country agribusiness international cooperation can support this agriculture-based industrial development through market demand and enhancing technology transfer and learning. Multinational enterprises are better able to integrate the activities of their foreign affiliate through the use of these technologies, and to respond more quickly to changing demand and supply conditions in the countries in which they operate. Taken together, these transaction-cost-reducing processes are enabling international production to be more efficiently organized (Narula and Dunning 2000). Environmentally sustainable development impacts on China's international cooperation of agricultural products in the long term. The international cooperation of agribusiness needs responsible enterprises to cooperate with smallholder farmers in China.

Environmental issues are not only important for China's sustainable development, but also to the upgrading and transformation of its economic structures. Ecological agricultural production has impacted on technological change and development pattern of family agribusinesses in rural China. In recent years, China's rural transformation has progressed toward ecological living and sustainable environment. The rural development strategy highlights rural environment and ecological management of agricultural production, including improvement of infrastructure, water irrigation, water sanitation, and road transportation. Under the 11th five year plan (2011–2016), the Chinese government made a commitment to protecting the environment by reversing current trends in energy consumption per GDP, as well as decreasing environmental pollution loads in the atmosphere (sulfur dioxide) and surface water bodies (chemical oxygen demand).

6.3 Inclusive Growth of Agribusiness and Industrial Development

Rural industrialization and industrial development can be achieved through the inclusive development of agribusiness and rural enterprises at a national scale of economic growth. China's farmers' income increased 130 times between 1978 and 2007 at a national level, and the income obtained from TVEs accounted for 34.8% of the total income on average (Sun 2008). The inclusive development of rural enterprises, e.g. TVEs, contributed significantly to industrial development at the time of take-off of China's rural industrialization. In 1984, 67.46% of TVE employment and 85.63% of TVE output came from collective firms (Zou 2003). By 2007, there were more than 150 million employees working in TVEs, 29.13% of the total rural labor force (ibid.).

The goal of industrialization is seen in the developing world as an essential ingredient of the expansion, diversification and modernization of their economies, and thereby of improving general living standards (Kirkpatrick and Nixson 1983). Nevertheless, the majority of the population in most developing countries is rural.

6.3.1 Industrial Development and Agricultural Transformation

Industrial development needs to impact on agricultural commercialization and large-scale economic development. It also needs to link with rural enterprises at a national level to bring about dynamic changes of rural industrialization in a transitional economy. A key challenge remains how to empower agriculture as an engine for economic growth and industrial development during the process of agricultural and rural transformation at a national scale, because the majority of agricultural producers in developing countries are smallholder farmers. Although some developing countries have been experiencing a fast economic growth, many of them still face serious challenges in tackling hunger, malnutrition and poverty. These challenges have generated continuing debates among policy makers, academics, international development organizations and NGOs. Meanwhile, there are opportunities to reduce poverty and eradicate hunger by empowering agribusiness and industrial development in the agricultural sector as an engine for economic development.

Many developing countries accelerated their agricultural transformation. The agricultural sector has traditionally been the backbone of economic development for developing countries, for instance China, India and other some south Asian countries, as well as many African countries. Most African countries have failed to meet the requirements for a successful agricultural revolution, and productivity in African agriculture lags far behind the rest of the world (Diao et al. 2010), this is the case, particularly, for low-income countries in sub-Saharan Africa (SSA).

In the past three decades, China has accelerated its agricultural transformation through different development strategies. Its development of industrialized production and rural enterprises accelerated its agricultural transformation. At present, industrial development is even more important because smallholder farmers are facing challenges to improve agricultural productivity, and their cultivated land areas are relatively small. Large numbers of young rural workers work in non-farming sectors, mainly the industrial sector. In addition, some small and middle sized enterprises (SMEs) and large-scale agricultural enterprises have developed value chains; these agro-enterprises have big agricultural production bases.

The share of industrial employment overall is going up in some developing countries. For example, in Vietnam it rose from 9% in 1991 to 25% in 2017. In the Lao People's Democratic Republic, the share of industrial employment rose from 3% to 10% over the same period (World Bank 2019b, World Development Report 2019).

Successful industrial development will help to solve the imperative problems, such as agricultural productivity, and environmental challenges. In remote areas and impoverished areas, infrastructure such as water system, is in poor condition. These smallholder farmers can hardly change environmental problems alone in their remote and impoverished rural areas. Innovative institutions and an active role for local government as well as enterprises are necessary for success. Therefore, industrial development needs to put agricultural development as a high priority in their strategy for transformation.

The term "industrialization" can mean either the organization of production in business enterprises in any sector of the economy, characterized by specialization and the division of labor and involving the application of technology and mechanical and electrical power to supplement and replace human labor, or it can mean the establishment of a modern, integrated, urban-based manufacturing sector (Kirkpatrick and Nixson 1983).

However, given that the majority of the population lived in rural areas before industrialization, the reallocation of the rural labor force to agribusiness enterprises is an initial stage of its industrial development. Importantly, the inclusive development of agribusiness enterprises is essential. The clustering and aggregation of agribusiness enterprises is important for increasing the employment opportunities of the majority of rural workers. Moreover, the development of rural enterprises is not limited to agricultural development, because rural enterprises specializing in the textile industry, the clothing industry and other industrial services can also help to absorb large numbers of rural workers. The textile and clothing industries also continuously demand raw materials from agriculture, such as cotton.

In order to promote industrial development and increase farmers' income, international trade and agribusiness are critical. Because international markets offer the strong possibility of higher prices than the local market, agribusiness and rural enterprises can make better profits and increase the income of rural households. When income increases for cumulative numbers of rural workers, demand for and consumption of goods and products will impel structural change at the earliest stages of economic transformation. In some developing countries, even though there may be rapid economic growth, the pace of economic transformation is slow. When the development path adopts clustering and aggregation of rural industrial development and inclusive growth of agribusiness at the onset of the development take-off stage, the efficient structural changes create more work opportunities for the many rural of poor.

In low-income countries, the proportion of the total labor force working in industry from 1991 to 2017 was consistently around 10%. The situation was stable in upper-middle-income countries as well, at around 23%. Lower-middle-income countries experienced an increase in the proportion of the labor force in the industrial sector over the same period, from 16% in 1991 to 19% in 2017. This increase may stem from the interplay of open trade and rising incomes, which generates more demand for goods, services, and technology. (World Bank 2019b, World Development Report 2019)

6.3.2 *China's Industrial Development and Technological Innovation*

China's technological innovation has helped its industrial development in different stages.

(1) In early agricultural transformation, China's commercialization and technological innovation helped to upgrade the value of agricultural products. Firms are a core factor in economic growth in respect of processing commercialization, and technological innovation facilitates the making of profits in market competition. In addition, China carried out effective economic policies to stimulate structural changes in its agricultural production during the 1980s and 1990s. Diversification in agricultural products was one of the

important strategies in its agricultural transformation. The farming sector produced the largest output of agricultural products between the 1950s and 1970s. The diversification of agricultural production—fishery, animal husbandry sector, fruit and vegetables—increased rapidly after the early 1990s.

(2) China carried out transformative technological change at unprecedented speed, now generated by the advancing wave of digital technology. This dynamic technological innovation drives rapid commercial and economic change, including information technology and application of new technology to industrialized agricultural production. The digital revolution is opening up new, undreamed-of opportunities, it is also closing down more traditional paths of rural development (the World Bank 2019b, World Development Bank Report 2019).

In recent years, adoption of digital technology has brought more opportunities to China's small family agribusinesses and farmers in domestic and international markets. Small family agribusinesses can access the market and gain better profits through the application of digital technology in business management, and the transaction costs of business and firm operation can be reduced through digital technology and e-commerce. China's technological innovation has contributed to its significant achievement in improvement of livelihoods and creation of work opportunities for farmers in the process of agricultural and rural transformation.

(3) Adoption of industrial development needs innovative institutions. In many developing countries a large number of workers remain in low-productivity jobs, often in informal sector firms whose access to technology is poor. Informality has remained high over the past two decades despite improvements in the business regulatory environment (The World Bank 2019b, World Development Report 2019). Innovative institutions are a precondition for successful implementation of industrial development at grass-root level.

The adoption of new technology and technological progress are important factors in industrial development, and institutional innovation helped industrial development toward modern agricultural production pattern and rural industrialization in China. If developing countries are to develop their own technology, there needs to be the right institutional environment, including an incentive structure through patents, sound infrastructure, political stability to attract investment funds, and the availability of credit (Thirlwall and Pacheco-López 2017).

Meanwhile, institutions and policies foster the appropriate social and economic environment. Entrepreneurship is not just a spiritual aspect accepting risk in the market and the competitive social environment. It is also important to understand that entrepreneurship includes the ability to develop, to change an unsatisfactory current situation to meet market competition in a local social and economic environment. Institutions and policies must support inclusive and sustainable business development so that every stakeholder can have opportunities for sharing prosperity through profits and their chance to develop. Industrial development and technological innovation facilitate growth of small-scale family agribusinesses, and institutional support for innovation can help such businesses upgrade their technology to adopt industrial development at an economic scale.

6.4 Perspectives of Theories in Development Economics

Development economists have paid attention to the role of dualistic economic structure in the process of economic transformation. Economic transformation needs structural change to transfer surplus rural labor from the agricultural sector to the industrial sector in developing countries. Before substantial economic transformation in developing countries or transitional economies, the majority of the population live in rural areas and large numbers of the rural labor force will be living on subsistence wages of US$1.90 or less per day, extremely poor by the standards of the international standard poverty line of the World Bank. In fact, large numbers of farmers have no regular income and live on US$1.90 a day or less. Lewis (1954) explained the role of dualism in the process of economic transformation. Unlimited supplies of labor ensure that capital accumulation is sustained over time, but the dynamic of the economic forces at play lead toward economic transformation (Lewis 1954; Kirkpatrick and Barrientos 2004).

The question is how to success economic transformation from the traditional agricultural production mode to industrial development? Lewis (1954) pointed out that the economic structure in developing countries with a large rural labor force, must transfer surplus labor from the agricultural sector to the industrial sector. The lower the cost of industrial labor, the faster the rate of industrial expansion is likely to be, but this depends on the rate at which the agricultural sector is releasing labor. Industrial development today in many of the rapidly growing countries of southeast Asia is being fueled by cheap labor drawn from agriculture. In this respect, China's industrial potential was enormous (Thirlwall and Pacheco-López 2017).

In developing countries, because the majority of workers engage in agricultural and rural labor, economic growth and development needs be complementary at different development stages. The development process needs to create suitable work opportunities for a large numbers of rural surplus labor at the right time and the right stage of development stage. The path of economic growth needs to solve a key development dilemma in economic transformation: in order to mitigate the income gap between rural and urban, it is crucial to sustain cumulatively large numbers of rural workers in industrial development to increase their income. It is also important to reduce disparities of social, economic, and environmental aspects. The level of technological progress is also a factor in the development process that may mitigate inequality between the rural and the urban economy. Importantly, both economies need strong integration development strategies.

On the basis of these initial considerations, it appears difficult, if not impossible, to use a single model to explain the entire development process of a single country. Rostow (1966) pointed out that, "the stages of economic growth are an arbitrary and limited way of looking at the uniformities in the sequences of modernization but also the uniqueness of each nation's experience." If our aim is to analyze the development of a whole region we can easily conclude that using one model will lead nowhere, but that we need rather a combination of models, each explaining specific aspects of the process.

There are common economic phenomena in developing countries, although there are different paces of economic growth and development paths at different development stages. In the initial stages of the transformation process, the sectorial shift in labor is mostly a shift from self-employment on the farm to self-employment off the farm in informal household enterprises (International Fund for Agricultural Development 2019). But as incomes rise and markets expand, firms begin to appear that are capable of hiring people and putting them to work while also bringing in new technology (capital) and expanding their production. By boosting overall productivity, these firms become key agents in the rural transformation process. New products and new technology are important for firms to improve productivity during a time of structural change.

Lewis's dual-sector model has been extensively applied to the issue of structural changes in developing countries. His model assumes that a developing economy has a surplus of unproductive labor in the agricultural sector. He suggests that surplus labor can be used instead of capital in the creation of new industrial investment projects, or it can be channeled into nascent industries that are labor-intensive in their early stages. Fei and Ranis (1964) extended Lewis's model. They recognize the presence of a dual economy comprising both a modern and a primitive sector, taking the economic situation of unemployment and underemployment of resources into account, unlike many other growth models that consider underdeveloped countries to be homogenous in nature. According to this theory, the primitive sector consists of the existing agricultural sector, and the modern sector is the rapidly emerging but small industrial sector.

Inclusive growth is a concept that advances equitable opportunities for economic participants during economic growth with benefits incurred by every section of society. Inclusive growth adopts a long-term perspective and is concerned with sustainable growth. (1) For growth to be sustained in the long run, it must be broad-based across sectors. Issues of structural transformation for economic diversification therefore take a center stage. (2) It must also be inclusive of a large part of the country's labor force, where inclusiveness refers to equality of opportunity in terms of access to markets, resources and unbiased regulatory environment for businesses and individuals (Ianchovichina and Lundstrom 2009).

Lin (2011) suggested that the market is the basic mechanism for effective resource allocation at each level of development. In addition to an effective market mechanism, the government should play an active role in facilitating structural changes. Efficient organization entails the establishment of institutional arrangements and property rights that create an incentive to channel individual economic effort into activities that bring the private rate of return close to the social rate of return (North and Thomas 1973).

Endogenous growth theory holds that investment in human capital, innovation and knowledge are significant contributors to economic growth. Romer developed endogenous growth theory, emphasizing that technological change is the result of efforts by researchers and entrepreneurs who respond to economic incentives (Romer and Jones 2019). Technological progress—improvements in the ways that goods and services are produced, marketed, and brought to market—is at the very heart of human advancement and development (Thirlwall and Pacheco-López 2017).

Effective complementary modes of economic growth and economic development can be coordinated by agribusiness and firms to response market demand at different growth stages. The neo-classical school assumes that markets seek to coordinate the behavior of individual agents through the price mechanism, i.e. prices are set so as to bring demand and supply into equilibrium within each market.

However, inclusive growth brings to the fore stakeholders in business firms that increase profits cumulatively, in terms of the returns from every individual producing revenues and increasing productivity. The share of profits proportionally given to stakeholders is based on individual contributions that include capability, knowledge and technology, tangible and intangible properties to grow productivity and revenue. Inclusive growth is an effective development strategy to increase income for the stakeholders of the agribusiness and farmers' business in a long term.

6.5 Governance and Bottom-Up Development Approach on China's Agribusiness

Governance is defined as the manner in which power is exercised in the management of a country's economic and social resources for development. Good governance is synonymous with sound development management (World Bank 1992). Local government rather than just national government has played a key coordination role in the practical process of agricultural development during the economic transformation of China. Bottom-up development is commonly known as the "farmer-first approach," or "bottom-up" development and has greatly influenced the way that rural development is practiced today. The farmer-first approach came to be recognized as an established approach in research, education and extension (Chambers et al. 1989).

China's decentralized governments helped the effective implementation of bottom-up development, because the agricultural projects of industrial development needed a scale-economy to succeed with local industrial development, according to indigenous and comparative advantages of local natural resources and specified local social and geographic environmental conditions, as well as cultural and historical contexts. China's decentralized governments still facilitate coordination of tasks of development when new development projects are implementing new technology at grass-root level, particularly when the local government supports agricultural projects of industrial development and the take-off of TVEs implementing national economic policies in local rural areas.

6.5.1 Local Governance and Business Development for Technology Progress

Some suggest that government has impacted on technology both directly and indirectly through, for example, public expenditure, public policy and preferential tax systems. Government can also impact economic growth through direct (tax) or indirect expenditure channels on R&D (Crafts 1996). Public spending is an important factor for self-sustaining productivity gains and long-term growth (Barro 1990). Technology plays an important role in agricultural growth. Nevertheless, firms transform technology into profits and productivity for sustainable development. All R&D operations need an external environment and institutional framework. Moreover, project implementation, diffusion of applications and information need coordination between internal and external environments. Therefore, governments can effectively implement public expenditures on R&D. In China, decentralization facilitates governance functions on bottom-up development, in which local governments have public expenditures to support the implementation of R&D projects and agribusiness development.

In China's case, prior to the reforms, the effects of government investment were largely restrained by many policy and institutional barriers. The reforms reduced these barriers, making it possible to achieve high levels of agricultural growth and poverty reduction (Fan et al. 2001). More importantly, the fundamental importance of innovative institutions was providing a freedom of environment to smallholder farmers for development, so that individual farmers could pursue their own profits through hard work and operation of their small agricultural businesses and small-scale family agribusinesses.

Technological change involves new technologies, technological transfer and technical innovation, and new management approaches to adapt to technological change. Implementing technological change in structural transformation needs appropriate policies to introduce new technology and technical innovation into farmers' and agribusiness managers' practice. Therefore, the decentralization of government and the bottom-up development approach can increase effectiveness of practice in adopting new agricultural technology and new agricultural products.

Importantly, China's decentralization has facilitated effective coordination of local government in technological progress and innovation in small-scale household agricultural production. Under decentralization, synchronization has the advantage that decisions can be made locally and can be fully responsive to information received from others in the system. China's decentralized structure facilitated the role of local government in implementing new technology.

In China, different functioning bureaux have been set up from the national level to the grass-root level. Oi (1999) describes China's local state corporatism as constituted and coordinated by local government—specifically counties, townships, and villages—not central authorities. In rural areas, the local specialized bureaux are responsible for coordinating economic activities within their regions. At present, the specialized functional bureaux at county level or technical stations at town level are mainly responsible for technology and innovation. Technical staff and professionals help to implement technological innovation and introduction of new technology into practice, for instance when national policies need to implement new technology or new agricultural products at local level. These local officials provide public services for local governments to coordinate the implementing of practical approaches of technological innovation between rural village communities or towns, technical stations and farmers.

At county level, there are several trained technical professionals working at specified bureaus of economic units at county level, such as the County Bureau of Agriculture and County Bureaux of Fishery respectively, and there are similarly functioning town technical stations, meaning that rural village communities can be coordinated with the town technical stations at a horizontal level for specialized technical support for the production of diversified agricultural products, such as a town fishery station or town livestock station. Each town has specialized-function stations, at the same administrative level, reporting to the county administrative level. Introduction of heterogeneous technologies in different agricultural products into smallholder farms can be coordinated by the technical professionals at the different specialized stations within each town.

China's innovative institutions have created conditions for implementing new technology and new products into smallholder farms. The reform of property rights has been an important part of the innovation: the two different systems of property rights are co-existent in one small-scale rural household. The reform of property rights has been associated with the household contracting system (HRS) that has different features than the system of equally allocated cultivated land areas. The household contracting system leases land to non-farm agricultural production. The household contracting system allocates land and resources by market price, and it encourages capable farmers to run family agribusinesses. Therefore, the family agribusiness management needs to improve technology and quality in order to gain better profits in the market.

Babu et al. (2015) pointed out that China has adopted a bottom-up development approaches beginning with reforms within the agricultural sector. In contrast, economic growth in India has been impelled by top-down reform. China's agricultural research system has grown to be the largest and most decentralized in the world (Babu et al. 2015). Improvement of agricultural technology and the high rate of self-sufficient food suppliers have benefited from China's public finance and investment in agricultural scientific research, as technological innovation has been directly associated with scientific research. The total R&D project expenditure within universities and research institutes increased from CNY 2361 million in 2002 to CNY 11,680 million in 2012 at 2005 constant prices, and its annual growth rate reached 17%. Both agricultural R&D expenditure in institutes and universities in China are mainly funded by the central government (Babu et al. 2015). There are agricultural universities in almost every province in China. Under the decentralized economic units of governments in China, local governments have more flexibility and greater incentive to handle public expenditure and R&D projects on development and poverty reduction in rural areas. China's decentralized governmental structures have helped the output of R&D, and produced technology and science with a practical effect on business development at grass-root level. The decentralized structure can help the research's outcome to transform productivity and profits for local business development projects and for the commercialized agroindustry and food industry.

Governance function is one of key contributors to development and poverty reduction. Effective governance can help to solve embedded problems and indigenous backwardness in impoverished and poor rural areas. The embedded problems and indigenous backwardness can be an obstruction to development. Besides the decentralization of China's governance, China's national government works on important strategies of development and policies for economic growth at a macro-level. China's government has put hunger reduction and food security as its top priority in the national development agenda. In order to target hunger reduction, China's central government established the Leading Group of Poverty Alleviation and Development of the State Council in 1986; its main function is to solve the problems of development and poverty reduction in China. There are similar governance functions at province level and local level. Development aid (poverty-relief funds) and public expenditure have been a part of the combination with economic development initiatives to target poverty alleviation. Governmental agricultural expenditure has also been used for poverty reduction, the eradication of hunger and development in China's rural areas.

China's fiscal organizational structures have five layers: the Ministry of Finance, the Department of Finance at provincial level, the Bureau of Finance at prefectural level, the Bureau at County level and the Sub-office at town level. Fiscal bureaux have been established in provinces, counties and prefectures. Moreover, by 1985, fiscal offices had been set up at town and county levels in rural China (Sun 1995). Local governance functions can be coordinated and managed by the Prefecture Finance Bureau, the County Finance Bureaus, and the Sub-offices. The Ministry of Finance of China has been operating separate taxation systems at local level since 1993. Under the separation of taxation systems, the local Financial Bureaus can keep a certain proportion of taxation for local government after submission of a fixed proportion to the Finance Ministry. Further, the decentralization of China's fiscal management effectively empowered the development of local governance's functions for local economic development, including the development of TVEs.

6.5.2 Governance and the Bottom-Up Development Approach to Agribusiness Growth

Rocha (2004) suggested that the impact of entrepreneurship on development—i.e. focus on capabilities rather than on output—is key, and he defined entrepreneurship as the creation of new organizations. Entrepreneurial initiative is one of the main—if not the main—ways to drive technological change and catalyze sustainable growth, hence the motivation to better learn from past entrepreneurial initiatives aimed at fostering economic development (Carayannis et al. 2006). China is used to arguing that poverty reduction comes through entrepreneurship. It is an internal process which helps the poor to undertake positive actions to reduce their poverty (Wu and Si 2018). China's analysis emphasizes that endogeneity and sustainability, social networks rooted in nostalgia are a determinant of the successes of entrepreneurial poverty-reduction initiatives.

There are two categories of central government departments. The first has direct power down to the level of the local government departments. The governance functions at local level include supervision and management enterprises with different freedom degrees at different economic development stages. The other category of central government departments are only responsible for giving policy guidelines; detailed management is operated by local governments. China's governance has facilitated a bottom-up development approach to accelerate industrial development, commercialization and rural industrialization. Governance has fostered grass-root technological updates that fit local needs when policies are put into, sometimes experimental, practice. Governance has also fostered non-governmental local organizations such as farmers' associations and co-operatives in rural areas.

6.5.2.1 Governance and Development of Local Rural Enterprises

Governance has to create an enabling environment for entrepreneurship, which has significantly driven business development in rural areas, where large numbers of poor lived in the 1980s. Private enterprises hardly survived in the early social and political environment. In the middle of the 1980s, the Chinese government carried out a development strategy, a plan that aimed to accelerate structural transformation in the agricultural sector, accelerate rural development and increase farmers' income through technological and institutional innovation. Many emerging private enterprises took the "red-cap" of collective economy in towns and countryside in the 1980s.

The pattern of rural industrial development has been market-driven, and development of rural enterprises is the key development strategy for rural industrial development. The TVEs have been pioneers of Chinese private enterprise. China's rural industry, which stemmed from rural subsidiary production, has been an important part of China's economy for centuries (Chen 2018). There were rural industrial units in the form of "village collectives corporations," in China, and former commune and brigade enterprises were a major composition of the rural industrial units of "village collectives corporations" in China before economic reform in 1979. Between 1978 and 1996, the former commune and brigade enterprises became township and village collective enterprises, while new enterprises, collective or individual/ private, were established (Chen 2018). On the one hand, in the later stage of the economic transformation, since 1999, the private enterprises have become the main kind of TVEs (Zhu and Elbern 2002). Fu and Balasubramanyam (2003) suggested that TVEs are much more efficient than comparable state-owned enterprises. They are also competitive in the international markets. Their management, which responds to market forces, and their outward orientation have contributed to their productive efficiency (Fu and Balasubramanyam 2003). On the other hand, the majority of small-scale household agricultural production management is de facto private family agribusiness. Chinese farmers' entrepreneurship was likewise a key factor in economic development (Du 1998). Therefore, the development of rural enterprises is an effective development path to rural industrial development.

Entrepreneurship impacts on sustainable and inclusive development. China has adopted inclusive development of agribusiness and rural enterprises in a sustainable way. Inclusive agribusiness development is a feature of public and private business partnership between local officials/ stakeholders and smallholder farmers under the aegis of innovative institutions. The public and private business partnership is a key feature of inclusive development, consistent with enterprises, village communities and farmers.

The rural industries had a rapid development in China from 1978 to 1996. The population employed in the rural industries increased from 28.27 million to 130.58 million, and the added value of the rural industries increased from 20.8 billion RMB to 1.766 trillion RMB from 1978 to 1996 (Li 2014). During this period, the robust development of rural industrial contributed to China's structural transformation in its agricultural sector from a traditional production pattern to a modern and commercial one. Since 1985, the government-initiated measures have adjusted the structure of agricultural production to increase production of high-value agricultural products: cash crops, aquaculture and husbandry. The governance and bottom-up development approach needed to combine with policy and social development.

Importantly, the dynamic development of China's TVEs has significantly contributed to the rural industrial development and rural transformation as well as agricultural transformation in China's take-off in economic growth in the 1980s and 1990s. The TVEs have survived and thrived by being extremely aggressive in implementing new technology and adapting it to their operational environment (Xie and White 2006). China's dynamic development of TVEs has absorbed enormous numbers of surplus workers and created huge opportunities for employment since the 1980s. Farmers have shifted into rural enterprises and manufacturing and services in the rural enterprises, which were TVEs.

In 1978, the total number of rural workers in enterprises run by the communes and brigade accounted for about 10% of the rural labor force. By the end of 2012, the employed population in TVEs reached 164 million, accouting for 40% of total employed persons in rural China (Li 2014). The employees of TVEs are mainly drawn from the rural labor force. Therefore, the TVEs are still a major part of China's rural economy, and play an important role in increasing income and creating job opportunities in the non-farm sector for smallholder farmers and in the linkage between agriculture and rural industry, and rural and urban integration.

6.5.3 The Bottom-Up Development Approach and Local Governance

Governance and the bottom-up development approach can effectively develop the inclusive growth pattern. The village communities maintain public order, manage welfare services, and oversee agricultural development projects within their affiliated villages. Unlike the governors of the formally five-level administrative hierarchy (central, province, prefecture city, county and town), a village committee structure falls below the township level and does not belong to the formal administrative hierarchy. Nevertheless, leaders and members of village communities actively participate in all decision-making on social, economic and environmental relevant development issues at the grass-root rural areas within their affiliated villages.

China has promulgated the Law of the Villagers' Committee Organization. The heads of village communities have adopted the grass-root election system. Each village is autonomous, and heads of village are elected by farmers from the village. The chairmen, vice chairmen and members of a village committee are directly elected by the farmers of their affiliated villages. Each term of office of the villagers committee shall be three years, and at the end of the term of office, a new election, using anonymous voting, must be held. The village election committee includes chairman and members of the village committee, and the candidates of members of villages committees are recommended at meetings of the local farmers of a village. In order to be elected as a head of a village community, candidates need to demonstrate their capability in improving the economy and livelihood of farmers.

Inclusive growth has strengthened the build-up of entrepreneurship, and China's democratic election system in village communities has nurtured the inclusive growth of agribusiness and the rural enterprises. Inclusive growth enhances public and private agribusiness and firms' development pattern in the take-off of economic growth through accelerating industrialization.

A key task of the chairman of village community is to develop the business and economy of affiliated villages. Chairs of village communities can coordinate local resources efficiently, and managers of large sized local agribusiness enterprises can create agribusiness opportunities for smallholder farmers. Compared with the entrepreneurs of large or small and middle-sized local agribusiness enterprises, most farmers lack access to capital and technology of industrialized production as well as the international market. In addition, the head of village communities may need to produce new products initially, and the village communities empower local resources and human capital as well as coordinating supporting funding to organize the products of industrial development based on the size of the village economy. Many farmers will follow up once they realize new products are profitable. Further, some farmers realize that their neighbors have obtained profit from new technology or new products, and follow up. Zhang et al. (2006) and Djankov et al. (2006) showed that entrepreneurship is more likely if the entrepreneur is a member of a network with friends or family who are entrepreneurs.

Institutional changes include incentive property rights and effective governance for inclusive and sustainable development. Incentive ownership is important for agricultural and rural transformation. China's reform of land ownership is incentive-based, which has contributed to its successful agricultural and rural transformation. Before reform, the village committee owned property rights. Farmers normally sign contracts with village communities for a length of tenancy up to 30 years. The government has carried out policies to lease another 30 years of land property rights to farmers. The farmers have the right to lease out their land to small and medium-sized agribusiness firms, and they can share the profits from agricultural businesses. Some farmers can also derive land-rent from local agribusiness firms. However, a majority of smallholder farmers use arable land areas for their household grain production; they are normally self-sufficient, and derive a substantial living.

The collective production system was replaced first by the joint-venture contract system that several rural households worked as a team in earlier stage of the transformation. The household contracting system then substituted the joint-venture contract system when individuals have developed their capability in management of agri-business and are more confident to gain more profit alone in market.

When farmers improved their capability to run their family agribusiness in a competitive market, the household contracting system then substituted the joint-venture contract system. Some farmers and rural workers developed their capabilities in the management of agribusiness, and are more confident in their ability to win profit unaided. Enlightened governance has helped to implement a bottom-up development approach, and has also facilitated rural industry and inclusive agribusiness development in a large-scale economy.

Notwithstanding the market being a driving force in consumption, product and resource allocation, it can also be "merciless," especially when poor smallholder farmers are unable to change their technology and products in response to market demands, due to lack of developments capabilities and a discouraging social and economic environment in the transitional economy. Therefore, feasible policies should be given priority in implementing new technology and technical innovation at a micro-level. Governance needs to strengthen development capabilities for smallholder farmers in adopting technical changes.

Entrepreneurship is important for rural industrial sustainable development and for transformation to modernization and industrial agricultural development. There are tangible and intangible development resources for agricultural growth. Intangible development resources include entrepreneurship and technical skills and knowledge. A lack of funds is not the only reason that people cannot get out of the poverty trap. Tangible development resources include production inputs such as land, labor, machinery, starting funds and infrastructure. Intangible development resources are also critically important to grow agroindustry with a scale economy. The power behind changing products, processes and services comes from individuals—whether acting alone or embedded within organization—who make innovation happen (Bessant and Tidd 2011). Smallholder individual farmers hardly work alone to develop the agroindustry with a scale economy. Governance and the bottom-up development approach may help indigenous agroindustry and agribusiness by association with a large-scale economy.

Inclusive agribusiness development involves a group of stakeholders, including smallholder farmers, rural communities, entrepreneurs and relevant governments. Success in innovation—whether an individual first timer or a global corporation—is not just about having a good idea and assembling the resources to make it happen. It also about having the capabilities to manage them—and these are the hardest to get a handle on; they can make or break the process (Bessant and Tidd 2011).

Effective local governance should facilitate smallholder farmers to access new technology. In addition, it needs to help develop a value chain with local, regional and national linkages. Institutions and policies also foster entrepreneurship in development capabilities. Institutions and policies determine the economic and political environment within which individuals accumulate skills, and firms accumulate capital and produce output (Besley and Burgess 2003). An efficient system of property rights of land is needed to minimize transaction costs in adopting new technology and new products for smallholder farmers. Local governments can create the local social environment for promoting or undermining sustained development (Tsakok 2011). The role of government is not to intervene in the market directly, because the role of government cannot substitute for the market function, but it can make up market deficiency. Local government plays a coordinating role in economic activity to foster market function in resource allocation. Strengthening institutional capability at the local level is essential, if decentralization is to be effective in implementing technical changes and innovation for fitting in local embedded culture and indigenous industry. Yet, decentralization alone is not a panacea: the role of central government in drawing up big plans and policies as well as institutional formulation is irreplaceable.

China's decentralized organizational structure helps local officials to play an effective and efficient coordination role. In China's transitional economy, the information flow was made more difficult by sheer geographical distance, and local officials have better local information about resources and local conditions. Importantly, China's decentralization has facilitated effective coordinating role of local government in technological progress and innovation. Besides, the local technical professionals have better information from smallholder farmers and have effective communication with them directly. Under decentralization, synchronization has the advantage that decisions can be made locally and can be fully responsive to information received from others in the system in China.

6.6 Conclusion

China has been through different development stages in poverty reduction and increasing income and improving livelihoods for farmers as well as creating more work opportunities in rural areas. China's government has emphasized technological innovation and institutional innovation to transform the structure of the agricultural sector and to upgrade agricultural modernization and rural industrialization. Decentralization facilitates coordination of local government in implementing technological innovation for farmers. Efficient property rights and feasible policies are important in allocation resources and in balance subsistence sector in agricultural production and capital accumulation sector in rural industrialization. Coordination of local government can enable smallholder farmers to participate in local agribusiness and industrial development with a scale economy. Institutional innovation helps smallholder farmers to share the profits from local industrial development and clusters of agribusiness, and thoughtful governance and the bottom-up development approach can foster farmers' ability to develop their family agribusinesses. The stakeholders in local agribusiness and enterprises have income or profit-sharing proportionally, following principles of every individual's contributions to output value and market profits. Local governance has strengthened local development environment, where local public and private management partnerships can facilitate smallholder farmers to access new technology market and value chain. These will be helpful for inclusive growth. A solution for poverty not only needs to improve agricultural productivity for smallholder farmers, but also the business opportunities to participants in the value chain of the business. China's governance and bottom-up development have fostered inclusive growth. The local stakeholders' firms enjoy sustainably inclusive growth.

Finally, global governance is important for coordination of different institutions and policies in different countries. Tailor-made feasible policies should also take account of cultural, social and political systems. An advantage of globalization is that there are more opportunities to share lessons among countries and regions. The valuable lessons not only come from successful development experiences, but also failed ones. Developing countries have worked on different development paths in respect of their cultural, economic and political aspects. Many developing countries have increased international cooperation of their agribusinesses and use of their own approachable development strategies. Therefore, global governance is very important for the development and empowering of agricultural growth in creating ample work opportunities for young rural workers and other poor in developing and underdeveloped countries. There is a great need for effective global governance to solve the problems of food safety and social and environmental development.

References

Babu, S. C., Huang, J. K., Venkatesh, P., & Zhang, Y. M. (2015). A Comparative Analysis of Agricultural Research and Extension Reforms in China and India. *China Agricultural Economic Review, 7*(4), 541–572.

Barro, R. J. (1990). Government Spending in a Simple Model of Endogenous Growth. *Journal of Political Economy, 98*(5), 103–125.

Besley, T., & Burgess, R. (2003). Halving Global Poverty. *Journal of Economic Perspectives, 17*(3), 3–22.

Bessant, J., & Tidd, J. (2011). *Innovation and Entrepreneurship*. Chichester: Wiley.

Blom, J. C. (2018). Environmental Polices in Europe and the Effect on the Balance of Trade. In M. E. Bredahl, N. Ballenger, J. C. Dunmore, & T. L. Roe (Eds.), *Agriculture, Trade, and the Environment – Discovering and Measuring the Critical Linkages*. New York: Routledge.

Carayannis, G., Popescu, D., Sipp, C., & Stewart, M. (2006). Technological Learning for Entrepreneurial Development in the Knowledge Economy: Case Studies and Lessons Learned. *Journal of Technovation* 26(4): 419–443. Accessed https://www.sciencedirect.com/journal/technovation/vol/26/issue/4

Chambers, R., Pacey, A., & Thrupp, L. A. (1989). *Farmer First: Farmer Innovation and Agricultural Research*. London: Intermediate Technology Publications.

Chen, H. Y. (2018). *The Institutional Transition of China's Township and Village Enterprises: Market Liberalization, Contractual Form Innovation and Privatization*. New York: Routledge Revivals.

China Business News. (2013). Macro-implications of the Incomes of have doubled for China's Residents, Shanghai, 11th September 2013, https://www.yicai.com/news/3003582.html

Crafts, N. (1996). Post Neo Classical Growth Theory: What Are the Policy Implications. *Oxford Review of Economic Policy, 12*(2), 30–48.

De Feis, G. L. (2018). Business Youth for Engaged Sustainability to Achieve the United Nations 17 Sustainable Development Goals (SDGs). In S. Dhiman & J. Marques (Eds.), *Handbook of Engaged Sustainability*. Cham: Springer International Publishing.

Diao, X. S., Hazell, P., & Thurlow, J. (2010). The Role of Agriculture in African Development. *World Development, 38*(10), 1375–1383.

Djankov, S., Qian, Y., Roland, G., & Zhuravskaya, E. (2006). Who Are China's Entrepreneurs? *American Economic Review Paper and Proceedings, 96*(2), 348–352.

Dollar, D. (2008). *Lessons from China for Africa*. The World Bank Policy Research Working Paper WPS4531. Washington, DC: The World Bank.

Du, R. S. (1998). *Du Rui Sheng Collections Papers 1980–1998*. ShanXi: Shanxi Economic Publishing House.

Fan, S. G., Zhang, L. X., & Zhang, X. B. (2001). How Does Public Spending Affect Growth and Poverty in China? *World Economy and China, 9*(4), 9–19.

Fan, S. G., Nestorova, B., & Olofinbiyi, T. (2010, April 27–28). China's Agricultural and Rural Development: Implications for Africa, China-DAC Study Group on Agriculture, Food Security and Rural Development, Bamako.

Fei, J. C. H., & Ranis, G. (1964). *Development of the Labour Surplus Economy: Theory and Policy*. Homewood: Richard A. Irwin.

Fu, X. L., & Balasubramanyam, V. N. (2003). Township and Village Enterprises in China. *Journal of Development Studies, 39*(4), 27–46.

Han, C. F., et al. (2019). New China's Agricultural Development with 70 Years-Policies Achievement Volume (Beijing: China's Agricultural Publisher).

Ianchovichina, E., & Lundstrom, S. (2009). Inclusive Growth Analytics, Framework and Application. Policy Research Working Paper 4851. Washington: The World Bank.

International Fund for Agricultural Development. (2019). *IFAD's 2019 Rural Development Report-Creating Opportunities for Rural Youth*. Roma: IFAD.

Jones, C. I. (2019). Paul Romer: Ideas, Nonrivalry, and Endogenous Growth. *The Scandinavian Journal of Economics, 121*(3), 859–883.

Juma, C. (2011). *New Harvest: Agricultural Innovation in Africa*. Oxford: Oxford University Press.

Katayama, R., & Wadhwa, D. (2019). Half of the World's Poor Live in Just 5 Counties. *The World Bank Data Blog*. Accessed 9 Jan 2019.

Kirkpatrick, C., & Barrientos, A. (2004, September). Development Economics and Public Policy. *Working paper series*, Paper No.9. Manchester: University of Manchester.

Kirkpatrick, C. H., & Nixson, F. J. (Eds.). (1983). *The Industrialization of Less Developed Countries*. Manchester: Manchester University Press.

Lewis, W. A. (1954). Economic Development with Unlimited Supply of Labour. *The Manchester School, 22*(2), 115–227.

Li, X. Y. (2014). China's Industrialization: Overview-Implications for Africa's Industrialization, November 2014. Beijing: International Poverty Reduction Center in China. https://www.tralac.org/images/docs/6676/background-report-chinas-industrialization-overview.pdf

Li, X. Y., Tang, L. X., Xu, X. L., Qi, G. B., & Wang, H. M. (2013). What Can Africa Learn from China's Experience in Agricultural Development. *IDS Bulletin* 44(4). https://doi.org/10.1111/1759-5436.12040. Assessed 28 Jun 2013.

Lin, J. Y. (2011). New Structural Economics: A Framework for Rethinking for Development and Policies. *The World Bank Research Observer, 26*(2), 193–221.

Lin, Y. F. (2013). *City Competitiveness and Sustainable Growth.* Beijing: National School of Development, Peking University. https://en.nsd.pku.edu.cn/news/238977.htm. Accessed 26 Nov 2013.

Narula, R., & Dunning, J. (2000). Industrial Development, Globalization and Multinational Enterprises: New Realities for Developing Countries. *Journal of Oxford Development Studies, 28*(2), 141–167.

National Bureau of Statistics of China. (2019). *National Economy and Social Development Statistic Bulletin in 2018.* Beijing: National Bureau Statistics of China. http://www.stats.gov.cn/tjsj/zxfb/201902/t20190228_1651265.html. Accessed 28 Feb 2019.

National Bureau of Statistics of China. (2020a). *Statistical Bulletin of China's National Economy and Social Development in 2019.* Beijing: National Bureau of Statistics of China. http://www.stats.gov.cn/tjsj/zxfb/202002/t20200228_1728913.html

National Bureau of Statistics of China. (2020b). *Statistical Bulletin of China's National Economy and Social Development in 2019.* Beijing: National Bureau of Statistics of China. http://www.stats.gov.cn/tjsj/zxfb/202002/t20200228_1728913.html

North, D. C., & Thomas, R. P. (1973). *The Rise of The Western World: A new Economic History.* New York: Cambridge University Press.

Oi, J. C. (1999). *Rural China Takes Off: Institutional Foundations of Economic Reform.* California: University of California Press.

Ravallion, M. (2009). There Lessons for Africa from China's Success Against Poverty? *World Development, 37*(2), 303–313.

Rocha, H. O. (2004). Entrepreneurship and Development: The Role of Clusters. *Small Business Economics, 23*(5), 363–400.

Rostow, W. W. (1966). *The Stages of Economic Growth: A Non-communist Manifesto.* Cambridge: Cambridge University Press.

Sun, T. Z. (1995). *Contemporary China's Rural Fiscal Study.* Beijing: Economic Science Publisher.

Sun, Z. C. (2008). *China's Agricultural and Rural Reform and Development with 30 Years.* Beijing: China's Agricultural Publishing House.

Sun, H. L. (2015). China's Town and Village Enterprises and Its Implication for Sub-Saharan Africa. *International Journal of Technology and Globalization, 8*(1), 29–49.

The National Bureau Statistics of China. (2019). *National Economy and Social Development Statistic Bulletin in 2018*. Beijing: National Bureau Statistics of China. http://www.stats.gov.cn/tjsj/zxfb/201902/t20190228_1651265.html. Accessed 28 Feb 2019.

The National Bureau of China's Statistics. (2020). Incomes of Rural Residents at Impoverished Rural Areas in 2019 at China. http://www.stats.gov.cn/tjsj/zxfb/202001/t20200123_1724697.html. Accessed 23 Jan 2020.

The United Nations. (2015). *Millennium Development Goals Report 2015*. New York: United Nations. https://www.un.org/en/development/desa/publications/mdg-report-2015.html. Accessed 6 Jul 2015.

The World Bank. (1992). *Governance and Development*. Washington, DC: The World Bank. http://documents.worldbank.org/curated/en/604951468739447676/Governance-and-development. Accessed 30 Apr 1992.

The World Bank. (2016). *World Development Indicators 2016*. Washington: International Bank for Reconstruction and Development/The World Bank.

The World Bank. (2018). *Atlas of Sustainable Development Goals 2018: From World Development Indicators*. Washington: World Bank.

The World Bank. (2019a). *Poverty Continues to Decline, but Pace of Poverty Reduction Is Slowing in Central Asia, Infographic: Poverty in Central Asia*. Washington, DC: World Bank.

The World Bank. (2019b). *World Development Report 2019: The Changing Nature Work*. Washington, DC: The World Bank.

The World Bank. (2019c). *Understanding Poverty*. Washington, DC: World Bank.

The World Bank. (2020). *China-Overview*. Washington, DC: The World Bank. https://www.worldbank.org/en/country/china/overview

Thirlwall, A. P., & Pacheco-López, P. (2017). *Economics of Development*. London: Palgrave Macmillan.

Trankmann, B. (2019). *What Changes After China Defeats Poverty*. Beijing: ChinaDaily. http://www.chinadaily.com.cn/a/201912/23/WS5dfffb82a310cf3e3557fd9f.html. Accessed 23 Dec 2019.

Tsakok, I. (2011). *Success in Agricultural Transformation, What Its Means and What Makes It Happen*. Cambridge: Cambridge University Press.

UNDP. (2020). UNDP-Overview *Inclusive Development*. https://www.kz.undp.org/content/kazakhstan/en/home/ourwork/inclusivedevelopment/overview.html

United Nations. (2014). United Nations Committee for Development Policy. *Global Governance and Global Rules for Development in the post-2015 Era*. New York: United Nations Publication, ISBN 978-92-1-104689-2.

United Nations Industrial Development Organization. (2017). *Agribusiness and Human Capital Development*. Vienna: UNIDO.

United Nations Industrial Development Organization. (2020). Agribusiness and Rural Entrepreneurship Development. Accessed at https://www.unido.org/our-focus/creating-shared-prosperity/agribusiness-and-rural-entrepreneurship-development

Wu, J., & Si, S. (2018). Poverty Reduction Through Entrepreneurship: Incentives, Social Networks, and Sustainability. *Asian Business and Management, 17*(4), 243–259.

Xie, W., & White, S. (2006). From Imitation to Creation: The Critical Yet Uncertain Transition for Chinese Firm. *Journal of Technology Management in China, 1*(3), 229–242.

Zhang, J., Zhang, L., Rozelle, S., & Boucher, S. (2006). Self-Employment With Chinese Characteristics: The Forgotten Engine of Rural China's Growth. *Contemporary Economic Policy, 24*(3), 446–458.

Zhu, Q. X., & Elbern, S. (2002). *Economic Institutional Evolution and Further Needs for Adjustments: Township Village Enterprises in China*. Bonn: Zentrum für Entwicklungsforschung (ZEF).

Zou, W. (2003). The Changing Face of Rural Enterprises. *China Perspectives* [online] Revues,org, http://chinaperspectives.revues.org/773. Accessed Nov–Dec 2003.

CHAPTER 7

China's Economic Development and International Cooperation

7.1 Introduction

International trade and investment have contributed to the economic growth of developed and developing countries. A report from the International Monetary Fund in 2001 stated that the growth of world trade has averaged 6% per year over the past 20 years, twice as fast as world output. The impact and potential gains from trade liberalization may differ based on a country's level of economic development (Leibovici and Crews 2018). Studies foresee that agricultural trade will play a large role in securing the food needs of developing countries as well as being a source of foreign exchange (Bruinsma 2003). In some developing and underdeveloped countries, commodities like agricultural products and primary products help to accumulate foreign exchange earnings in the early economic transformation phase, because the agricultural sector is the large component of a pre-industrial country's gross domestic product.

Some developing countries have experienced a moderate level of economic growth in the past two decades, but their poverty reduction has progressed slowly. In addition, food insecurity remains a serious problem in impoverished regions of underdeveloped countries. Many developing countries have undertaken an economic transformation in which urbanization and industrialization have made progresses at different levels. In some transitional countries a majority of the population lives in at rural areas, where smallholder farmers mainly depend on their agricultural

L. Sun, *Economic Growth and Development*, Palgrave Studies in Economic History,
https://doi.org/10.1007/978-3-030-46099-0_7

production for subsistence. Some developing countries have had sustained GDP growth over the past decade, but their agricultural productivity did not increase at the same rate, and rural poverty remained pronounced. Crop production was more than 70% of total agricultural output in sub-Saharan Africa (Fuglie and Rada 2013). In 2012, sub-Saharan African countries spent $37.7 billion on food imports (Montpellier Panel Report 2014). A report of FAO in 2019 revealed that the majority of the world's undernourished population (more than 500 million) live in Asia.

Rethinking domestic economic development strategies and policies is necessary to solve development barriers when developing and underdeveloped countries have economic growth, although international trade of agricultural products can help to supply demand. International trade of agricultural products plays an important role in economic development. The functions of economic development include international trade of agricultural products contributing to industrial development in some developing countries and transitional economies, in part by accumulating foreign exchange earnings at an early stage of economic transformation. International trade is becoming more important for developing countries and transitional economies that are progressing toward becoming upper-high income and high-income countries. Agricultural growth was the precursor to the industrial revolutions that spread across the temperate world from England in the mid-eighteenth century to Japan in the late nineteenth century (Mcmichael 2009). More recently, rapid agricultural growth in China, India and Vietnam has been the precursor to the rise of industry (Mcmichael 2009).

Developing countries have been the locus of a trend of investment by multinational enterprises (MNEs). Some MNEs are trading companies that engage in international agribusiness; others invest directly in developing countries. Globalization is often charged with shifting power away from national governments to MNEs, and MNEs in food and agriculture operate across many country borders. They are increasingly vertically integrated, carrying out the whole sequence of operations from producing and marketing seed, through purchasing the crop, to food processing and distribution. They can and do move operations from country to country in search of lower costs, including wage rates, and lower labor rights and environmental standards (World Investment Report 2019).

The benefits from MNEs have been demonstrated: they include technological transfer, creation of work opportunities for local workers and help in building value chains from advanced to developing countries. MNEs promote technological innovation and R&D in innovative programs, because they gain profits from long-term growth of businesses. Technological innovation is a key factor to the growth of businesses in competitive markets. Compared with private enterprises, role of governments is to foster inclusive agribusiness development and carry out feasible economic policies to facilitate processes of industrial development in agribusiness and rural enterprises.

In this chapter, Sect. 7.2 analyzes the role of China's international trade in economic development; Sect. 7.3 analyzes China's economic development and international trade as it affects the agricultural sector; and Sect. 7.4 analyses China's international cooperation in trade and investment. Section 7.5 presents a summary.

7.2 The Role of China's International Trade in Economic Development

China has increasingly imported agricultural products, including staple foods, from international markets during its economic transformation. The proportion of total international trade of China's manufacturing sectors has accelerated over a long period. Further, in terms of comparative advantage, China exported its agricultural sideline products and traditional commodities when its level of industrial development was low. The dynamic changes to China's international trade include categories of commodities, and the ratio of imports and exports in total value. Another dynamic change is the distribution of international trade of commodities in different regions over time. All these dynamic changes in China's international trade have been driven by its rapid domestic economic development, both industrial and enterprise development.

The share of agriculture in GDP and national economic composition declines as developing countries make progress toward industrialization and urbanization. In the process of industrialization, the relationship between trade policy and progress of industrialization is important in economic development.

Siddiqui (2018) analyzed free trade and its impact on the industrial and agricultural sectors and showed how the performance of both sectors could have a long-term impact on local industrialization, food security, employment and well-being of the population of developing countries.

Industrial development is not only a matter of developing economies progressing toward industrialization per se; it also it refers to industrial development in forming rural enterprises and family agribusinesses at a time of economic transformation. Industrial development has featured in association with a scale economy, commercialization of agribusinesses and technological innovation as well as management of agribusinesses in the process of economic transformation. Therefore, national economic policies can impact on the rural industrialization through the development of rural enterprises, and the dynamic development of rural enterprises at a national scale can impact on the structure of international trade in commodities during the process of economic transformation. Developing countries need to adjust their polices of domestic economic development and industrial development, which can help their planning through a strategy of international trade according to different stages of economic development. There is an approach to trade policy reform which differentiates between countries according to their level of development, industrial base and individual characteristics, and emphasizes the need for building up supply capacity (Shafaeddin 1994).

Lower trade barriers alone may not suffice for developing countries. In many developing countries agriculture has not only suffered from trade barriers and subsidies abroad but has also been neglected in domestic policies (Bruinsma 2003). Industrial countries maintain protection of their agriculture through an array of very high tariffs: average tariff protection in agriculture is about nine times higher than in manufacturing (International Monetary Fund 2001). These policies foster structural changes in production of commodities and the development strategy of domestic trade.

Agricultural commodities are fundamental to economic composition, unlike service industries. Without sufficient production of agricultural products and foods, the population faces starvation. Developing countries are projected to provide most of their domestic consumption growth by expanding their own agricultural production through improvement of agricultural productivity. International trade in agricultural products to meet domestic food demand and gain foreign currency is an alternative development approach to development via structural changes in economic transition. In a market economy, individuals can exchange what they own for other commodities either through trading, or through production, or through a combination of the two (Sen 1981).

7.2.1 Multinational Enterprises and Global Value Chains

Global value chains (GVCs) powered the surge of international trade after 1990 and now account for almost half of all trade (World Development Report 2020). Trading for development in the age of GVCs examines whether there is still a path to development through GVCs and trade. The issue of GVCs and development should also address the challenges and opportunities between developed and developing countries. Opportunities are partly driven by multinational enterprises, which will bring new commercial opportunities to smallholder agricultural producers profit from international trade in the future, following application of technology to commercial trade transactions, such as e-commerce agribusiness.

There are also challenges in that there are information asymmetries on markets in developing countries. China has increased its imports of some agricultural products in the past ten years, the prices for several agricultural products in domestic markets in China were higher than their imported agricultural products, such as the domestic prices of several key staple food products have been higher than the imported prices in the period of 2012–2017 in Table 7.7. China imported higher-priced agricultural products than domestic prices from both developed countries and developing countries. In the market for information and knowledge, potential customers are typically ignorant of potential gains from obtaining services outside their circle of awareness. Private production or supply of information may be inhibited because potential purchasers find it difficult to evaluate information prior to its acquisition (Kristiansen 2003).

There are potential opportunities for smallholder farmers' business development where inclusive agribusiness development and management by stakeholders of agribusinesses may help the improvement their profits through local value chains. Some local firms are closely linked with global partners, both upstream and downstream; this is characteristic of firms in the final stages of value chains and of dynamic suppliers (Chiarvesio et al. 2010).

This needs policies to implement industrial development at grass-root level, and numbers of China's private local enterprises have upgraded their industrialization level and the quality of their agricultural products, driven by GVCs. Despite the fact that agriculture is experiencing profound

Box 7.1 Multinational Enterprise in Heilongjiang Province
Multinational enterprises usually upgrade local skills, methods, standards and technologies as they expand in a country. For example, in the late 1980s, in China's Heilongjiang province, the multinational Nestle built rural roads, organized milk collection points and trained dairy farmers in basic animal health and hygiene.

MNEs have advantages in linking with local firms to upgrade in order to remain competitive.

Source: *World Agriculture: Towards 2015/2030*, FAO 2002

changes in most developing countries, not all localities have shifted from a traditional to a modern productive sector (Soundarrajan and Vivek 2015). Effective management of multinational agribusiness can bring business opportunities for the stakeholders in local agribusinesses to make profits from home countries indirectly to gain profits in a GVC. Multinational enterprises' cooperation can help to transfer technology, and can also exchange experience of business management as a platform among different countries. Box 7.1 illustrates the example of multinational enterprises in Heilongjiang province in the early stage in 1980s when its economic transition was in its early stages.

In the past three decades or more, China's great market demand for agricultural commodities has driven its international agribusiness to upgrade the value chains of and with both developed and developing countries. In European agro-food value chains source globally but supply locally. By contrast, those of China have a greater span in both sourcing inputs and supplying other markets. For the United States, sourcing is narrower and more regionally focused, but supply is global (Greenville et al. 2017).

Industrial development accelerates the upgrading of a value chain of agribusiness in domestic markets in China. Simultaneously, inclusive development of agribusiness and application of informational technology in e-commercial development are important to help local rural enterprises and smallholder farmers to have more lucrative agribusiness opportunities in domestic markets. The materialization of GVCs and the change in the trade paradigm require a new set of policies able to attenuate or overcome current domestic constraints and allow small and medium-sized producers to become more competitive and participate in national and international value chains in a sustainable manner (Montalbano et al. 2015).

7.2.2 *Investment in Industrial Development and Sustainable Agribusiness*

In 2018, global flows of foreign direct investment fell by 13%, to $1.3 trillion (World Investment Report 2019). The numbers of the undernourished and sufferers from food insecurity are still serious at present. More than 820 million people suffered hunger in 2019 (FAO 2019). FAO estimates that US$83 billion dollars per year of additional investment in food, agriculture and rural development are required for the world to feed its growing population in 2050—in other words, investment needs to rise by 50%. Investment in agriculture is imperative in developing countries. In most developing countries, agriculture accounts for between 20 and 60% of GDP, and employs up to 65% of the labor force, providing a livelihood for approximately 2.6 billion people globally (UNCTAD 2012).

Previously, development aid was a major factor in poverty reduction and eradication of hunger, whereas foreign direct investments (FDI) tended to develop agribusiness projects to gain returns of commercial profits. Today, there are more FDI development projects to invest in agribusiness and firms, which have advantages for industrial development with a scale economy. Epaphra and Mwakalasya (2017) analyzed the effect of foreign direct investment (FDI) on the agricultural sector in Tanzania. They suggest that the sector is inefficient and therefore needs to make efforts to attract more FDI, aiming to improve productivity in the agriculture sector, which in turn may reduce poverty.

There are some 570 million farms worldwide, of which the majority are small farms. In some countries, small-scale food producers account for up to 85% of all food production (FAO 2019). In China, smallholder farmers are a majority of agricultural producers, and rural households have small cultivated land areas. Further improvement of agricultural mechanization and modernization as well as commercialization will be important for industrial development.

Government investment will be necessary to promote the industrial development of sustainable agribusiness in the future. Industrial development can improve agricultural productivity and generate better returns from agribusiness. Productivity of small-scale producers is systematically lower on average than for larger food producers and, in most countries, the incomes of small-scale food producers are less than half those of larger food producers (FAO 2019). Industrial development helps smallholder farmers to improve profits through upgrading integration with horizontal and vertical business chains.

However, a majority of smallholder farmers lack capital to invest. Industrial development and agribusiness value chains need capital investment. Government investment in industrial development can help smallholder farmers to increase incomes and create more agribusiness opportunities in a sustainable manner. In some rural areas, investment in industrial development includes infrastructure (road, water distribution systems, etc.) and market value chains (from individual agricultural producer, retailer, to export), and extension and regulations on import and export (knowledge of international markets, means of access and standards required). Investment in agricultural extension develops systems through which technologies can be extended to and adopted or adapted by farmers, and several studies have shown the positive impacts of such investments on agricultural productivity and incomes (Alston et al. 2000).

Industrial development can help farmers increase returns from their family business. For instance, small scale family businesses in the Chinese aquaculture sector have increased income for farmers. Government investment helped this development: total investment for aquaculture development was 389.2 million RMB for year 2000, of which 244.2 million RMB was spent on training and research, and 145 million RMB on project loans (*Chinese Fishery Statistic Yearbook* 2003). Investment in industrial development is important in increasing the incomes and profits of family and small-scale agribusinesses. For instance, the industrialized production of leather catfish yield per unit is extremely high compared with other carp-species output. The output per unit of intensive aquaculture is several dozens or even 100 times higher than ordinary fishing. Investment in industrial production is also higher than in extensive production systems. To maintain appropriate water conditions, a high water-exchange rate and / or mechanical aeration is required. Most small-scale farmer households cannot afford to invest in leather catfish production for reasons of increased costs, although the profits are high. Therefore, government investment is important for the industrial development of small-scale agribusiness.

7.3 China's Economic Development and International Trade

China has enjoyed rapid economic growth in the past four decades, and has accelerated progress toward industrialization from its agricultural-backbone economy of the 1950s. China exported agricultural products before the economic reform in 1979. Its economic policies were centered on industrial development; the export of agricultural products accumulated foreign exchange earnings to support industrial development. China's dynamic development of enterprises and businesses now contributes to economic growth. In particular, the remarkable development of rural enterprises is China's pioneering industrial development. China has implemented the opening-up of economic policies on development, including international trade and markets as well as enterprise development based on the policies outlined earlier—including, as a core proposition, to sustain food security by improvement of agricultural productivity and the supply of domestic markets.

China's international trade has experienced three development stages during its industrial and agricultural development. Industrial sectors have increased their weight in international trade since 1990s. This section analyzes the role of rural enterprises in the structural changes in China's international trade in commodities. Many developing countries have substantially increased their exports of manufactures and services relative to traditional commodity exports: manufactures have risen to 80% of developing countries' exports. Trade between developing countries has grown rapidly, with 40% of their exports now going to other developing countries (International Monetary Fund 2001).

7.3.1 *International Trade and the Accumulation Stage of Industrial Development*

In the first stage of industrial development, the agricultural sideline products and processing agricultural sideline products were the most important commodities in international trade to gain foreign exchange earning to support domestic industrial development. Economic development needs resources for growth at different development stages. The system of modern commercialized agriculture, upon which many developing countries depend for their export earnings, is often terms agribusiness (Thirlwall and Pacheco-López 2017). China had already adopted export strategies for the agricultural sector to accumulate capital to help its industrial development even before the 1970s. Agricultural exports' contribution to foreign exchange receipts were higher than other sectors well before China's economic reform.

Table 7.1 shows that China imported mainly production materials between 1952 and 1978. These imported materials improved China's industrial development, because the government accentuated the importance of industrial development for its national economic growth. In 1952, the agricultural sector accounted for 57.7% of China's GDP (Yu 2018), and the agricultural sector labor force accounted for 83.5% of the total number of employed workers. China was a backbone agricultural economy and a low-income country in the 1950s. MaoZeDong highlighted the principle of China's economic development in the relations between agricultural sector and industrial sector between 1952 and 1975: the industrial sector was a key driver to economic development, and the agricultural sector was a fundamental part of that economic development (Sha 2009).

Table 7.1 shows that China exported agricultural and sideline products between 1952 and 1978. The share of agricultural and sideline products in total exports declined during this period. China also significantly exported the processed agricultural products between 1952 and 1978:

Table 7.1 China's Agricultural Products Import and Export Status 1950–1978 (%[a])

Years	*Sideline product exports*	*Processed agricultural products exports*	*Import of production materials*
1950	57.5	33.2	83.4
1952	59.3	22.8	89.4
1957	40.1	31.5	92.0
1962	19.4	45.9	55.2
1965	33.1	36.0	66.5
1970	36.7	37.7	82.7
1975	29.6	31.1	85.4
1978	27.6	35.0	81.4

Source: *China Agricultural Development over 70 Years*

[a] Agricultural and sideline product exports as a proportion of total exports

59.2% of total exports were agricultural and sideline products was, processed agricultural products were 22.8% of total exports. China's staple grain production was kept for its domestic consumption between 1950 and 1978.

China's economic development was at the accumulation development stage between 1950 and 1980, and large numbers of the population were living on very low or subsistence income. Structural changes in the agricultural sector started to lead to diversification during this period.

China participated in international cooperation on agricultural technology and exchanged development experiences for a long period It started international communication and cooperation on agricultural technology with Russia, Romania, Bulgaria, Korea and Poland in the period of 1950s–1960s (Hao et al. 2019). There were also technological exchanges on agricultural development between China and other developed countries, including Japan, Denmark, the United Kingdom in that period. China had international exchanges on agriculture with some developing countries, including a few countries from Africa, and Middle Eastern countries during the 1960s and 1970s (Hao et al. 2019).

In terms of international trade and market, China had already started to build up economic cooperation with Western countries in the early of 1970s, including bilateral trade cooperation with the United States starting in 1971. China was marginal to world trade in 1971 when President Richard Nixon announced his visit to China, and Nixon officially ended the US trade embargo on China, sweeping aside the legal barriers which had hindered significant economic interaction between the two nations since 1950 (Wang 2013). Wang (2013) explained that the decade 1971–80 witnessed rapid institution-building and the lifting of some of the barriers to the flow of goods, technology, and people between China and the United States. China became a permanent member of the United Nations Security Council in 1971 and established diplomatic and economic relations with Western countries and other developing countries, including the United Kingdom and West Germany, in 1972. West Germany became China's most important trading partner in Europe (Kundnani and Parello-Plesner 2012).

In 1952 the population of China was 574.82 million, of which 503.19 million (87.54%) were rural population (Han et al. 2019). Labor-intensive agricultural production included agricultural sideline products and the processing of agricultural products. Some rural workers were members of production teams (work groups) engaged in the production of agricultural sideline products and the processing of agricultural products.

Table 7.2 China's export composition between 1953 and 1981 (%)

Classification	*1953*	*1957*	*1981*
Primary products	79.4	63.6	49.6
Food	30.9	27.2	14.7
Beverages and tobacco	7.9	3.9	0.4
Non-food materials	33.3	28.3	9.9
Fossil fuel	0.8	1.1	24.2
Fats and vegetable oils	6.5	3.1	0.4
Manufactured goods	20.6	36.4	50.4
Chemical products	8.3	10.1	18.2
Textile products	12.3	26.3	32.2

Source: *China Agricultural Development over 70 Years*

Table 7.2 shows that China's agricultural products were the largest contributor to its exports commodities between 1953 and 1957. By 1981, the manufactured goods had come to predominate, though agricultural products were still important. China's textile products as a proportion of total export commodities also increased between 1953 and 1981.

7.3.2 *International Trade of Agricultural Products and Industrial Development*

Rapid industrial development accelerated China's international trade in the second economic development stage. China's rural industry took off on a national scale between 1979 and 2001. The successful inclusive development of China's town and village enterprises (TVEs) and family agribusinesses contributed to rapid industrial development on a national scale, and international trade helped to upgrade the value chain during this period. The industrial development of agricultural production impacted on agricultural products for international trade: China's aquaculture sector became one of the country's highest foreign exchange earners, and the industrial development of small-scale pond fish production has helped smallholder farmers to make bigger profits and higher output value.

Family agribusiness and industrial development of the off-farm sector impacted on China's international trade in agricultural products. Table 7.3 shows that aquaculture and vegetables achieved high values of exports between 1994 and 2001. International trade is based on comparative advantage in international markets, in terms of price and quality. China's structural changes and markets contributed to its output value of

Table 7.3 China's net exports of agricultural products between 1994 and 2001 (Units: US$100 million)

Agricultural products	*1994*	*1995*	*1996*	*1997*	*1998*	*1999*	*2000*	*2001*
Grain products	2.82	-34.7	-22.08	4.03	8.58	6.62	11.03	4.68
Cotton	-7.73	-14.38	-12.62	-14.05	-3.22	1.81	1.7	-0.35
Edible oil seeds	7.25	5.33	2.8	-4.31	-8.02	-10.11	-23.04	-24.92
Edible vegetable oil	-12.7	-19.74	-12.7	-10.47	-11.03	-10.37	-6.18	-4.39
Sugar	-0.87	-7.1	-1.45	-0.96	-0.16	-0.07	-0.32	-2.57
Vegetables	17.02	21.53	20.51	19.24	18.93	18.90	20.03	22.57
Fruits	3.18	4.49	3.39	3.59	3.20	3.54	3.11	4.08
Livestock	10.57	13.65	14.52	13.70	11.34	3.81	-0.82	-1.23
Aquaculture	17.33	23.28	18.27	19.32	18.17	18.33	19.80	22.99
Beverages	6.01	5.84	5.91	7.25	6.96	6.25	5.69	6.48
Tobacco	6.54	6.40	5.19	4.03	4.72	2.49	0.97	1.19
Others	23.45	20.40	12.84	8.77	5.67	11.03	10.12	11.61
Total	72.87	25.00	31.58	50.14	55.14	52.23	42.09	40.14

Source: *China's Agricultural Development over 70 Years*, 2019

Table 7.4 China's Gross Domestic Production Value Composition by Sectors (%) 1978–2000

	Agricultural sector	*Industry*	*Services sector*
1978	27.7	47.7	24.6
1990	26.6	41.0	32.4
2000	14.7	45.5	39.8

Source: *China's Statistic Yearbook* 2001

aquaculture products with a significant growth between 1994 and 2001. China's aquaculture production contributed heavily to foreign currency earnings during this period. The high output value of aquaculture development was characterized by the family agribusiness pattern and industrial development.

There is a strong relation between the progress of industrial development and international trade. Table 7.4 shows that the industry sector's share of GDP in 1978 was 47.7%, and was 45.5% in 2000. Therefore, the growth of the industrial sector contributed to economic transformation in China at the accumulated economic development stage between 1952 and 1978. In addition, Table 7.4 shows that the agricultural sector's share of

GDP in 1978 was 27.7%, and that it had declined to 14.7% by 2000. The agricultural sector's share of GDP in 1952 was 57.7% (Yu 2018). The services industries' share of GDP increased to 39.8% in 2000 from 24.6% in 1978. The different economic sectors changed in their relative contributions to China's GDP between 1978 and 2000, while China significantly increased its international trades.

The agricultural sector remained important in China's international trade during this second development stage. China's agricultural exports value accounted for more than 50% of China's total exports value in 1980 (Yu 2018). By 2009, agriculture's proportion of China's total exports value had decreased to 5.25%, from 20% in 1992, and agriculture's share of China's imports had increased to 29% in 2009 from 17% in 1992 (Yu 2018).

On the one hand, the growth of China's agricultural imports has been even faster than the growth of agricultural exports during this period because China's domestic market demand increased. China's rural enterprises and agribusiness have developed rapidly during this period. China's international trade in agricultural products increased to US$28.042 billion in 2001 from US$15.408 billion in 1993 (Han et al. 2019). Although the share of agricultural exports to total exports declined between 1992 and 2009, the value of exports increased from US$11.454 billion in 1993 to US$16.029 billion in 2001, while import value increased from US$3.954 billion in 1993 to US$12.013 billion in 2001 (Han et al. 2019).

On the other hand, the shares of industrial sector and other sectors have increased international trade. Table 7.5 shows that the industrial sector's share of China's total exports increased significantly to 95% in 2009 from less than 50% in 1980, while the industrial sector's share of imports rose to 71% in 2009 from 65% in 1980.

In its early economic development, China's rural industrial development contributed heavily to China's industrial sectors and its international trade. The development of TVEs was a key component of China's rural industrial development. China's rural industry has made a remarkable contribution to the commercialization and transformation of agriculture and China's international trade is an important part of its commercialization.

The industrial development has been a gradual economic transformation from pre-industrial commercial commodities, and goods and services. The value of the agricultural sector increased 4.1% annually on average, the growth rate of industrial sector grew 17.3% annually on average, and the services sector increased 9.5% on average annually between 1991 and

Table 7.5 China's export and import composition by sectors 1980–2009

Year	*Agriculture (%)*	*Industry (%)*	*Mineral & fuel & lubricating oil (%)*	*Light industrial manufacturing (%)*	*Machinery & Transportation Equipment (%)*
			Exports		
1980	50.30	49.70	23.62	22.07	4.65
1985	50.56	49.44	26.08	16.43	2.82
1992	20.02	79.98	5.53	19.00	15.56
1995	14.44	85.56	3.58	21.67	21.11
1996	14.52	85.48	3.93	18.87	23.38
2001	9.90	90.10	3.16	16.46	35.66
2009	5.25	94.75	1.70	115.38	49.12
			Imports		
1980	34.77	65.23	1.01	20.75	25.57
1985	12.52	87.48	0.41	28.16	38.43
1992	16.45	83.55	4.43	23.92	38.86
1995	18.49	81.51	3.88	21.78	39.85
1996	18.32	81.68	4.95	22.61	39.45
2001	18.78	81.22	7.17	17.22	43.94
2009	28.81	71.19	12.33	10.71	40.54

Source: Yu (2018)

1995 (*China National Statistic Yearbook* 1996). Industrial development helped to effect structural changes between 1952 and 1978. In 1952, the agricultural labor force was more than 83.5% of the total (Yu 2018), which had declined to 70.5% by 1978.

The progress of industrial development and international trade has helped structural changes in the relation of agricultural sector to the industrial sector. Low production costs and low prices of some processed products helped China's exports from TVEs at the take-off stage of economic development on a national scale in the 1980s and 1990s. The composition of the rural economy included the agricultural sector and TVEs in the 1980s (Liu et al. 2018). The rise of industrial sector included the industrial development of China's urban areas in 1990s, though a big proportion of industrial development remained at the level of town and village areas in China in the 1990s (Liu et al. 2018). China's rural industry's contribution to the growth of China's industrialization was less than 20% in the early 1980s (Liu 2003), but it experienced a rapid growth from the middle 1980s. In 1992, rural industry contributed to 71.15% of the growth of China's industrial sector. In 1997, industry in villages and towns added value of RMB 1250 billion, which accounted for 50% of national industrial added value (Liu 2003).

7.3.3 International Trade and Structural Changes in the Agricultural Sector

China accelerated its international trade in its third development stage. In 2001, China gained access the World Trade Organization, which was a milestone for international market of Chinese commodities and trade. China's imports and exports played an important role in the development of global trade (Ministry of Commerce of China 2019). According to Customs statistics, China's total import and export value reached US$4.62 trillion in 2018, with an increase of 12.6% year on year. Exports reached US$2.48 trillion, with an increase of 9.9%, and imports reached US$2.14 trillion, with an increase of 15.8% (Ministry of Commerce of China 2019). International trade has impacted on China's economic transformation at an increasing scale. The development of foreign trade powerfully promoted the construction of China's open economy and speeded up the process of industrialization and urbanization (Ministry of Commerce of China 2019).

Many Chinese enterprises have increased their economic and business cooperation under multi-institution and international regulation. Bhattasali (2004) assessed the impact of the reforms associated with WTO accession on poverty in China, particularly in rural areas, which now lag so badly behind urban areas. Trade reforms increased the range of enterprises eligible to trade in specific commodities and led to the development of new indirect trade instruments, such as duty exemptions. Comprehensive liberalization measures in China's World Trade Organization (WTO) accession package will help ease this problem as tariff reduction reduces the costs of domestic inputs to exporters (Ianchovichina and Martin 2001).

Since 2002, China's the value of China's imports has increased rapidly. Since 2011, the China's share of total world import value was kept at 10%. Since 2009 China has become the second largest importer in the world after the United States, and it is the largest importer of all the developing countries. Moreover, the import value of agricultural products was US$ 216.81 billion in 2018, with an increase of 7.7% over the previous year; in the same year the export value of its agricultural products was US$79.71

billion (Ministry of Agriculture and Rural Affairs of China 2019). The average annual rate of increase of China's agricultural products' export value was 6% between 1993 and 2001. At the same time, the average annual rate of increase of China's agricultural products' import value was 16% over the same period (Chen et al. 2018).

International trade has affected China's agricultural production for four decades, and international trade has driven the structural change of China's agricultural production. Its upgrading living standards have demanded more high value-added food products. The livestock feed industries need high imports of corn as well as other agricultural products. The cost of some Chinese domestic agricultural products is sometimes higher than the international market price. Huge demand is a major factor. For instance, the poultry industry needs feed resources, such as maize. Cultivated land area has been declining, because of China's development of rural and urban integration, and progress of urbanization. Additionally, the production costs of producing agricultural products have been raising. These phenomenon can cause an increase in the price of some agricultural products.

Table 7.6 shows that China's grain exports have declined between 2001 and 2017, and its imports declined from 5.29% in 2001 to 2.61% in

Table 7.6 Composition of China's Exports and Imports of Agricultural Products after Accession to the World Trade Organization (%)

	Exports				*Imports*			
	2001	*2006*	*2011*	*2017*	*2001*	*2006*	*2011*	*2017*
Grain products	6.88	3.74	1.34	1.05	5.29	2.61	2.15	5.21
Cotton	0.51	0.08	0.13	0.05	0.97	15.47	10.17	1.89
Edible oilseeds	4.51	3.58	3.04	2.91	26.76	24.73	33.01	34.64
Edible vegetable oil	0.29	0.76	0.35	0.28	4.04	9.82	9.46	4.56
Sugar	0.35	0.19	0.08	0.12	2.61	1.71	2.04	0.87
Vegetables	14.85	17.47	19.11	20.49	1.02	0.49	0.36	0.45
Fruits	4.67	7.44	8.58	8.77	2.84	2.37	3.23	4.89
Livestock	16.40	11.8	9.75	8.25	22.91	14.04	14.02	15.84
Aquaculture	26.04	29.71	28.95	27.34	15.6	13.36	8.4	8.74
Beverages	5.53	5.13	3.72	5.46	1.98	2.56	3.57	5.26
Tobacco	2.41	1.8	1.88	1.76	2.23	1.44	1.2	1.41
Other agri-products	17.56	18.29	23.07	23.52	13.76	11.39	12.38	16.23

Sources: *China's Agricultural Development over 70 Years*

2006, though they have more recently increased from 2.15% in 2011 to 5.21% in 2017. China's edible oilseed imports increased significantly between 2001 and 2017. China's livestock products exports declined between 2001 and 2017, and though livestock products imports decreased from 21.91% in 2001 to 14.04% in 2006 they have slightly increased more recently from 14.02% in 2011 to 15.84% in 2017. Aquaculture's products share of exports has increased slightly from 26.04% in 2001 to 27.34% in 2017, and its share of imports has declined to 8.74% in 2017 from 15.6% in 2001. Vegetable exports' share of the total increased between 2001 and 2017. Domestic structural changes have impacted on international trade. China's aquaculture production has been one of the fastest growing of its agricultural sectors between 2001 and 2017, and China is the largest aquaculture producer in the world. Technological innovation has contributed to the rapid growth of its aquaculture production.

China is the largest importer of many agricultural products from the international market, notably soybean and oilseed. For instance, China consumes 25% of the world's soybeans: its imports accounted for 60% of the global market in 2010. Further, high demand from the agricultural processing and livestock feed industries may cause a tightening of the domestic supply of corn. China's international agricultural trade (import and export) increased by 26.7% annually on average between 2002 and 2008. Caporale and Sova (2015) found a significant change in China's trading structure associated with the growth of foreign trade. In particular, shift from resource- and labor-intensive to capital- and technology-intensive exports.

China has passed a milestone development stage of international trade and business. Table 7.7 shows that between 2012 and 2017 the price of some imports became lower than China's domestic prices for several key agricultural products. China has increased its imports of several important grain products, even though the output of rice, wheat and corn per hectare increased in China between 1996 and 2017: The output of rice per hectare was 6916.9 kilogram in 2017, an increase of 11.3% over the output per hectare in 1996; the output per hectare of wheat was 5481.2 kilogram in 2017, an increase of 46.8% over 1996; and the output per hectare of corn was 6110.3 kilogram in 2017, an increase of 17.4% over 1996 (Information Office of the State Council of China 2019).

Following from the general and consistent improvement in living standards in China, a healthy food industry and an ecologically aware, technological agro-industry has grown up. Food industry and agribusiness enterprises have largely driven the improvement of technology and

Table 7.7 China's Domestic Prices and Imported Prices for Major Agricultural Products (Unit: RMB/Kilogram)

Product categories	*Items*	*2012*	*2013*	*2014*	*2015*	*2016*	*2017*
Wheat	Domestic price	2.15	2.44	2.50	2.97	1.42	1.47
	Import price	2.06	1.94	1.87	1.99	0.92	1.07
	Price variance	0.09	0.50	0.63	0.98	0.50	0.40
	Import volume[a]	368.86	550.67	297.12	297.17	337.43	429.65
Rice	Domestic price	3.80	3.94	4.00	4.16	2.07	2.11
	Import price	3.45	3.22	2.56	2.60	1.56	1.59
	Price variance	0.35	0.72	1.44	1.56	0.51	0.52
	Import volume[a]	234.46	224.43	255.65	334.99	353.39	399.28
Corn	Domestic price	2.29	2.26	2.33	2.38	0.92	0.88
	Import price	1.87	1.61	1.25	1.60	0.81	0.84
	Price variance	0.42	0.65	1.08	0.78	0.11	0.04
	Import volume[a]	520.71	326.49	259.85	476.86	316.66	282.56
Soybean	Domestic price	3.94	4.8	4.42	3.84	3.41	3.74
	Import price	4.45	4.19	3.90	3.07	3.33	3.34
	Price variance	-0.51	0.16	0.52	0.77	0.08	0.40
	Import volume[a]	5838.26	6337.78	7140.31	8168.97	8391.33	9553.42

[a] Import volume unit is 10,000 tons

Domestic prices of wheat, rice, corn refer market prices of wholesale by average, price variance is gap between domestic price and international price

Source: *China's Agricultural Development over 70 Years.*

productivity. China has a giant market of urban consumption that has moved toward a pattern of high value, high-quality and diversified food consumption in the past two decades.

Further, a large number of China's private agribusiness firms have increased integration with international markets. The product costs of agribusiness and firms have increased over the past decade and more. Further, China has enormous demand for food and agricultural and natural resource commodities and has become the world's largest importer of several agricultural commodities. The agribusiness enterprises have increased its demand so that china has become the world's largest importer agricultural input commodities such as oilseed, and is set to increase these imports, as well as those of vegetable oil, palm oil, soybean and rapeseed. China is also increasing its imports of fruit and vegetables as well as processed-food products.

7.4 China's International Cooperation in Trade and Investment

7.4.1 International Cooperation in Enterprise Development

A deepening market-oriented economic transformation has provided a foundation for the swift development of agribusiness and trade, and private rural enterprises, family agribusiness and international corporations. These enterprises' development has accelerated China's rural industrializing progress and agricultural transformation. Schumpeter (1965) defined entrepreneurs as individuals who exploit market opportunity through technical and/or organizational innovation". China's government carried out a series of policies to encourage well-established Chinese enterprises and private companies to undertake agricultural investment and development projects in developing and developed countries. Table 7.8 shows that the number of Chinese companies engaged in international trade increased throughout the 19080s and 1990s.

Table 7.8 Number of Chinese Companies Engaged in Trade Overseas, 1978–2001

Year	*Number of Companies*
1978	12
1985	800
1986	1200
1988	5000
1996	12,000
1997	15,000
1998	23,000
1999	29,258
2000	31,000
2001	35,000

Sources: Lardy (1994)

Prebisch (1950) suggested that countries import articles that can be paid for by means of exports or, in the case of capital goods, by foreign investments, within a general program of economic development in Latin-American countries. In Brazil, there are high growth and largely export-oriented agricultural enterprises co-existing with smallholder household farms, either subsistence- or domestically oriented (Tsakok 2011). Whatever the achievements of land redistribution, dualism has not been removed from Brazilian agriculture. Terms of trade, however, have benefited the mainly large farms that use imported inputs. Large-farmer agriculture has grown for decades but the level of poverty reduction is modest. The challenge for labor productivity remains serious for the dual structure economy of the agricultural and industrial sectors in Brazil (Tsakok 2011).

Over recent decades, China has demonstrated a successful practical case of economic development combined with economic growth, development and business. China has lifted 700 million rural people out of poverty, which accounts for more than 70% of global poverty reduction since early 1980s (The World Bank 2018). China's international businesses and trade help to upgrade GVCs through technology transfer and markets. Agribusiness enterprises are important for economic development by balancing economic structures between agricultural and industrial sectors during economic transformation.

Domestically, China's inclusive agribusiness development pattern includes firms, cooperatives and farmers. Social services and organizations play important roles in providing services such as information and coordination, and participating in cooperation with local agribusiness enterprises, cooperatives and farmers. Inclusive business management has better capital, resources and technology as well as markets. This inclusive business management has advantages for the industrial development of agribusiness and agro-industry as well as agricultural production in general. Firstly, firms have advantages in technology, capital and social welfare and human capital. Cooperatives are associated with village communities. Moreover, cooperatives have advantages in local resources and public services. In addition, farmers have the lease rights of lands. Farmers can share profits from inclusive agribusiness development with "firm and cooperatives and farm management" or "firm and farmers." Agribusiness enterprises can develop into large-scale agribusinesses, because farmers have lands to rent to agribusinesses and so are stakeholders in the inclusive enterprises. The inclusive agribusiness development pattern helps the growth of agricultural products in terms of comparative advantages in local resources and a market supply chain for high-quality agricultural products.

China's agribusiness enterprises' development has significantly contributed to rural-based industrialization and has helped large numbers of small family agribusinesses to access a value chain both domestically and internationally. Importantly, local social enterprises and inclusive agribusiness development help sustainable, long-term economic growth. Local social enterprises are characterized as profit-sharing, public responsibility and inclusive business enterprises. Smallholder farmers in developing countries often find it difficult to start their agribusiness enterprises and to access a GVC.

In China, local social enterprises lead to inclusive agribusiness development that enables smallholder farmers to become stakeholders of agribusiness enterprises through innovative institutions. A substantial change of agricultural transformation happens at a national level, while innovative institutions are preconditions for China's development of agribusiness and rural enterprises from local farmers to international markets. Innovative institution has played an important role in China's agricultural transformation. During the process of agricultural transformation, China's local governments have forged capacity in coordinating meager markets and helping farmers upgrade primary products with less industrialized technology and low prices to progress to rapid rural industrialization.

Further, China's innovative institutions help local farmers to share profits from agribusiness enterprises that have accessed GVCs. This is important for a successful agricultural transformation and rural industrialization, because small-scale household agricultural production systems and family agribusinesses remain the majority in China at present. Often there is a barrier to development in developing countries, such as in many African countries and Brazil, and the majority of farmers are unable to profit from a global agribusiness value chain. Smallholder farmers need more help to invest and handle the risks associated with investment. And small family-based agribusiness enterprises need more help to access international markets.

7.4.2 China's Financial Investment in Development

Financial assistance is needed in order to improve agricultural output and reduce poverty in underdeveloped countries. After a temporary recovery in 2017, FDI flows to the 32 landlocked developing countries (LLDCs) declined again in 2018 (World Investment Report 2019). China has enhanced international cooperation in agricultural development, including multilateral and bilateral agreements with more than more than 60 countries as well as international organizations (Information Office of the State Council of China 2019). Chinese MNEs are increasingly active sources of investment and are present in practically all LLDCs. Prospects for FDI vary according to LLDCs level of development and industrialization, with the fastest growth expected in those with most potential for economic diversification (World Investment Report 2019).

China's foreign direct inward investments have been expanding at a fast pace. China has been a large foreign investment recipient over the past more than two decades and is the largest FDI recipient country among all emerging economies. Box 7.2 shows the FDI recipient regions between 2016 and 2018. The United States remained the largest recipient of FDI, followed by China and Singapore in 2018 (World Investment Report 2019). In addition, China has accelerated its international economic cooperation in emerging markets. The international market structure became more diversified, and the proportion of imports and exports with emerging markets increased by 1.3 percentage points, reaching 57.7% (Ministry of Commerce of China 2019).

Box 7.2 Inflow of FDI in Different Regions (2016–2018)

1. Asia is the world's largest FDI recipient region, absorbing 39% of global inflows in 2018, up from 33% in 2017. FDI inflows to developing Asia rose by 4% to $512 billion in 2018. Growth occurred mainly in China, Singapore, Indonesia and other ASEAN countries, as well as in India and Turkey.
2. FDI flows to Africa defined the global downward trend in 2018. They rose to $46 billion, an 11% increase after successive declines in 2016 and 2017. Rising prices of and demand for some commodities led to sustained resource-seeking investment.
3. FDI flows to Latin America and the Caribbean decreased by 6% in 2018 to $147 billion.

World Investment Report 2019, UNCTAD

China's financial resources are significantly increasing to support agribusiness cooperation. The China Development Bank (CDB), and the ExIm Bank of China, China's Asian Infrastructure Investment Bank, provide loans to support agribusiness and development projects in developing countries. In recent years, the Export–Import Bank of China (China Eximbank), the China Development Bank (CDB) and other financial institutions have also provided commercial loans to support private enterprises in China. The private enterprises have been increasing the multinational businesses in developing countries. The rapid development of private enterprises have played the important role for sustainable development through markets and technological innovation as well as management, because the development of business and profit of enterprises can facilitate the sustainable development in a long term. For instance, Zimbabwe and China signed an agreement worth $585-million aimed at reviving the southern African country's agriculture, health, mining and sectors, which are supported by the CDB.[1] China's agricultural FDI in Africa was USD $30 million in 2009, according to the Ministry of Commerce of China. China's FDI in African agriculture increased by more than 13% in 2010 and its agricultural trade increased more than 20% in the same year. China's agricultural trade and investment are expected to achieve sustainable growth in the near future. China has increased its agribusiness investment in many developing countries in the past 10 years: its investment is on the rise in agro-processing, resource-based agriculture and agricultural commodities in developing countries.

7.4.2.1 International Cooperation and Investment

China has been increasing its participation and cooperation on development projects in developing and developed countries as well as in association with international development organizations. Firstly, China's government has been accelerating international cooperation and development projects. China's government proposed the development of "the Belt and the Road" in 2013, aiming to enhance international cooperation on inclusive development and sharing prosperity from development from the perspectives of economy, business and trade. under the cooperative frameworks of "the Belt and the Road" China has successfully developed bilateral agreements with developing and developed countries, and has increased the scale of

[1] Zimbabwe, China Sign $585 million Trade Agreements, 21st March 2011, Action for Southern Africa. www.actsa.org/newsroom/2011/03/zimbabwe-china-sign-585-million-trade-agreements/

imports from the countries of 'the Belt and the Road' since 2013: the total value of imports from the countries of "the Belt and the Road" was US$ 677.974 billion in 2013, accounting for 34.77% of China's total import value. By 2018, China's import value from the countries of "the Belt and the Road" had increased to US$861.867 billion, accounting for 40.36% of total import value (Jin 2019). China has been playing an important role in international cooperation, and the country has effectively integrated with GVCs through development and international trade in the past decade or more. For example, China's Belt and Road Initiative (BRI) is international cooperation on transport infrastructure, which has impacted on development and multilateral and bilateral international trade. *The World Development Report 2020* of the World Bank describes the Belt and Road Initiative (BRI) as an example of international cooperation in the context of infrastructure and GVCs to tackle development issues.

> Although the scope of the BRI is still taking shape, it is structured around two main components, underpinned by significant infrastructure investments: the Silk Road Economic Belt (the "Belt") and the New Maritime Silk Road (the "Road"). The overland Belt will link China to Central and South Asia and onward to Europe, and the maritime Road will link China to Southeast Asia, the Gulf countries, East Africa and North Africa, and on to Europe.

Secondly, In terms of the agreement between China and the WTO, China has reduced the tariff applied to member countries of the Association of Southeast Asian Nations (ASEAN) to below 50%. The agreement was implemented with different countries after 2015 and 2018 (Chen et al. 2018). The members of ASEAN include Thailand, Singapore, Philippines, Malaysia, Indonesia, Brunei, Myanmar, Laos, Cambodia and Vietnam. China has accelerated its agricultural product exports to the member countries of ASEAN since 2001. The growth rate was 17.3% for agricultural product exports to members of ASEAN between 1999 and 2001, and 27.3% between 2002 and 2005 (Chen et al. 2018).

The China and ASEAN free trade area started to operate in 2010. The total trade of ASEAN and China is more than 10% of the world total. The majority of the world's undernourished population (more than 500 million) live in Asia (FAO 2019). The China and ASEAN free trade area is the one of the largest free trade areas in the world and the largest free trade areas in developing countries. Agricultural products are susceptible to comparative advantage. China has retained labor-intensive practices in some rural areas, and has advantages in primary products and agricultural raw material production, such as cotton for the textile industry. Domestic prices for some of China's high-demand agricultural products are higher than import prices.

Intraregional agricultural trade has rapidly increased, and it will further impact on development issues in the future. Since 2002, when China signed the first Free Trade Zone agreement with ASEAN, developing countries and emerging economies have taken comparative advantage of development opportunities through international economic cooperation through free trade zone and cross-countries free trade zone and cross-country regional economic cooperation. ASEAN countries, where regional hubs have a significant role, have a higher share of direct investment covered by the agreement than the share of investment of the ultimate owner (World Investment Report 2019). Regional investment hubs play an important role as conduits in indirect investment flows through multinational enterprises, and development projects of technological transfer in agribusiness and agro-industry development.

Thirdly, China's government has implemented 20 South–south cooperative projects, cooperating with the Food and Agriculture Organization of the United Nations since 1996 (Information Office of the State Council of China 2019). The development cooperation includes training and development assistance on agricultural production technology (Han 2019). The share of South–South investment in total investment to developing economies drops from 47% (when measured on the basis of standard FDI data) to 28% when measured on the basis of ultimate ownership in 2018 (World Investment Report 2019).

In strengthening South–South cooperation targeting rural poverty reduction and ensuring food security in developing countries, international organizations have sought to ensure that developing country partners can support this process by broadening the scope of engagement beyond extractive sectors and enhancing technology transfer and learning (UNCTAD 2010).[2] International organizations have strengthened the importance of technology in South–South cooperation in food security and eradicating hunger and alleviating poverty. There is now a need for strong South–South cooperation and transfer of technologies when

[2] "Africa and the New Forms of Development Partnership", United Nations Conference on Trade and Development, 2010, https://unctad.org/en/pages/PublicationArchive.aspx?publicationid=75

responding to the challenges of food insecurity. Climate change is having a severe impact on the Asia-Pacific region, particularly on the agricultural and water sectors (UNESCAP 2009).[3] International development's cooperation and South-South cooperation need to enhance on the sustainable development and climate change in developing countries in the future. According to the FAO, emerging economies could provide appropriate technologies that will help to improve agricultural production. This is expected to lead to a rapid improvement in the livelihood of small-scale rural producers, through an increased number of experts and technicians and technical coverage through a supporting program of South–South cooperation (FAO 2010).[4] South–South development cooperation has been receiving greater attention, as developing countries gain increasing weight in the development of trade and investment.

7.4.2.2 China's Agribusiness Enterprises and International Investment

China has accelerated its international economic cooperation on agricultural investment in developing countries, including the African, Asian and Latin American regions. Chinese investment on overseas ventures in agriculture, forestry and fisheries soared from $300 million in 2009 to $3.3 billion in 2016 (Gale and Gooch 2018). China' had over 1300 agricultural, forestry, and fisheries enterprises with registered overseas investments of $26 billion, at the end of 2016; 51% of China' overseas agricultural investment went to Asia in 2014 (Gale and Gooch 2018).

Internationally, according to theories of comparative advantage in perspectives of multinational companies, big and well-established FDI enterprises may have a place to play monopolistic role or oligopolistic role. These international companies have advantages in free markets and worldwide competition in value chain through reducing the global costs of production. Buckley and Casson (2009) showed that multinational corporations can derive more profits when the market for intermediate products is incomplete; then it is possible for such companies to replace external markets with internal markets.

[3] "Technological Transfer and South–South Cooperation Key to Food Security in Asia Pacific", UNESCAP, 25 August, 2009, http://www.unescap.org/unis/press/2009/aug/g58.asp

[4] "Supporting Programmes for Food Security-South South Cooperation", http://www.fao.org/spfs/south-south-spfs/ssc-spfs/en/

Private enterprises have increased the import and export of commodities, their role in import and export of agricultural products has been increasing. As business entities developed together, the proportion of export of private enterprises increased by 1.4 percentage points, reaching 48.0%, and continuing to maintain the status of the largest export business entity (Ministry of Commerce of China 2019). China had set up more than 851 agribusiness enterprises in 100 countries by 2017 (Information Office of the State Council of China 2019).

China's agricultural enterprises' foreign investments include different types of enterprises. Table 7.9 shows that limited liability companies are the largest category, followed by shareholder cooperative enterprises. State-owned enterprises and private enterprises were also important categories in 2017.

Table 7.9 shows the different types of China's agricultural enterprises' foreign investment in 2017.

In the early period, the Chinese state-owned enterprises were mainly doing their agricultural business in developing countries. Many private agricultural enterprises had taken an initiative to seek profit from the mid-1990s onward. Most of the private companies were scattered small-scale enterprises. China's overseas farming investments are mainly two key categories of enterprise management: private companies are one of the key economic driving forces in China's rapid economic development. Reform and opening-up policies have encouraged private agricultural firms to run businesses abroad and participate in international competition.

Table 7.9 China's Agricultural Enterprises' Foreign Investments in 2017

State-owned enterprises	85
Collectively owned enterprises	2
Shareholder limited enterprises	163
Shareholder cooperative enterprises	6
Limited liability companies	492
Private enterprises	77
Joint-venture enterprises	2
Foreign investment enterprises	4
Hong Kong Macao and TaiWan investment enterprises	7
Other enterprises	13
Total numbers of enterprises	851

Source: *Report on China's Agricultural Foreign Investment Cooperation* 2018

Multinational enterprises include foreign investment operating their business within China, and China's domestic agribusiness enterprises running business abroad. In order to maintain sustainable development in the long term, many developing countries have accelerated multinational cooperation, especially for technology investment. The value chain of food consumption has involved new technology, new products and new management. Technological processes in production of livestock food has become a key trend in high-value food production, notably for the beef industry. Moreover, a GVC has been forged by the demands of the livestock industry; for example, McDonald's Beijing branches import beef from Scotland, and supply to local customers in Beijing. Market demand is significant. The businesses of multinational enterprises include livestock industrial feed production, livestock food processing, breeding species of poultry, importing food products and biotechnological agricultural products.

The case of China's multinational agribusiness enterprise shows that international cooperation brings development of agribusiness opportunities in supply chain, industry chain and value chain, both for the domestic and the international market. The WellHope Agri-Tech Joint Stock Co. Ltd. was founded in 1985. It is the biggest agribusiness company in northeast China (Yu and Liu 2018), one of China's leading agribusiness companies in feed for husbandry and aquaculture. The firm exports products to international markets, including Nepal and other South Asian countries. Globally, the company has shareholder enterprises with a Dutch agribusiness company. Capital, technology and market are important for the successful management of multinational enterprises (Yu and Liu 2018). The company is expanding its agribusiness with "Belt and Road" countries. The principle of multinational enterprises is to shares profits. International cooperation, however, is not only for company profits. It can nurture international sharing of information and knowledge.

7.5 Conclusion

Economic growth impacts on the pace of development of developing countries. Many developing countries have a similar development barrier to their progress to an industrial economy from a backward agricultural economy. International trade is important to growth at the early stage of economic transformation. Developing countries need policies and development strategies to export primary products and agricultural products to accelerate industrial development in this early stage. Food security mainly relies on a country's own policies and improvement of agricultural productivity. Imports of agricultural products can only be a small part of the solution for food insecurity, if such is necessary. The import of agricultural products needs to revive agribusiness markets through competition. In many developing countries, small-scale agricultural production is a major proportion of the rural economy. Inclusive development of agribusiness helps to scale up industrial development. Developing countries need to upgrade the local value chain through rural industrial development.

China is increasing its imports of many key products. It relies on improvement of agricultural productivity, technology and market to maintain its food security. International trade helps industrial development. Importantly, China has strategies to develop its rural industry at a national level. TVEs have contributed significantly to its exports, helped by comparative advantages of price and scale in 1980s and 1990s. Rapid industrial development and inclusive agribusiness have also upgraded local value chains across China. As the largest food consumer in the world, Chinese agricultural enterprises are increasing their cooperation with foreign companies.

China has been one of the largest FDI recipient countries in past two decades or more. FDI has facilitated agricultural growth. China has received significant inflows of FDI in agriculture from the 1990s up to now. Meanwhile, China is also one of the largest investors in foreign development projects and business. Its foreign agricultural investment has been diversified through different approaches, including aid-projects, investments in both government- and company-promoted in infrastructure, technology demonstration and training programs. China has enhanced its international cooperation on agribusiness and development. China's international development cooperation highlights infrastructure and economic cooperation as well as multinational cooperation on agribusiness. China has been a contributor to development projects alongside international organizations and governments of developing countries under the initiative of South–South cooperation. And China's international cooperation also has enhanced its international trade in free trade zones and regional trade cooperation, as well as development through economic cooperation with developing countires. A decline in agricultural investment in developing countries in recent years has significantly hindered those countries and the global community in achieving the Sustainable Development Goals. Large-scale investment in agriculture and efforts to boost livelihoods is needed, as is more international cooperation.

References

Alston, J. M., Chan-Kang, C., Marra, M. C., Pardey, P. G., & Wyatt, T. J. (2000). A Meta Analysis of Rates of Return to Agricultural R&D: ex pede herculem? *International Food Policy Research Institute, Research Report 113.* Washington, DC.

A Montpellier Panel Report. (2014). *Small and Growing - Entrepreneurship in African Agriculture.* London: Agriculture for Impacts, Imperial College London. https://www.mamopanel.org/media/uploads/files/SMALL_AND_GROWING-_ENTREPRENEURSHIP_IN_AFRICAN_AGRICULTURE_2014.pdf

Bhattasali, D. (2004). China's Accession to the World Trade Organization, Policy Reform, and Poverty Reduction: An Introduction. *The World Bank Economic Review, 18*(1), 1–2.

Bruinsma, J. (2003). *World Agriculture: Towards 2015–2030.* London: Earthscan Publications Ltd.

Buckley, P. J., & Casson, M. C. (2009). The Internalisation Theory of the Multinational Enterprises: A Review of the Progress of a Research Agenda after 30 Years. *Journal of International Business Studies, 40,* 1563–1580.

Caporale, G. M., & Sova, R. (2015). Trade Flows and Trade Specialisation: The Case of China. *China Economic Review, 34,* 261–273.

Chen, Y. Y., Liu, H. G., & Cai, H. Y. (2018). *Research on the Agricultural Products Trade between China and USA.* Beijing: China Economic Publishing House.

Chiarvesio, M., Maria, E. D., & Micelli, S. (2010). Global Value Chinas and Open Networks: The Case of Italian Industrial Districts. *Journal of European Planning Studies, 18*(3), 333–350.

China National Statistic Yearbook (1996).

Chinese Fishery Statistic Yearbook. (2003).

Epaphra, M., & Mwakalasya, A. H. (2017). Analysis of Foreign Direct Investment, Agricultural Sector and Economic Growth in Tanzania. *Modern Economy, 8*(1), 111–140.

FAO. (2002). *World Agriculture: Towards 2015/2030.* Rome: Food and Agriculture Organization of the United Nations. http://www.fao.org/3/y3557e/y3557e00.htm

Food and Agriculture Organization of the United Nations. (2019). *Tracking Progress on Food and Agriculture-Related SDG Indicator.* Rome: FAO.

Food Security, Governance, Aid and Investment Needs. (2010, March 17). WTO Workshop on Aid for Trade. https://www.wto.org/english/news_e/news10_e/aid:17mar10_fao_e.pdf
Fuglie, K., & Rada, N. (2013). Resources, Policies, and Agricultural Productivity in Sub-Saharan Africa, United States Department of Agriculture Economic Research Service [online]. http://www.ers.usda.gov/media/1037838/err145.pdf. Accessed Feb 2013.
Gale, F., & Gooch, E. (2018). *China's Agricultural Investment Abroad is Rising*. United States Departments of Agriculture, Economic Research Service. https://www.ers.usda.gov/amber-waves/2018/april/china-s-agricultural-investment-abroad-is-rising/. Accessed 24 Apr 2018.
Greenville, J., Kawaski, K., & Beaujeu, R. (2017). How Policies Shape Global Food and Agriculture Value Chains. In *OECD Food, Agriculture and Fisheries Papers No. 100*. Paris: OECD Publishing.
Han, C. F. (2019). *New China's Agricultural Development with 70 Years-Policies Achievement Volume*. Beijing: China's Agricultural Publisher.
Hao, W. P., Ke, X. H., & Zhang, H. J. (2019). International Cooperation and Exchange on China's Agricultural Science and Technology. In C. F. Han (Ed.), *New China's Agricultural Development with 70 Years- Science and Technology Volume*. Beijing: China's Agricultural Publisher.
http://www.oecd.org/industry/ind/global-value-chains.htm
Ianchovichina, E., & Martin, W. (2001). Trade Liberalization in China's Accession to the World Trade Organization. *Policy Research Working Paper Series 2623*. The World Bank.
International Monetary Fund. (2001). *Global Trade Liberalization and the Developing Countries*. Washington, DC: International Monetary Fund.
Jin, H. (2019). China Has Ranked The World Second Largest Importer of in 10 Years. (*Beijing: Economic Information Daily*). http://xiaofei.people.com.cn/n1/2019/1113/c425315-31452197.html. Accessed 13 Nov 2019.
Kristiansen, S. (2003). Information Asymmetry and Economic Concentration: the Case of Hens and Eggs in Eastern Indonesia. In *ESA Working Paper No. 03-21, December 2003, Agricultural and Development Economic Division*. Roma: The Food and Agriculture Organization of the United Nations.
Kundnani, H., & Parello-Plesner, J. (2012). China and Germany: A New Special Relationship? *Why the Emerging Special Relations Matters*. European Council on Foreign Relations, Policy Brief. https://www.ecfr.eu/publications/summary/china_and_germany_a_new_special_relationship. Accessed 15 May 2012.
Lardy, N. R. (1994). *China in the World Economy*. Washington, DC: Institute for. International Economics.
Leibovici, F., & Crews, J. (2018). Trade Liberalization and Economic Development. *Economic Research, Federal Reserve Bank of St. Louis*, No.13. Assessed 20 Apr 2018.

Liu, H. (2003). *Research on Rural Industrialization and Regional Development*. HuNan: Research of Agricultural Modernization.

Liu, X. H., Zhang, P., & Zhang, P. (2018). *Economic Growth and Structural Transformation in China's Reform Period*. Shanghai: Gezhi Press/Shanghai People's Publishing House.

Mcmichael, P. (2009). Banking on Agriculture: A Review of the World Development Report. *Journal of Agrarian Change, 9*(2), 235–246.

Ministry of Agriculture and Rural Affairs of China. (2019). China's Agricultural Products Import and Export Statues in 2018. http://www.moa.gov.cn/ztzl/nybrl/rlxx/201902/t20190201_6171079.htm. Accessed 1 Feb 2019.

Ministry of Commerce of China. (2019). Scale of Import and Export Hit a Record High and the High-Quality Development of Foreign Trade Achieved Positive Results. http://english.mofcom.gov.cn/article/zt_yearlyoverview2018/news/201902/20190202837961.shtml. Accessed 24 Jan 2019.

Montalbano, P., Nenci, S., & Salvatici, L. (2015). Trade, Value Chains and Food Security. In *The State of Agricultural Commodity Markets 2015–16, Background Paper*. Roma: Food and Agriculture Organization of the United Nations.

Prebisch, R. (1950). *The Economic Development of Latin America and Its Principal Problems*. New York: United Nations Economic Commission for Latin America.

Report on China's Agricultural Foreign Investment Cooperation. (2018). *Compiled by Ministry of Agriculture and Rural Affairs of China*. Beijing: China Agricultural Press.

Sen, A. (1981). *Poverty and Famines: An Essay on Entitlement and Deprivation*. Oxford: Clarendon Press.

Sha, J. (2009, August 16). MaoZeDong and Founding of New China and its Development, QSTHOERY.CN, Beijing.

Shafaeddin, M. (1994). *The Impact of Trade Liberation on Export and GDP Growth in Least Developed Countries*. Geneva: United Nations Conference on Trade and Development.

Siddiqui, K. (2018). David Ricardo's Comparative Advantage and Developing Countries: Myth and Reality. *Journal of International Critical Thought, 8*(3), 426–452.

Soundarrajan, P., & Vivek, N. (2015). A Study on the Agricultural Value Chain Financing in India. *Agricultural Economics-Czech, 61*, 31–38.

The Information Office of the State Council of China. (2019). *China's Food Security*. Beijing: People's Publisher House.

The World Bank. (2008). Agriculture and Economic Growth. *World Development Report 2008*. Washington, DC: The World Bank.

The World Bank. (2018). Press Release: Consensus Reached at the International Forum on Reform and Opening Up and Poverty Reduction in China, November 5, 2018, https://www.worldbank.org/en/news/press-release/2018/11/05/consensus-reached-at-the-international-forum-on-reform-and-opening-up-and-povertyreduction-in-china

The World Bank. (2020). *World Development Report 2020: Trading for Development in the Age of Global Value Chains*. Washington, DC: The World Bank.

Thirlwall, A. P., & Pacheco-López, P. (2017). *Economics of Development*. London: Macmillan Palgrave.

Tsakok, I. (2011). *Success in Agricultural Transformation, What Its Means and What Makes It Happen*. Cambridge: Cambridge University Press.

UNCTAD. (2010). Economic Development in Africa Report 2010 - South-South Cooperation: Africa and the New Forms of Development Partnership. Geneva: United Nations Conference on Trade and Development. https://unctad.org/en/pages/PublicationArchive.aspx?publicationid=75

UNESCAP. (2009). *Economic and Social Survey of Asia and the Pacific 2009, Addressing Triple Threats to Development*. Bangkok: the United Nations Economic and Social Commission for Asia and the Pacific.

United Nations Conference on Trade and Development. (2012). *Agriculture at Crossroads: Guaranteeing Food Security in a Changing Global Climate*. Geneva: United Nations Conference on Trade and Development. https://unctad.org/en/Docs/presspb20108_en.pdf. Accessed 18 Dec 2012.

United Nations Conference on Trade and Development. (2019). *World Investment Report: Special Economic Zones*. Geneva: United Nations Conference on Trade and Development.

Wang, D. (2013). The United States and China. *The Asia-Pacific Journal, 11*(24), Number 4, Article ID3958.

World Development Report. (2020). *Trading for Development in the Age of Global Value Chains*. Washington: The World Bank Group, https://www.worldbank.org/en/publication/wdr2020

Yu, M. J. (2018). *Miracle of China's International Trade – 40 Years Opening Up Towards the Way to Power*. Shanghai of China: Truth and Wisdom Press/Shanghai Peoples' Publishing House.

Yu, X. D., & Liu, B. (2018). The Success of Wellhope Agri-Tech Joint-Stock, Co. Ltd. *Journal of China Animal Husbandry and Veterinary*, http://news.wugu.com.cn/article/1452830.html. Accessed 2 Dec 2018.

CHAPTER 8

Conclusion

This book has analyzed the important role of China's agribusiness and rural enterprises in its economic growth and sustainable development. It suggests that the combination development approach of agribusiness and rural enterprises has facilitated China's inclusive growth and sustainable development between 1990 and 2019. China's inclusive growth features the development of rural and social enterprises. Social enterprises can facilitate inclusive growth in developing countries, where large numbers of the population have an income below the World Bank's international standard poverty line. Growth of the agriculture sector is two to four times more effective than any other action in raising incomes among the poorest. Analyses in 2016 found that 65% of poor working adults made their living through agriculture (World Bank 2020). China's dynamic development of agribusiness and rural enterprises has increased incomes for a majority of farmers and rural migrant workers in recent decades. The effective way of dealing with the development barrier is to implement policies that secure profits for the poor through inclusive development. Farmers can increase their income through connecting to an industrial chain and developing rural enterprises through a sustainable and inclusive development approach. Inclusive approaches require the matching of public and private investment to achieve good commercial and public outcomes (Woodhill 2016). A sustainable approach requires the upgrading industrial chain of agribusiness and enterprises at micro level and upgrading economic development at macro level. Stakeholders, including smallholder farmers and

L. Sun, *Economic Growth and Development*, Palgrave Studies in Economic History,
https://doi.org/10.1007/978-3-030-46099-0_8

entrepreneurs, can share prosperity from profits of agribusiness and enterprises at the micro level. From a macro-level perspective, China has upgraded from a low-income country to an upper-middle income country through rapid economic growth.

1. The rapid development of agribusiness and rural enterprises has significantly contributed to China's economic growth in recent decades. During this period, structural changes in agricultural production and the diversification of agricultural products have contributed to improvement of agricultural productivity. New agricultural products have led to the adoption of new technologies to produce high output of agricultural products, contributing to the improvement of agricultural productivity and growth. High-output production and new agricultural products demand changed technology. In other words, technological change has been an important factor in the improvement of agricultural output.

The management of agricultural commercialization and the development of agribusiness have upgraded a value chain from China's local markets to domestic and international markets. Increased consumption of high-value agricultural products and the growth of the food-processing business have significantly increased the prices of food, and profits to agribusiness, in the past 20 years, following and reflecting the significant increase in China's middle-income population. Value chain management is a key instrument of strategic business analysis and planning, used for coordination of value chain components and resources. Effective management of a value chain directly affects profitability of the involved stakeholders and the satisfaction of consumers (Keshelashvili 2018).

In recent years, the information technology and e-commerce technology have been applied to agribusiness management and the development of rural enterprises. Biotechnological applications have helped the process of sustainable development and success in the market for agribusiness management. E-commerce applied in the field of agriculture—agricultural e-commerce (Zhang and Du 2004)—penetrated into agriculture at the end of twentieth century, providing existing customers with a new avenue to product information and a link to a new customer base (Zhang and Du 2004). E-commerce technology has brought new business opportunities for rural enterprises and agribusiness, and has created more work opportunities. It has brought business opportunities to small and medium-sized rural enterprises, opening access to global value chains in domestic and international markets.

Further, inclusive business development can help small and medium-sized rural enterprises and smallholder farmers to cooperate. Information technology can improve management of business and markets, and reduce transaction costs. China's agribusiness development pattern has accelerated the application of e-commerce in expanding the market and supply chain. Serving as an advanced productive force, e-commerce has great potential for improving industrialization of agriculture, agriculture structural adjustment, reducing transaction costs in agriculture and expanding the market and scale of agriculture production (Wang et al. 2016).

2. The book analyzed allocation efficiency, which has significantly contributed to agricultural growth. China adopted different ownership management and property rights of farming and non-farming sectors. Allocation efficiency is related to features of public and private management of leasing rights of farmland, and helped inclusive economic growth in agriculture during China's economic transition. China's institutions facilitated the privatization and marketization of rural enterprises. The system of property rights is an incentive for private families' agribusiness management and collective business management. The collective business management helps the development of rural enterprises and big companies to drive local industrial development. The leasing rights of non-grain sector's farming land has been allocated through prices and markets mechanism, which has secured private profits return from private families' agribusiness. Compared with the leasing rights of non-grain sector's farming rural land, the household responsibility system on grain sector helps smallholder farmers to maintain subsistence livelihoods, because through the household responsibility system the village committees allocated a very small size cultivated land area equally to each rural household.

In addition, in the international context, a "farmer–enterprises" partnership for industrialization of agriculture can be interpreted as the model of contract farming that is widely practiced in many countries (Asian Development Bank 2015). China's property rights to farmland have helped farmer–enterprises partnership over the past 30 years. The property rights of farmlands are collectively owned, but farmers have long-term leasing rights. Leasing rights on farmlands have been characterized by private management by farmers. Smallholder farmers have the right to assign land to local farmers' cooperatives. In addition, local rural enterprises can make contracts with farmers for management of farmland, which helps inclusive growth and increases the economic scale of agribusinesses. The property rights of farmlands have helped allocation efficiency in markets and business development. The 12th Five-Year Plan for National Economic and Social Development of China stresses the promotion of the industrialization of agriculture based on farmer–enterprises partnership (Asian Development Bank 2015).

3. China's inclusive development of agribusiness and rural enterprises has helped a large number of smallholder farmers to access a value chain from local rural areas. Institutions haves played an important role in China's agricultural transformation: during the process of agricultural transformation, China's local governments played a coordinating role, helping farmers to upgrade their industrial chain and optimize structural changes in agricultural development.

Further, China's government has carried out polices to accelerate agricultural and economic transformation as well as developing rural and urban integration. Urban–rural transformation and rural development are issues at the forefront of research on the topic of the urban–rural relationship in the field of geography, as well as important practical problems facing China's new urbanization and its overall planning of urban and rural development (Liu et al. 2016). China had a large numbers of surplus labor during its agricultural and rural transformation. To encourage rural labor to move out of rural areas, local governments began to provide free information, job-search assistance and consultation services for migrant workers (Li 2008). Local economic development made significant progress in providing employment opportunities in the developing rural enterprises and agribusiness in towns, and in rural and urban linkage areas for the large numbers of rural workers in China between 1990 and 2019.

China's town and village enterprises (TVEs) characterize social enterprises and the inclusive development pattern. They have extended their role to become inclusive local enterprise organizations, which emerged as special enterprise organizations located in villages and towns in the early 1980s (Sun 2015). The development of TVEs successfully promoted large-scale rural industrialization, which enabled farmers to transform into skilled specialized workers and employees in rural areas. The TVEs expanded rapidly in towns, villages and rural–urban linkage areas during the accelerating rural industrialization and take-off of economic development in China in the 1980s and 1990s. China has undergone a remarkable transformation, with the movement of over 260 million migrants from rural to urban areas. These migrants have seized the opportunities offered by urbanization, leaving their agricultural jobs and taking up more productive and higher-paying jobs in cities (World Bank 2016).

Some rural migrant workers are mobile rural workers in cities, maintaining their farming lands in rural areas. The number of rural migrant workers increased spectacularly from an estimated 30 million in 1989 to about 130 million in 2006 (Li 2008). The development of rural enterprises contributed to industrial and business economic development in parallel with the strategy of rural-urban integration. Importantly, China's rural enterprises are located in rural *and* urban areas, where rural enterprises provided enormous work opportunities for skilled rural workers in local rural areas during the years of economic transformation. The rapid development of TVEs has helped the process of structural change during agricultural transformation and has propelled industrial development as part of economic development and rural–urban integration.

The role of rural communities and local government is important in fostering inclusive development of rural enterprises. China's TVEs were usually collectively owned and operated by village communities, which were responsible for their profits and losses (Li 2014). Rural land constituted the major source of investment in TVEs as factories were largely built by farmers (ibid). The development of TVEs was an important feature of inclusive growth in the early stage of economic transformation, when private rural enterprises were not well developed.

The book analyzed the combination development approach of agribusinesses and rural enterprises. The inclusive growth of agribusiness and rural enterprises has been a key factor in the acceleration of rural industrialization and sustainable development as well as mitigating inequality between rural and urban development. The development of rural enterprises has played a vital role in a successful rural–urban integration at a national level, which is important to mitigate inequality of development. China has accelerated its urbanization in the past four decades. The indicators of economic development contain signs of the changes of economic composition in regard to the integration of town and country. In the early stages of economic transformation, rural economic growth included some economic contribution from towns. In later stages, rural industrialization and agro-industrial development have incorporated combined agricultural, service and industrial sectors driving industrialization and enterprise development in towns. This has brought about a development pattern of rural and urban integration. The dynamic development of agribusinesses and rural enterprises has played a pivotal role in economic development with rural–urban integration. Kassiola (2017) studied a new social spatial reorganization plan for urbanization, migration and rural development in China. The plan is for rural–urban development that is comprehensive, concentrated and coordinated.

4. The inclusive development of rural enterprises has significantly contributed to industrial development in China. Rural enterprises have played a pivotal role in creating work opportunities and increasing incomes for a majority of rural workers during China's transformation from a low-income to an upper-middle income country.

On the one hand, the rising incomes of a large numbers of rural workers increases consumption of high-value agricultural products, and the increased demand of markets for diversified agricultural products can upgrade a local value chain. On the other hand, the inclusive development of rural enterprises has helped local industrial development and agricultural commercialization on an economic scale. As a result, smallholder farmers have the chance to profit from their economic upgrading.

Industrial development and rural industrialization creates plenty of work opportunities for large numbers of skilled rural workers and surplus rural labor in the early stage of economic transformation. In the pre-industrial period in most developing countries, a majority of rural labor is employed in the agricultural sector. Industrial development needs to highlight agro-industrialization and rural enterprise. And industrial development also needs a multivariate development pattern combined with agricultural development and growth of industrial and service sectors during the acceleration of industrialization.

China's TVEs have characteristics of inclusive, local social enterprises. Such enterprises had advantages in the prices of local resources during the early stage of economic transformation, when markets were meager contributors to development of new products and changes in production and firms' business. Production costs were lower in collective rural enterprises during the early development stage in the 1990s. One reason was the local government and village communities had an advantage on the allocation of local resources at low cost. Another reason was the income of rural workers was lower than the income of workers in cities, on average, in the 1990s. These price advantage helped the rapid development of TVEs, which included manufacture of textile products and clothing. TVEs contributed significantly to China's exports in the 1990s. A lot of TVEs engaged in manufacturing and other industrial sectors, and they recruited a large number of rural workers. This helped to reduce the surplus labor force and transferred rural workers into the manufacturing and industrial sectors. The inclusive development of TVEs helped to upgrade value chains through international trade from locally to globally connected. Rural workers engaged in non-agricultural rural enterprises increased their incomes, leading to a higher demand for diversified foods. Therefore, rural development of inclusive and local social enterprises in the non-agricultural sector reduced poverty in rural China.

5. The book analyzed a case study of China's rapid economic growth and inclusive development in poverty reduction and increased incomes for a large number of farmers in the past several decades. The scale and the pace of rural industry development effectively provided the solution to the development dilemma of dual structure: traditional agricultural production and industrial development. In the traditional agricultural economy, there are a large number of surplus rural workers in grain production, and the level of commercialization and modernization is low. China's TVEs contributed to international trade, which helped the process of structural change and the permeation of industrial development and technological progress. In the third economic development stage, China enhanced its international cooperation, reflected in its economic development in respect of international trade and investment between 2001 and 2019. China cooperated economically with developed and developing countries. China's government proposed inclusive development and sharing prosperity through international economic cooperation, and it has significantly increased its agribusiness cooperation with developing countries, its international cooperation projects strength through South–South cooperation, and regional economic cooperation. China has large domestic markets and international access; it is a large importer of many agricultural products at international market prices. In addition, China has increased international cooperation and agribusiness development projects with developing countries, including the Association of Southeast Asian Nations (ASEAN), African development cooperation and international development cooperation with the global south. There are increasing development opportunities for international economic coopera-

tion through free trade zones and cross-country free trade zones and regional economic cooperation.

China's agribusiness enterprises have also gradually accelerated the country's import and export trade since the 1990s. The numbers of private agribusiness enterprises cooperating with developing countries continues to increase because production costs are rising domestically, and some private agribusiness enterprises are looking for new agribusiness opportunities in developing countries. In responding to the acceleration of globalization and the demand of international markets, China's agribusiness enterprises also increase business cooperation with developing countries through technological transfer.

International trade and global markets have helped China's growing agribusiness enterprises. And China has been the largest importer of many agricultural products, such as soybean and corn in the past a decade. Global market and international trade have helped to upgrade structural change of China's agriculture. The phenomenal growth in global value chain-related trade has translated into significant economic growth in many countries across the globe over the last two decades, fueled by reductions in transportation and communication costs and diminishing trade barriers (World Bank 2019). China's capital-intensive agribusiness enterprises have been increasing international cooperation in the past two decades. A gradual transition from collective-led to private-led rural enterprises and family-based agribusiness enterprises have facilitated the building up of global value chains from local to international markets based on commercial competition. Institutions are playing an important role in forging inclusive growth of agribusiness enterprises.

6. The development of agribusiness and rural enterprises is even more important in respect to international development. There are common economic phenomena on agricultural transformation, rural industrialization and urbanization in all developing countries and transitional economies. In terms of economic development stages, China, India and many African countries as well as some Asian developing countries have accelerated agricultural transformation and processes of urbanization and industrialization.

There are other similar development challenges among transitional economies and developing countries, including economic growth path, development experiences in poverty reduction, and processes of agricultural transformation, inclusive and sustainable agribusiness enterprises, rural industrialization and urbanization.

China has made rapid progress in agricultural and economic transformation in the past more than four decades. Its growth in international trade has stimulated structural change in agriculture, through the activities of China's agribusiness and trade enterprises. China has speeded up its unprecedented urbanization since the 1990s, while the country has implemented rural–urban integration to mitigate the inequality between the two areas.

7. The book sheds light on the institutional reform, including consideration of the pre-economic reform period in China. The economic development path is a continuously accumulative process: institutional reform needed adjustment to correspond with China's market-oriented economic development "trajectory." China's economic transition is classified into two development stages in respect of a market-oriented economic development "trajectory." Ownership of agribusiness enterprises has undergone reform, including establishment of cooperatives, joint-venture and private firms within China's domestic market during economic transformation. In the first development stage, China's rural enterprises were mainly collectively managed businesses. In the second stage, family agribusinesses and private rural enterprises have developed rapidly.
8. China's agribusiness and rural enterprise development is facing new challenges. Agribusiness enterprises are meeting high production costs in some regions of China, there are obstacles in the way of smallholder farmers seeking to upgrade their technology, and smallholder farmers face challenges arising from the risks of market uncertainty and price competition. Upgrading technology and changing the environmental–ecological production pattern will be important for business development and market competition. Local government needs to help smallholder farmers in improving environmental conditions and infrastructure. Development of ecologically sound production and business management patterns will be even more important in the future. Industrial development in the agricultural sector should improve technological standards of food production and modernize environmental management of production patterns.

Commercial operation patterns impact on agricultural development: commercial management highlights perspectives of agribusiness enterprises, cooperative, e-business enterprises and farmers' associations. Intelligent agriculture uses technology and science to manage agricultural production, and can help to improve the efficiency of agricultural production. Agribusinesses and rural enterprises should adopt digital production technologies.

9. China's economic growth and development strategy has made significant progress on poverty reduction. There were different development strategies for hunger eradication and poverty reduction. For the first stage, China's strategy on poverty reduction centered on pro-poor policies and institutional reform in agricultural development. This path was chosen to deal with the fact that smallholder farmers in less developed rural areas were often unable to change their technology and products in response to market demand due to shortage of funding, lack of knowledge and technological skills, and restricted infrastructure.

In order to reduce poverty, inclusive growth in developing countries should highlight increasing income and creation of ample work opportunities for a mainly poor rural labor force. Inclusive growth needs to strengthen both the role of government and the development of enterprises. Market access and prices are important growth factors. The successful development of China's local inclusive agribusiness enterprises has been driven by domestic and international markets in recent decades.

Additionally, institutions are important for the inclusive development of family agribusinesses. China's grassroots governments of town and collective village committees have played a coordinating role in local industrial and business development. Inclusive agribusinesses can take advantages of success to upgrade industrial chain development in the agricultural sector. Importantly, inclusive agribusiness development involves stakeholders, including smallholder farmers, rural communities and entrepreneurs.

Coordination by and with local government can help inclusive and sustainable development in developing countries. Local officials can provide incentives for local economic development. Private enterprises have no obligations of social responsibility to reduce farmers' poverty, unless entrepreneurs are willing to take social responsibility. Often, private enterprises give priority to profits. However, local government alone cannot overcome development barriers. For instance, local government cannot afford to support a large number of unemployed. Therefore, inclusive and local social enterprises are important for the creation of work opportunities.

Last but not the least, global governance is important for international cooperation on economic development and poverty reduction in developing countries, emerging economies and transitional economies. Developing countries have been characterized by different development paths in the context of their cultural, economic and political characteristics. Many developing countries have increased international and regional cooperation in agribusiness and enterprises cooperation. As well as different political systems there are different institutions and policies, as well as different economic development stages. Multinational agribusiness enterprises will be more important for international development through inclusive development patterns and application of advanced technology to commercial management in the future.

References

Asian Development Bank. (2015). Contract Farming For Better Farmer-Enterprise Partnerships. *ADB's Experience in the People' Republic of China*. Philippines: Asian Development Bank.

Kassiola, J. J. (2017). Coordinated Rural-Urban Development in China: A New Social Spatial Reorganization, Migration, and Rural Development. *Journal of Chinese Political Science, 22*, 77–95.

Keshelashvili, G. (2018). Value China Management in Agribusiness. *International Journal of Business and Management, VI*(2), 59–77.

Li, S. (2008). Rural Migrant Workers in China: Scenario, Challenges and Public Policy. Working Paper No. 89. Geneva: International Labour Office.

Li, X. Y. (2014). China's Industrialization: Overview-Implications for Africa's Industrilization. Beijing: International Poverty Reduction Center in China. https://www.tralac.org/images/docs/6676/background-report-chinas-industrialization-overview.pdf

Liu, Y., Long, H. L., Chen, Y. F., Wang, J. Y., Li, Y. R., Li, Y. H., Yang, Y. Y., & Zhou, Y. (2016). Progress of Research on Urban-Rural Transformation and Rural Development in China in the Past Decade and Future Prospects. *Journal of Geographical Sciences, 26*, 1117–1132.

Sun, H. L. (2015). China's Town and Village Enterprises and Its I for Sub-Saharan Africa. *International Journal of Technology and Globalization, 8*(1), 29–50.

The World Bank. (2016). Inclusive Urbanization and Rural-Urban Integration: Lessons from China. https://olc.worldbank.org/content/inclusive-urbanization-and-rural-urban-integration-lessons-china

The World Bank. (2020). Agriculture and Food. https://www.worldbank.org/en/topic/agriculture/overview. Accessed 1 Apr 2020.

The World Bank; World Trade Organization. (2019). *Global Value Chain Development Report 2019: Technological Innovation, Supply Chain Trade, and Workers in a Globalized World (English)*. Washington, DC: World Bank Group. http://documents.worldbank.org/curated/en/384161555079173489/Global-Value-Chain-Development-Report-2019-Technological-Innovation-Supply-Chain-Trade-and-Workers-in-a-Globalized-World

Wang, J., Zhu, X. L., & Zhang, C. (2016). Model of China's E-Commerce in the Agricultural Sector: An Exploratory Study. *International Journal of u-and e-Service, Science and Technology, 9*(4), 389–400.

Woodhill, J. (2016). *Inclusive Agribusiness: The State of Play Background Working Paper*. Global Donal Platform for Rural Development.

Zhang, J. L., & Du, X. F. (2004). A Study on the Application Model of B2B E-Commerce in Agricultural Sector. *Journal of Electronic Science and Technology of China, 2*(3), 134–139.

Index[1]

[1] Note: Page numbers followed by 'n' refer to notes.

L. Sun, *Economic Growth and Development*, Palgrave Studies in Economic History,
https://doi.org/10.1007/978-3-030-46099-0

F

S

The manufacturer's authorised representative in the EU is Springer Nature Customer Service Centre GmbH, Europaplatz 3, 69115 Heidelberg, Germany. If you have any concerns regarding our products, please contact ProductSafety@springernature.com

Printed and bound by CPI Group (UK) Ltd, Croydon, CR0 4YY

30/09/2026

02225645-0002